Every Morning New

Blessings always...

Coreane

COVER PHOTO

Mossebo Church, near the border between the provinces of Västergötland and Småland, was founded in the 14th century. The current building was constructed in 1773. Josef Hansson, a member of the congregation and its organist, was instrumental in securing offerings from churches all over Sweden for its construction. The interior paintings are unique to this congregation. It is the "mother church" from which the Chilstrom (Kjöllerström in Sweden) families originate.

The photo was taken by Bengt Kjöllerström, retired professor of physics at Lund University in Sweden and a distant cousin of Herbert Chilstrom. Bengt's wife Annika Molander was a Swedish exchange student at Gustavus Adolphus College in 1963–64.

Herbert W. Chilstrom and E. Corinne Chilstrom

EVERY MORNING NEW

Worship references and hymns are identified by:

(*ELW*) *Evangelical Lutheran Worship*, copyright © 2006 Evangelical Lutheran Church in America, Augsburg Fortress, Publishers.

(*WOV*) *With One Voice*, copyright © 1995 Augsburg Fortress.

(*LBW*) *Lutheran Book of Worship*, copyright © 1978.

(*SBH*) *Service Book and Hymnal*, copyright © 1958.

The Hymnal, The Hymnal of the Evangelical Lutheran Augustana Synod, copyright © 1923.

Gather, copyright © 1994 GIA Publications, Inc.

Cover image: Bengt Kjöllerström
Publishing consultant: Huff Publishing Associates, LLC
Cover and book design: Hillspring Books, Inc.

ISBN 978-0-9676573-2-5

Sixth Printing

Foreword

❖ ❖ ❖

More than thirty years ago I started rising early for a morning walk. At first I did it to maintain good health. I soon discovered, however, that those early dawn treks were also good for my soul. Among other things, I memorized several morning hymns that became my dawn light liturgy. Among them was "Again Thy Glorious Sun Doth Rise" from the pen of the prolific nineteenth century Swedish hymn writer Johan Olaf Wallin.

After I retired, my wife Corinne and our dog, Jonah, joined me on these daily excursions. When Corinne agreed to coauthor this volume we pondered over an appropriate title. It came to us on one of those morning walks that the last phrase of Wallin's hymn had the right words: "thy bounteous grace is *every morning new.*"

One of the blessings we reaped from our efforts has been to bring to memory many who have touched our lives, both directly and indirectly. What they have in common, whether they are well-known or ordinary, is that each fulfilled in a very natural way the calling God gave them. We hope that as you read you will call to memory many who have been a blessing in your life as well.

While there are a few instances where the writing for a particular day relates to those that precede and follow, in most every case each day stands by itself. Because some seasons of the year—Lent, Easter, and Pentecost, for example—are "moveable" on the calendar, we refer to those times only in general. When the date is "fixed"—New Year's Day, Epiphany, and Christmas, for example—we write for that day.

We have also included reflections for "Commemoration Days." These are the dates when the church remembers outstanding believers who have influenced the world by their unusual lives. We are indebted to our long-time acquaintance, Dr. Philip H. Pfatteicher, for his book, *Festivals and Commemorations,* which has aided us for these particular days.

We have included no prayers with these writings. There are several options.

Given its completeness, simply using the Lord's Prayer is appropriate.

Others may want to use conversational prayer, speaking informally to God and employing the suggested pattern of praise, confession, thanksgiving, and intercession. Keeping a prayer list is helpful.

One might also use these prayers from *Evangelical Lutheran Worship* on a daily basis:

MORNING

Almighty and merciful God, you have brought us in safety to this new day. Preserve us with your mighty power, that we may not fall into sin nor be overcome by adversity. In all we do, direct us to the fulfillment of your purpose; through Jesus Christ our Lord. Amen.

EVENING

We give thanks to you, heavenly Father, through Jesus Christ your dear Son, that you have graciously protected us today. We ask you to forgive us all our sins, where we have done wrong, and graciously to protect us tonight. For into your hands we commend ourselves: our bodies, our souls, and all that is ours. Let your holy angels be with us, so that the wicked foe may have no power over us. Amen.

Readers will note that we have attached our initials for each day's writing— "ecc" for Corinne and "hwc" for Herbert.

We are grateful to the Augustana Heritage Association (AHA) for sponsoring this book, to Dr. Arland Hultgren, chair of the AHA Publications Committee, to Susan Niemi for editing the text, and to William Huff, publisher, for his assistance in bringing our efforts to completion.

Finally, we offer these writings in the hope that every reader will be drawn into the stories we have shared, seeing yourself in the lives of others. Above all, we pray that the words of Scripture will be a daily source for insight, inspiration, and encouragement.

- Herbert W. Chilstrom

EVERY

Morning
NEW

❖ Certainty for a New Year ❖

Maybe you've had a good year. You look back on the past twelve months and realize you have much for which to give thanks, dozens of reasons to be grateful for all the pleasant memories you carry with you into the new year. Wonderful!

Maybe last year's resolutions went down in flames before the end of January. Friends you thought you could rely on seemed to abandon you. Each month brought some new reason to wonder, "Where is God?"

Regardless of what kind of year we leave behind, the truth is that none of us has any idea what this dawning year will bring. Maybe you've had a bad year, one you would even like to forget. Nothing seemed to work out as you had hoped. We can hope for the best, we can try to be optimistic, but who knows?

There is one point of stability in the uncertainties of these coming months. It is the bedrock promise that God will be with us every day.

My father-in-law, a devout Dane, gave us a good word when we were married. We don't necessarily get grace in advance, he said, but we do get grace when we need it. This was the seasoned wisdom of one who had farmed the land for many decades through drought and heavy rain, high and low prices, illness and health.

We look back and wonder how we made it through dark nights of the soul. We thought we might not make it. But in each time of calamity, each moment of doubt, each test of endurance, God was with us—the Holy Spirit did not abandon us.

A good promise we might grasp hold of this first day of the year and repeat each morning is this word from Jeremiah: "[God's] mercies never come to an end; they are new every morning" (Lam. 3:22-23).

~ hwc

❖ LAMENTATIONS 3:19-26 ❖

❖ YOU ARE MINE ❖

A woman from India told about being afraid that after delivering her baby in the hospital, she might be sent home with the wrong baby. Having heard of this happening to others, she decided to devise a plan. She went to the store, bought a pen with indelible ink, and took it with her to the hospital.

She felt so much love looking into his eyes as she held him for the first time. Then and there, she took the pen and put a mark on the palm of his little hand. She had marked her signature, YOU ARE MINE. When leaving the hospital, she was sure he was hers because she saw the mark she had placed on his hand.

God claimed us with the cross of Jesus at our baptism. We were sealed with the Holy Spirit and marked with the cross of Christ forever. "In Baptism God forgives sin, delivers from death and the devil, and gives everlasting salvation to all who believe what he has promised."

When assailed by the devil, the world, and our own flesh, God sees the mark and defies those powers that lure us away. We are claimed by Almighty God who made us. By Jesus Christ who died and rose from the dead to save us. By the Holy Spirit who guards and protects us. Father/Mother God embraces us with parental, possessive, eternal love, which will never let us go.

Luther says we need to retrace that cross, reclaiming our gifts in baptism every day. And remember whose we are. God remembers, but we need help to remember. Let us pray:

> Stir up in me the gift of your Holy Spirit; confirm my faith, guide my life, empower me in serving, give me patience in suffering, and bring me to everlasting life. Amen (*LBW*, p. 201).

Like a loving mother, God says, "I have called you, YOU ARE MINE."

~ ecc

❖ ISAIAH 43:1-7 ❖

❖ LIGHT FOR THE NEW YEAR ❖

One of the first things I noticed when I started walking in the early morning hours was the power of light.

On winter mornings in Minnesota it was still dark when I stepped out of our home. On overcast days only the dim streetlights illuminated my way. But as I made my turn toward home, the first rays of light began to appear on the eastern horizon. "Nothing," I would say to myself, "can stop the light from coming." Even on the darkest mornings, when heavy clouds blanketed the earth, the light of the sun still penetrated the gloomy landscape. If I had shouted at the top of my lungs, "Stop! Don't rise today!" it would have been silly and useless.

That, I said to myself, is how God's grace comes day after day. I can't stop it. If our sun, a small flaming orb in the vast reaches of the universe, can have such power, what about our Christ, the Sun of God? He has "rescued us from the power of darkness" (Col. 1:13). Even to the darkest corner of my soul, I can't stop God's light from coming to me. And as we think of the darkest corners of our world, where war, poverty, riot, and unrest often seem to be raging out of control—yes, even there God's sun is rising, God's Son is present.

One of my favorite services in *Evangelical Lutheran Worship* is Vespers. Now we are at the other end of the day. Darkness is descending on the world again. The long hours of the night can be threatening. But we need not fear. Why? Because

> Jesus Christ is the light of the world,
> the light no darkness can overcome. . . .
> Let your light scatter the darkness and illuminate your church
> (*ELW*, p. 309).

~ hwc

❖ 1 JOHN 1:5-10 ❖

Sing a New Song unto the Lord

It's a new year—time for a fresh start and celebrating. Israel was rejoicing with a new king, God's representative to lead them to victory. It was also time to celebrate their annual covenant renewal with God. Old songs wouldn't suffice. They needed to sing a new song to the Lord. It must have sounded like our Easter Sunday with trumpets leading the singing. So much joy that even the floods were clapping their hands and the hills were singing. In fact, all creation was joining in praise to God.

One day an unchurched young man was prompted to come to worship. He wasn't sure why. But the Holy Spirit connected the proclamation of the gospel to his needs, and on Monday morning he called, needing to talk out his anger at God and the story of his mother dying when he was ten. Now after ten more years, he was shedding his first tears.

Beneath all of the anger was a beautiful tenderness received by Jesus as we prayed together. I simply used all of his words and feelings, giving them to Jesus who heard all and embraced him with love he longed for. He said, "I never knew you could pray like that," and left relieved with new peace and a resolve to get better acquainted with Jesus by reading the Gospel of Mark.

As we enter this new year, let's recount all God has done for us, especially remembering his steadfast love and faithfulness. For Israel, a new king and new hope. For the young man, relief from his burdens and a new start with the Lord. For us, Jesus is here to carry our worries and grudges and give us a new start.

> Sing a new song unto the Lord;
> let your song be sung from the mountains high.
> Sing a new song unto the Lord, singing alleluia (*Gather* #384).

~ ecc

PSALM 98

❖ All Things New ❖

"See, I am making all things new" (Rev. 21:5). What good news for a new year! "See, the home of God is among mortals" (Rev. 21:3). God is here. So it is not glibly, but with prayerful confidence that we say to one another, "Happy New Year!"

Revelation was given as a vision to John with instructions from God to write it—preserve for us this important message of hope. This vision must not be taken literally, Barbara Rossing insists, or we will miss the power of God's message. The key theme is Jesus the Lamb. And he is a person not a sheep. In her book *The Rapture Exposed*, she cites Kathleen Norris: "a poet's book doesn't tell, it shows over and over again, language engaging the listener in a tale that has the satisfying yet unsettling effect of a dream."

A vision, like a dream, comes with images and symbols that expose reality to make us certain of change that must happen and gives us courage to act. John's images exposed the terrible reality of Christians being persecuted and made them certain God was there giving courage to persevere.

Rossing (*The Rapture Exposed*, p. 171) writes, "Revelation's story is about seeing the Lamb beside us every moment of your life—in the car, at the shopping mall, at work or school. . . . The Lamb is leading you even now into a world of joy and healing." Lamb power is available for us now, helping us heal a broken world as we walk into the new year.

This song expresses for us new beginnings:

> God is here! As we your people meet to offer praise and prayer,
> May we find in fuller measure what it is in Christ we share.
> Here, as in the world around us, all our varied skills and arts
> Wait the coming of the Spirit into open minds and hearts
> (WOV #719).

~ ecc

❖ REVELATION 21:1-6 ❖

❖ Remember Your Baptism ❖

We call this day "The Epiphany of our Lord." Next to Easter and Pentecost it is the most ancient of Christian holy days. Because it seldom falls on a Sunday, it gets lost for most of us in Western Christian churches.

In the Eastern churches, however, this day is a time to remember the baptism of Jesus. I happened to be in Addis Ababa, Ethiopia, on January 6 in the early 1990s. Coptic Christians by the tens of thousands flocked to public parks for a gigantic celebration of this day. Priests conducted open-air services. I watched as adult men and women leaped into large pools of water with shouts of joy and ecstasy.

I like the idea of remembering our baptism near the beginning of a new year. Luther, in fact, thought it a good idea to remember it every morning. We may not jump into an open-air pool—especially if we live in places where water is covered with a layer of thick ice! But surely pausing to think about the grace of God that blessed us on our baptism day with a gift that lasts for a lifetime—how better to begin a new year as well as a new day?

Yes, and this gift reaches beyond this life and into eternity. Each time I visit my son's gravesite I repeat the words I used when he was baptized: "Andrew John, child of God, you have been sealed by the Holy Spirit and marked with the cross of Christ forever."

If baptized in infancy, take a moment to recall your baptism. Give thanks for parents and godparents who made certain this gift—like good food and loving care—was given to you before you understood it. If they are still living, this would be a good day to give them a call and thank them directly.

~ hwc

❖ EPHESIANS 2:2-6 ❖

❖ Jesus Loves Me, This I Know ❖

When I was a young lad our family lived at the edge of town. Between us and the open prairie that stretched to the west, there were only two or three other houses. One of my duties was to take my wagon in the summer or sled in the winter and walk to grumpy farmer Paulsen's place about a half-mile away. He had just one cow that he milked about seven in the evening. I often had to wait for him to pasteurize the milk before I was on my way home again. He obviously didn't like children. I was eager to hand him my coins and be on my way.

I didn't mind that chore on a lovely evening in July. But on a snowy, wind-swept January night it was a fearsome task. I was certain there were wild characters lurking in the dark woods along the path, ready to pounce on me. There was only one thing to do. As lustily as I could, I belted out the words of reassurance: Jesus loves me, this I know, for the Bible tells me so. . . .

Since then I've walked along many more dark and foreboding roads, always looking for an easier way home, but always knowing that the only way was to forge on through the darkness. And you, my reader friend, have had the same kinds of experiences, times when you wondered if you would make it to your destination.

But God never fails. There is always the promise that we are loved and that the Holy Spirit will be our Guide and Helper. We do as the hymn writer has suggested: "Your songs and prayers against the darkness hurling" (*ELW* #665).

What is your worst fear today? What fierce winds are blowing across your path? Follow the lead of that young lad. Keep moving. Keep praying. Keep singing.

~ hwc

❖ PSALM 23 ❖

❖ A Light to My Feet ❖

Growing up on a South Dakota farm before rural electricity, we knew how black the darkness could be on a moonless night. Especially in midwinter when we went out to do chores after supper. So we lit the lantern and carried it with us getting cows into the barn. Our lantern lit up the path, keeping us from stumbling or falling on stones or rough ice. While milking, the lantern hung on a rafter lighting up our work.

In the house we carried kerosene lamps at night from room to room. To save time it was easier to do errands in the dark, groping for what we needed. For me, as a child, those errands happened very quickly because I was afraid of the dark. That was, no doubt the reason when memorizing Bible verses, this one was particularly comforting—to know that God's word was a lamp for our feet and a light for our path. Like a good object lesson, this word taught me that we needed God's word with us always.

Stepping into a new year causes us to think about uncertainties that face us in the coming year. Because we can't see into the future, we wonder—will our lives unfold just as expected or will there be surprises? Will we be up to challenges? Looking at unknowns is like stepping into the dark night. We do need a lamp to light up our path—a light to guide us, protect us from danger, and show us the way. God's word is that light, giving us hope and courage. Because God is alive and present in the Word, it is God who will take away our fear of the dark.

> O Word of God incarnate, O Wisdom from on high,
> O Truth unchanged, unchanging, O Light of our dark sky;
> We praise you for the radiance that from the hallowed page,
> A lantern to our footsteps, shines on from age to age (*ELW* #514).

~ ecc

❖ PSALM 119:105 ❖

❖ FEAR OR CONFIDENCE ❖

Do you sometimes fear the future? That's the question I asked two friends over coffee one day. It opened a very interesting discussion as we each told our stories. But interestingly, the fear factor always was only the minor part of the greater story.

My story was about fear of being lonely. At age thirteen, preparing to leave home for my freshman year of high school at Augustana Academy, a residential school of the church, I knew I wouldn't get home often because we had gas rationing during the war. So I prayed earnestly for a special friend. No sooner had I arrived at my assigned dorm room on third floor when from across the hall came a cheerful voice saying, "Hi, I'm Audrey."

She was God's immediate answer—classmate and soon a good friend; roommate the next three years and again twice more, at LBI in Minneapolis and after that during nursing school; bridesmaids in each other's weddings; and always a helpful sharing friend from across the miles during our early years of motherhood. So much closeness until her untimely death at age forty. But somehow, even still, her friendship is a special part of me. God's answer was beyond all expectations.

Fear is common to the human experience, especially fear of the unknown. What's behind the next door of our life, we wonder. Darkness of the future. But Isaiah teaches us an important lesson—fear overtakes only when we forget to recall all that the Lord has done for us in the past.

> Look to the rock from which you were hewn, and to the quarry from which you were dug (51:1).

God, our maker, the one who stretched out the heavens and laid the foundations of the earth is the one who sees and knows beyond the closed doors of our lives. We can trust our loving God who even now is preparing the future.

~ ecc

❖ ISAIAH 51:1-3, 12-16 ❖

❖ Keep Life in Perspective ❖

I like to learn new words. That is, words that are new to me. Yesterday it was "hyperopia." My eye doctor knows it as far-sightedness. Some folks see clearly into the distance, but cannot see what is at hand. It is the opposite of myopia—near-sightedness. This applies to those who can see what is in front of their nose but cannot see what is at a distance. We also apply it to those who are self-centered and those who fail to make plans for the long run.

In our Christian walk we can easily become hyperoptic. We can be so concerned about what will happen a year or five years from now that we fail to enjoy the blessings God is giving us this day.

As we continue to move into these first days of a new year, we surely need to plan for our future and make provisions for ourselves and our families. But Jesus reminded us on several occasions that this can become a preoccupation. It can lead to a lack of trust in God and failure to see the good that is right before our eyes this very day.

We should ask ourselves: How many of the things I feared a year ago have actually happened? When the unexpected happened in the past year, did God forsake me? How might I have used all the energy I spent on worry in helping someone who needs my attention?

I have visited no place on earth as impoverished as India. Most Christians in that land come from the lowest caste. They have little of this world's goods. Our middle class in the United States lives like kings and queens by comparison. Yet, I found more joy and satisfaction among them than I have found among many Christian in our country.

So, "Count your blessings, name them one by one."

~ hwc

❖ MATTHEW 6:25-34 ❖

❖ Making Sense out of Chaos ❖

Today I learned another new word: "chaorder." There are theories about how order sometimes emerges out of chaos. So, a new word to describe it.

At times when we are asked what kind of day we have had, we feel like saying, "It was chaotic! Everything seemed to fall apart just when I put it together."

That's one of the good things about the beginning of a new day. We look back at what we thought was chaotic, messy, and nonsensical. But with more reflection we realize that some good things have come out of seemingly bad situations. Something new opened for us and we set out on a new path. A relationship breaks up and we think the world has come to an end. But a new one unfolds and we can't imagine how fortunate we are. In time we discover a new way to look at life. Talents we never knew we had come to the surface because we have to deal with new expectations.

God is good at bringing order out of chaos. That's the story of creation. "The earth was formless [chaotic] and darkness covered the surface of the deep. . . . And God said, 'Let there be light (Gen. 1:2-3)'" When God had created the human family—"God saw everything that he had made, and indeed, it was very good" (Gen. 1:31).

As we take one more step into the new year we may feel anxious, we may think that our life looks chaotic and confusing. This is a good time to remind ourselves that God brings order not only to all of creation but to our human family and to each one of us personally. This is a good day to say, "No matter how unsettled I may feel, I will cling to Jesus, the solid rock, and build my life on him."

~ hwc

❖ GENESIS 1:1-4; 26-27 ❖

❖ FORGIVENESS ❖

Forgiveness. That's something God promises to do for us. But when Jesus taught his disciples to do the same, Peter asked how many times we should forgive. The answer: "Seventy times seven." It sounds ongoing, even endless. And isn't that the way life is, as misunderstandings keep happening?

One morning in church a woman unintentionally took home the wrong snow boots. This was never confronted and because of this, years of great bitterness came between two women.

Some say, "Can't we just forgive and forget?" Or just say, "I'm sorry." The solutions are not that simple. Jesus suggests it is a process. We need first to go to the offender, pointing out the fault. If the person is unwilling to discuss it, we must ask trusted witnesses to listen and help.

Walt Wangerin, in *As for Me and My House*, helps us notice that forgiveness contains the important word *give*. Each must give something. One must give notice to the one who offended. Hopefully that person will realize he or she has hurt the other and change so it will not happen again. Both then, give something: 1. give notice of the offense; 2. give change so no further offense will happen; 3. give up holding a grudge.

This word *forgiveness* is pregnant with meaning—release, let go, liberation, leave in peace. All of this is what we need, what we hope for in the process of forgiveness. Does it always work? Unfortunately, not. We must remember two things. We cannot change another. But holding anger against an offender will only harm the one who retains the anger. Only by God's grace are we able to let it go.

In Jesus' parable, the king forgave his servant a debt worth more than fifteen years worth of service. He in turn would not forgive a miniscule debt. God asks us as we are continually forgiven, to extend the same to others. May God give us this grace again today.

~ ecc

❖ MATTHEW 18:15-34 ❖

❖ The Hand of God Has Touched Me ❖

Isn't it amazing, how we're led to new and deeper understandings of God by the people and events that come together in our lives? And how the timing of these things touch us so deeply just when we need it most.

Henri Nouwen, in visiting the Saint Petersburg Hermitage, was awed by Rembrandt's painting "Return of the Prodigal Son." A copy of it is on the cover of his book, entitled the same. Nouwen tells of how just when he needed it most, in his viewing of the painting, it became for him, the beginning of his journey to understand new depths of "God's perfect love beyond all paralyzing fears and the divine consolation beyond the desolation of human anguish and agony" (p. 16).

We're drawn into the painting particularly by the hands of the father—especially his right hand. We see both strength and compassion as his hand touches the back of his son. During my seminary training, I studied clinical pastoral education at the Hennepin County Home School with Chaplain Henry Taxis as my supervisor. He was wise, compassionate, and insightful in helping us know ourselves and also work with the juvenile delinquent residents.

When our son died, Henry Taxis came to the funeral. He was one of many bringing us special comfort. As he looked into my eyes, he placed his right hand with firm middle fingers on the center of my upper back. His hand became a direct channel of God's compassion and strength for me on such a difficult day. Remembering that moment, even years later, I experience again, God's strength.

The hand of God touched Job, bringing him at last out of terrible pain to witness powerfully, "I know that my Redeemer lives" (Job 19:25).

Today, I invite you to simply look at your hands as you ask God to use them. Your hands can be channels of God's compassion and strength for someone in need, just when they need it most.

~ ecc

❖ JOB 19:1-26 ❖

❖ What Are Your Chances? ❖

Do you ever feel that your life consists mainly of interruptions? No matter what your plans may be for a given day, you can be almost certain that something—indeed, many things—will happen in the course of the day to frustrate those carefully made agendas.

You may take some consolation in studying the life of Jesus. He is about to address a large crowd when a person with leprosy pleads for healing. Jesus is interrupted. He drops in at Peter's home for a visit and discovers that Peter's mother-in-law needs help. Jesus is interrupted. When he is weary and needs rest, the sick are carried to the door for healing. Jesus is interrupted. In the middle of his discourse, a runner comes with a request that Jesus come to raise a child thought to be dead. Jesus is interrupted.

Continue reading and you will soon see that the life of Jesus was mostly one of a constant stream of interruptions.

Possibly the best example of this maxim is the familiar parable of the good Samaritan. The text reads: "Now by *chance* a priest was going down that road" (Luke 10:31) and saw the beaten man in the ditch. But he had no time to be interrupted. And so with the Levite. But the Samaritan, who might also have excused himself for good reason, "went to him and bandaged his wounds" (v. 34). He might have turned aside from this interruption as easily as the other two. But the priorities of his life were different from theirs.

As you move through another day, take time to pay attention to the interruptions. In the very least expected places and at the most inconvenient times, you may discover a blessing that could easily slip away. Hidden in one of those interruptions may be an unexpected incident that could change not only someone else's life, but yours as well.

~ hwc

❖ LUKE 10:25-37 ❖

❖ The Devil Charges Me in Vain ❖

Anna had moved to be near her son's family because cancer was threatening and she was now hospitalized undergoing heavy chemotherapy. I met her for the first time when I made a pastoral call. Because she was in reverse isolation, I donned a scrub gown and mask. She was lying quietly in her silent darkened room. So I could be close, I sat on the arm of her chair with my hand on hers, asking what her night had been like when she was so ill.

"Oh, the devil's been here in this room all night," she said, "accusing me of wrongs from my whole life." Then she went on to explain how ordinarily she would have taken her Bible to read promises from God, but couldn't now because her eyes were blurred from therapy.

So I opened my Bible and the Holy Spirit enlivened us as together we heard promises. "There is therefore now, no condemnation to those who are in Christ Jesus. . . . It is that very Spirit himself bearing witness with our spirit that we are children of God. . . . that very Spirit intercedes with sighs too deep for words" (Rom. 8:1, 17, 26). Throughout the reading she hungrily grasped God's promises saying YES, YES, YES. And she kept saying YES, as I sang:

> How sweet the name of Jesus sounds in a believer's ear!
> It soothes our sorrows, heals our wounds, and drives away all fear.
> It makes the wounded spirit whole and calms the heart's unrest;
> 'Tis manna to the hungry soul and to the weary, rest.
> Dear name! The rock on which I build, my shield and hiding place;
> My never failing treasury, filled with boundless stores of grace.
> By thee my prayers acceptance gain although with sin defiled;
> The devil charges me in vain, and I am owned a child (*ELW* #620).

YES!

~ ecc

❖ ROMANS 8:1-17 ❖

Faith Is Falling into God's Hands

Walt Wangerin wrote an article some years ago in *The Lutheran* magazine, telling about Karen, a young woman who wrote asking him to tell her what faith is. Better than an explanation with words, a story would be better. And so he told his own story from boyhood.

In their back yard, Walt had a favorite tree to climb and on a summer day he would sit and daydream. One day, sitting high on a branch, a sudden thunderstorm rolled in, blowing hard on his branch. Yelling for help, he expected his father when he came running, to climb up to rescue him. But instead, he stood below with outstretched arms, calling for Walt to jump. Much too scared to jump, he clung ever more tightly to the weakening branch. Then with a terrible blast of wind, the branch started cracking. Down he fell. And into the arms of his waiting father. "And that, Karen, is faith," explained Walt.

In Hebrews 11 we have stories of such faith. Abraham. Sarah. Noah. Enoch. Isaac. Jacob. Each was clinging to a breaking branch when they couldn't see the way ahead. But God was there leading and guiding. If they could have seen, it would have been sight and not faith. But faith is "the assurance of things hoped for, the conviction of things not seen" (v. 1).

Until our branch is breaking, we cannot know faith. Faith comes only when we're helpless and there is nothing to which we can cling. When we're at the end of the rope. And falling. Then and only then do we know faith. We find God waiting for us with open arms. Loving us. Ready to catch us as we fall.

> Nothing in my hand I bring; simply to thy cross I cling.
> Naked, come to thee for dress; helpless, look to thee for grace;
> Foul, I to the fountain fly; wash me, Savior, or I die (*ELW* 623).

~ ecc

❖ HEBREWS 11:1-3 ❖

❖ Running Away from God ❖

Margaret Wise Brown gave us a most wonderful children's book, *The Runaway Bunny* (Harper & Row, 1942). Good for adults as well as for children. How beautifully it paints the gospel with pictures and words—original sin, our turning away, and always God pursuing us with love. Brown does it with warm pictures and poetic rhyme. Let me recap.

When a little bunny announces he wants to run away, his mother said she would run after him because he belonged to her. When he said he'd be a fish, she said she'd be a fisherman and fish for him. When he said he'd be a rock on a high mountain, she said she'd be a mountain climber and climb to him. When he said he'd become a crocus in a hidden garden, she said she'd be a gardener and find him. When he said he'd be a bird and fly away from her, she said she'd be a tree that he would come home to. When he said he'd be a sailboat, she said she'd be the wind and blow him where she wanted him. When he said he'd join the circus and fly on a flying trapeze, she said she'd be a tightrope walker and walk across the air to him. When he said he'd then become a boy and run into a house, his mother said, "Then I will become your mother and catch you in my arms and hug you."

Jesus painted a picture too. Another son who ran away. And all the while his father was pursuing him with love until he did return. God's love is like that—a love that will not let us go. Whether we think of God as mother or father, it is love beyond what we can know—following us, waiting for us, longing every day for us to come home. And we will receive an abundance of forgiveness, peace, and joy.

~ ecc

❖ LUKE 15:11-24 ❖

❖ Those Other Christians ❖

At this time of year Christians around the world observe the Week of Prayer for Christian Unity. It begins with the "Confession of St. Peter" and ends with the "Conversion of St. Paul."

It has always amused me a bit that we link these two apostles when we think of Christian unity. Why? Because from the Letter to the Galatians it is apparent that these two "type A" leaders, Peter and Paul, did not always get along as well as might be expected. Paul criticizes Peter (also known as Cephas) for being inconsistent, eating with Gentile Christians in one setting, but withdrawing from them when Jewish Christians show up.

Fortunately, this "dust up" between Paul and Peter did not alienate them. Instead, each leader sees that he is called to a special mission—Paul to the Gentiles and Peter to the Jews. Running deeper than their differences is a common bond. Whether Jew or Gentile, "We know that a person is justified . . . through faith in Jesus Christ" (Gal. 2:16).

Over more than a half-century as a Lutheran pastor and bishop I have been engaged in ecumenical dialogues, ranging from Roman Catholic to Episcopalian to Presbyterian to Assemblies of God and many others. In all of these settings I have had the privilege of representing the convictions of our Lutheran tradition. At the same time, I have discovered in all of these encounters that our differences do not divide when we stand together as brothers and sisters at the foot of the cross of Jesus Christ. And I have always felt at ease encouraging members of our Lutheran congregations to be in conversation and prayer with other Christians.

Before this week concludes, seek out someone who is of a different church tradition. You will learn things that may surprise you. You will be impressed at how much you share in common.

~ hwc

❖ GALATIANS 2:15-21 ❖

❖ It Didn't Start with Luther ❖

Not many Lutherans have heard of Henry, Bishop of Uppsala. Not even Swedes. Little wonder. First, there is little known about him other than that he probably died as a martyr to the faith. But also because Henry preceded Martin Luther by about 400 years, dying on this day in 1156.

It is good for us in Lutheran and other Protestant traditions to recall that though our churches took a sharp break from Roman Catholicism in the sixteenth century, the roots of our faith are buried deep in the church that preceded that time. Our ancestors in the faith would not have had anything to pass on to us were it not for heroes, such as Bishop Henry, who persevered even to giving their lives for us.

Sometimes I wonder if we have leaned too far in dismissing the importance of saints in the life of the church. We rightfully accent that every believer is a saint, as a forgiven child of God. But it is good to remember that over many centuries prior to the Reformation there were men and woman, mostly unknown, who kept alive the treasure of the gospel.

After I retired I did a study of my own family history. I was able to trace our roots in Sweden back to 1612. Most of the names on that list are unknown to me. Yet as I look at this genealogy I am filled with a sense of profound gratitude. It represents the passage of faith from one generation to the next. Though there are no notable saints in my family tree, I would not be a Christian were it not for their faithfulness in passing on this priceless treasure.

We may think of ourselves as rather ordinary Christians. But we have the privilege of letting the gospel flow on from us to future generations.

~ hwc

❖ 2 TIMOTHY 1:3-7 ❖

❖ Envy ❖

A woman pastor friend tells this story of a "Trudy" in her parish. Trudy was an efficient, faithful, and cheerful servant volunteer. So it was shocking one morning when she exploded in the face of her pastor. Although the anger was directed at her, the pastor sensed there were underlying issues and wisely drew out Trudy's anger, carefully asking her to say more. Finally when the anger seemed fully spent, they parted. It was not reconciliation, but the best that could have happened at the time.

About four months later, a three-page handwritten letter appeared on the pastor's desk. Trudy explained how after being a stay-at-home mom, she had followed her husband as he climbed his ladder of success. Each time they moved, she would be plucked from whatever momentum of her own she was achieving at the time. Then she came to the point writing, "I am so envious of you! You've followed your dream and become a good pastor." She went on to apologize for the anger she had dumped on her pastor and also erupted with so much sadness, long covered in the recesses of her soul. But now to have gotten it out, wonderful new health had come to Trudy. And there came a reconciliation with her pastor.

Envy, one of our most powerful sins is devastating both to the one who holds it and devastating when projected on others. It is one of the hardest feelings to cover. Unknown only to the one who carries it, envy wears no clothes. It is naked and plain to see. Envy breaks relationships, hurts God's kingdom, and messes up the church.

Jesus tells a story of envy as he pictures the elder son so envious of his prodigal brother when given a big welcome home by their father. Can we allow the searchlight of the Holy Spirit to root out the envy in our hearts today?

~ ecc

❖ LUKE 15:25-32 ❖

❖ Modern Heroes of the Faith ❖

One of the most courageous persons I've known is Medardo Gomez, bishop of the Lutheran church in El Salvador. His country has been torn about by civil war and oppression for decades. Gomez has been the lightning rod for his defense of the poor and helpless.

Gomez had so many death threats that he had to leave the country for a time. When he wanted to return he asked if I would go with him. I told him that I was not afraid to die, but asked if we would have any form of security. He looked at me without apology and said, "We must trust God."

Several weeks later we flew together to El Salvador. As soon as we landed I realized why he could make no promise about security. There was no way to protect anyone in a land where many had taken the law into their own hands.

Over the next several days we traveled across the country. Gomez's aim was to visit and encourage his people, to give them hope in the midst of chaos.

One night I ate dinner with two attorneys, both faithful members of the Lutheran church. They had acted fearlessly in advocating for the cause of those who had been unjustly accused of crimes. One said that he was assaulted one evening in his home. His attackers said that if he did not stop his work of advocacy they would come again and rape his daughter before his own eyes and then kill him.

I surely do not wish for such a situation for us who live in relative comfort and security. But this taste of a very different world gave me a new appreciation for all the saints and martyrs down the centuries who have risked their lives in order that we might live and worship without fear.

~ hwc

❖ 2 CORINTHIANS 11:23-29 ❖

❖ Our Shield ❖

For morning devotions at a bishop/spouse gathering in the early '90s, the late Bishop Herlof Jensen delivered a homily that was moving and unforgettable. He had served U.S. forces in World War II. In the thick of battle one day, a comrade beside him took a quick step in front of him. And just in that instant an on-coming bullet took his buddy down. It was the bullet that would have hit him. His buddy died as he became Jensen's human shield. And his name was Worthy.

Still, after so many years, Bishop Jensen was very emotional telling the story. In fact, he said that ever since that most memorable day, he fills with emotion every time when singing "Worthy is the Lamb" at communion. For him, it was a very powerful object lesson, because Worthy's body became his shield.

The image of God as our shield was given first to Abraham (Gen. 15:1), "I am your shield." Again in Isaiah 53:5, "He was wounded for our transgressions, crushed for our iniquities; upon him was the punishment that made us whole, and by his bruises we are healed." God so loved that he gave his only son to step in front of us to take our punishment so that we might live. He is our shield that we might have abundant life now and for all eternity.

Today you and I are in fierce battle against the wiles of the devil. We could not stand without Jesus Christ taking his place in front of us to take the blows. Since he descended into hell and rose from the dead gaining victory over the evil one, Jesus is our shield, our gift in baptism. So let us again today, take the shield of faith and be strong in the Lord. And live this day thankful that he has won for us the victory. "Worthy is Christ, the Lamb who was slain!" (*LBW*, p. 102).

~ ecc

❖ EPHESIANS 6:10-20 ❖

❖ Searching for the Lost ❖

On a lovely autumn afternoon when leaves were falling, I accompanied Herb to a rural parish where he spoke. Remembering getting out of the car and walking through heavy leaves, I wondered later if it were there that the diamond fell out of my ring.

But I didn't notice it was gone until much later. Coming home late that evening was like any other, with time to read the Sunday paper in the family room. But while getting ready for bed panic set in when I noticed my ring was empty of the diamond! We searched everywhere; but it was not to be found. I went to bed praying, and in the morning called the church secretary where we'd been. But that was like a stab in the dark. How do you find a needle in a haystack? All day I searched through the house, feverishly sweeping and inching through the carpet.

After school, our son came in, loaded a plate with cookies, and carried a tall glass of milk to the family room. Quickly he came up the stairs saying, "Mom, guess what I found," as he handed me my diamond. As he turned to sit in the chair where I had read the paper the night before, he saw something glistening in the carpet. The lost was found. And there were shouts of rejoicing.

In Jesus' story, the lost coin was something very precious. Worth a day's wage, the loss may have meant a family would go hungry. Or it could have been a romantic symbol, one of the ten coins a betrothed woman had saved to fill up the traditional headdress that would become her mark as a married woman. In her dark house, finding the coin was almost impossible. So, there was joy! But how much greater is God's joy each day when we offer up whatever separates us from his love.

~ ecc

❖ LUKE 15:8-10 ❖

❖ It's Not All Black and White ❖

Today we remember the legacy of the great Supreme Court justice, Thurgood Marshall. He stands tall among those who have served on that court since its founding. Over a quarter century on that bench his understanding of justice and equal rights led to enormous changes in the way all minorities are treated in our society.

I needed men and women like Marshall. Growing up in an entirely white community in Minnesota, I had absolutely no personal contact with a black person until I went to seminary in the fall of 1954. It was there that I met classmate Lee Wesley. Lee and I sat together in the bass section of the seminary male chorus. A bond of friendship soon developed, not only with Lee, but also between his wife Elaine and my wife Corinne.

I recall vividly the day our male chorus presented a concert in a smaller midwestern community. Lee and I were strolling together down Main Street. I noted that some local folks were giving us strange, furtive glances. At first I wondered why they looked at us that way. Then it dawned on me, "Lee is black and I'm white. These folks can't conceive of such a friendship."

Isn't it strange, yes, pathetic, that we so easily allow our view of the world to be so narrow, so restricted? Though the biblical world seems to have permitted separation of peoples by race and even allowed for slavery, the deeper currents of our Bible point to a world in which we stand on level ground as brothers and sisters in the faith. The apostle Paul, like Thurgood Marshall and Martin Luther King, Jr. envisioned a day when women and men, slave and free, would be equal before God.

Prejudice is never absent from our common life. As Christians we should be in the forefront in working for equality and justice.

~ hwc

❖ GALATIANS 3:23-29 ❖

❖ Be Faithful ❖

John Donne, seventeenth-century poet and clergyman of the Church of England, was dean of St. Paul's Cathedral and one of their acclaimed preachers. Even while his preaching always centered on sin and redemption through the death and resurrection of Jesus, he sorrowed to the point of despair over his own sin and that of his world.

Despairing like the apostle Paul if, after preaching to others, he himself might be disqualified (1 Cor. 9:27), he wrote:

> I have a sin of fear, that when I have spun
> My last thread, I shall perish on the shore;
> Swear by Thyself that at my death thy Sun
> Shall shine as it shines now, and heretofore;
> And having done that, Thou hast done.
> I have no more.
>
> (*Daily Readings from Spiritual Classics*, edited by Paul Ofstedahl, Augsburg Fortress, 1990)

Perhaps we, too, while walking in faithful service, suffer in this way. Despair might be for failing to accomplish more of our dream or because we could never do enough to right injustice and suffering. We may feel despair because of broken relationships and problems around us even in the church.

Despair is one of our greatest sins, withering us from receiving God's forgiveness and peace, paralyzing us from doing God's will, and maybe robbing us from joy in the Lord and from sharing it with others.

The book of Revelation was written to Christians in despair. It was a time of terrible persecution when many died witnessing to faith in Jesus. Revelation is a message of hope for them and for us. John Donne had hope knowing the shining of "thy Sun" would sustain him. God never promises that we will see the outcome of what the Spirit calls us to do. But God does promise, as to first century believers, to help us conquer despair. God promises to help us be faithful.

> Be faithful unto death, and I will give you the crown of life (Rev. 2:10).

~ ecc

❖ REVELATION 2:2-11 ❖

❖ THE MYSTERY OF SUICIDE ❖

Through history suicide has often been considered the ultimate sin, one for which there could be no forgiveness. But here and there one hears a voice that raises questions about this all too easy judgment. Thoughtful believers have realized that it may be more complex than it may seem on the surface.

One such was the great Russian novelist Dostoevsky, whose death we remember on this date. In *The Brothers Karamazov* he writes of an elder who is on his deathbed. He is sharing last thoughts about suicide with younger monks. The elder bares his soul:

> They tell us that it is a sin to pray for them, and outwardly the church, as it were, renounces them. But in my secret heart I believe that we must pray even for them. Love can never be an offense to Christ. For such as those I have prayed inwardly all of my life. I confess it, fathers and teachers, and even now I pray for them every day.

Those of us who have experienced suicide in our immediate family or among close friends know only too well that the reasons one is moved to do such a tragic and final act can be extremely complicated. At such times we, like the old priest, pray for those who have succumbed to the dark hell that has overpowered them.

More than that, we look to our merciful God whose love is infinite, and especially for those who fall into despair.

In his letter to the faithful in Rome, Paul writes about the folly of assuming we know the mind of God in all things. He urges them—and us—to be humble and to yield to a higher wisdom and a greater mercy. "Who has known the mind of the Lord?" Paul asks. "Or who has been his counselor?" (Rom. 11:34).

~ hwc

❖ ROMANS 11:33-36 ❖

❖ How Big Is Your God? ❖

Tomorrow marks the date of America's worst space tragedy, the day when several astronauts perished as their space vehicle scarcely rose from the launching pad. It was a sober moment for the entire nation, a time when we realized the high price some pay to lead us to new horizons.

I recall the day back in the early 1950s when an older friend gave me a copy of J. B. Phillips's book *Your God Is Too Small.* For one who thought in youthful hubris that he knew something about God and the world, the title itself was like a splash of cold water in my face. How small my faith, how little my knowledge, how insufficient my view of God's endless creation.

Surely one of the gifts of the space program, including the probes into distant planetary reaches, has been to expand our understanding of the nature of God. The moment we think we have reached some maturity in our faith, God breaks in with new wisdom from the world of exploration.

The view of the psalmist was that the earth was flat, that a huge canopy stretched over the land, that the earth rested on pillars, and that both above and beneath was a vast sea of water. The portals of heaven opened to give rain. When one dug into the earth there was water. It all seemed so logical.

Yet, even with such an elementary view of creation, the psalmist believed that the height of God's steadfast love and the measure of God's forgiving grace were beyond his greatest imagination.

How much more for us in this age of space exploration! As we learn of new planets millions of miles away we come back to earth and claim the good news that "The steadfast love of the Lord is from everlasting to everlasting" (Ps. 103:17).

~ hwc

❖ PSALM 103 ❖

❖ WHAT LOVE! ❖

Theologian Ken Bailey, after researching Mid-Eastern culture, shares great insight on the parable of the prodigal son. There is nothing like this story, he says, in all of the Old Testament, nor in any Arabic literature, oral or written. Their culture could not have imagined a son spurning a parent in this way. He could just as well have said, "Dad, why don't you just drop dead?" Bailey says Mid-Easteners think it is so terrible they would never tell a story like this. But Jesus did.

It's the story of a young man who took the freedom to reject his own father's love. Can you think of a greater human suffering than to have love for your child rejected? And what of our rejecting God's love?

In his dying on the cross, Jesus suffered great physical pain. But how deep his suffering as he cried, "My God, my God, why hast thou forsaken me?" What ultimate sorrow, forsaken by God. "A man of suffering and acquainted with infirmity" (Isa. 53:3). So Jesus surely understands us when our love is rejected. But in telling the parable, Jesus pulls us to the heart of God's love being rejected by us.

God so loved the world that he gave his son that we might have everlasting life. Jesus gave a parable to help us see God's love and what sorrow when we reject it. Rejection happens in our unbelief, our doubting God's promises. Our coldness in relationship to God. Our rejecting the Holy Spirit leading and guiding us. Our lack of joyful celebration in God's presence. Our unwillingness to suffer for justice. Our selfish working for our own success rather than putting our lives on the line for doing God's will. Our refusing to let the Holy Spirit cleanse us so that we can be open channels for God's love.

But God waits for our return again today, to receive us with a love that will not let us go.

~ ecc

❖ JOHN 3:14-21 ❖

❖ ADVOCATE, COUNSELOR ❖

The King's Speech tells of a king limited in carrying out his responsibilities by the stranglehold of stuttering. With his wife's urging he did reach for help, engaging a speech therapist who also became his counselor, advocate, and finally a true friend.

Disciplines his therapist demanded were extremely frustrating and caused the king anger while doing exercises and monotonous drills. Fortunately, the young king persisted in receiving help before the day of his greatest challenge. War had come and he needed quickly to galvanize his country into action. This time he couldn't rely on others. The king must give this speech. Ears were glued to radios everywhere as the broadcast opened. The king stood ready but fearful, speaking with his therapist beside him in the studio. Whenever he paused with panic, the therapist supportively gave an encouraging prompt that kept giving him confidence and strength to continue. It was an electrifying speech.

Scripture describes the work of the Holy Spirit for us in these same ways—counselor, advocate, and friend. Jesus promised after going away, he would send the Holy Spirit to be with us forever. When God calls us to do a kingdom task, we are promised the Holy Spirit to stand beside us, touching our God-given abilities, giving strength to accomplish what we are called to do.

So, why are we fearful? We believe God's word, don't we? Yes, and no, because our believing is so small compared to the strength God offers. What is it that looms too large for you today? If you ask, God will give you amazing strength to accomplish it as you pray.

> O Holy Spirit, enter in, and in our hearts your work begin,
> And make our hearts your dwelling. . . .
> Your strength in us upwelling.
> In your radiance, life from heaven now is given, overflowing,
> Gift of gifts beyond all knowing (*ELW* #786).

~ ecc

❖ JOHN 16:1-15 ❖

❖ How Original Is Sin? ❖

Citizens of the United States make up five percent of the world's population. Yet we consume eighty-five percent of antidepressants. I realize, of course, that these medications are sometimes used for purposes other than combating depression. Could they afford them, people in other parts of the world might consume their share.

Yet one must ask if there is another story in these statistics. Is it possible that our culture puts so much stress on being happy and successful that many cannot bear it when life gets tough? For us who claim to be Christian, is it possible that we have a hard time accepting what is called "original sin"?

I have always appreciated the realism of the apostle Paul. He understood the character of human nature. In his letter to the Romans he writes about the complexity of human nature. We set lofty goals, yet fall short repeatedly. We have good intentions at the beginning of the day yet look back in the evening over goals that were only half achieved at best. "I can will what is right, but I cannot do it," Paul says. "For I do not do the good I want, but the evil I do not want is what I do" (Rom. 7:18b-19).

Paul is not suggesting that we give up trying to grow in faith and in love. Rather, his accent is on accepting our brokenness, coming back to the cross for forgiveness, and then moving on to the next day, knowing we will fail again, but confident that out of our imperfect efforts some good will come.

After wrestling honestly with his shortcomings, Paul ends the passage in Romans with words appropriate for us as well: "Thanks be to God through Jesus Christ our Lord!" (v. 25).

As we sing in an old gospel song, "If I have walked in my own sinful way, dear Lord forgive." Forgiven, we rise to new life. What better antidote for depression?

~ hwc

❖ ROMANS 7:14-25 ❖

❖ Claiming the Power of God over Evil ❖

Exorcism? That sound "so Catholic" many would say. Yes, Roman Catholics have practiced exorcism throughout their history. In fact, after some neglect in recent years that church is giving it new attention.

But what about Lutherans and other Protestants?

Exorcism begins with the recognition that there is evil in the world. Whether we relate it to a personal devil or simply a vague sense that there are powers of evil beyond our comprehension, most Christians believe in the reality of evil. There are too many things that go wrong in our lives and the world around us that cannot be explained by calling them mistakes and errors of our own making.

Though some question the account about Martin Luther hurling an inkwell against the wall of his Wartburg cell, he certainly believed in the power of evil.

Exorcism involves using the Name of God, the Name of Jesus, and the power of the Holy Spirit to counteract those alien forces when we feel powerless in ourselves.

When a pastor blesses us with the benediction, it is done "in the Name of the Father, and of the Son, and of the Holy Spirit." We believe there is power in the Name. This is not magic. We believe that there is real power and protection in the Name.

More often than not it is in the hours of the night that we encounter our most strenuous battles with evil. I have found it helpful at such times to verbalize a prayer of exorcism by saying: "In the Name of Jesus, I demand that you leave me in peace." Then I claim the promises of Scripture, such as Philippians 4:7: "The peace of God, which surpasses all understanding, will guard your hearts and your minds in Christ Jesus."

As we sing in the Reformation hymn: "We tremble not, unmoved we stand; they cannot over pow'r us" (*ELW* #503).

~ hwc

❖ PHILIPPIANS 4:4-7 ❖

Getting It Right the First Time

Like most men, I used to resist asking for directions when on a trip. I wanted to prove that I knew how to find the destination without help. I paid for my stupidity in added miles and wasted time. Eventually I decided to do it the easier way—ask for directions.

It's a parable of life, isn't it? How often have we all had to retrace our steps because we didn't get it right the first time? Or even the second time?

In Epiphany season we have Bible readings from the book of Jonah. He was the kind of fellow who insisted he knew the way. Unfortunately, it ended in chaos in the belly of the fish. Then he decided to follow God's leading and go to Nineveh to call the citizens to repentance. The results were remarkable. The city repented and turned to God. Jonah should have been thrilled and satisfied.

But he still didn't get it right. He harbored the idea that when people sinned they should be punished. Somehow he couldn't get into his head that when God forgives the punishment is revoked, the sentence is stayed, the sinner is set free.

Judgment and mercy. Those are the key words that run through the Bible. We come under judgment when we run counter to the will and purpose of God. Jonah got that part right. But Jonah didn't remember the other part—mercy. The final purpose of God is not judgment, but mercy and grace.

This is why we say that folks are wrong who think the Old Testament is about judgment and the New Testament about mercy. Judgment and mercy are written in all parts of the Bible. We, like Jonah, may take some pleasure in pronouncing judgment on persons we think deserve it. But once we get the right directions we can only want what God wants—grace and mercy.

~ hwc

2 CHRONICLES 7:13-15

❖ LIFE'S SMALL HINGES ❖

I had injured my ankle playing basketball. That meant I would be a spectator instead of a player for a time. Just as I was about to enter the gymnasium balcony to watch a game I heard an authoritative voice from the second floor of the high school: "Herbert! Herbert!" There stood Jesse McClure, my eleventh grade social studies teacher. "Herbert," she called, "I want you to come up and join our extemporaneous speaking group."

I need to explain that Miss McClure was a combination of Eleanor Roosevelt and Margaret Thatcher. When she called, you answered. Though I had no idea at the moment what "extemporaneous speaking" was about, I turned on my heel and ascended the stairs. That night changed my life. I soon learned that I not only was able to speak on my feet after brief preparation, but that I actually enjoyed it. That, in turn, led to original oratory in high school, debate in college, and a lifetime of preaching and teaching.

These kinds of unexpected encounters are sometimes called the "small hinges" of life, moments when the doors of our lives swung open in a direction we could never have imagined at the time.

It certainly was that way with the disciples. They are simply going about their fishing business on the shores of Galilee. Along comes Jesus. Had they heard of him? Possibly so. But did they expect that on that day their lives would turn in completely unexpected directions? Certainly not. But it happened, and from that moment and on nothing would be the same.

This would be a good day to think about those "small hinge" experiences that changed your life. And it would also be a good time to reflect on how a word of encouragement from you to some young person in your congregation or neighborhood might be a "small hinge" for them as well.

~ hwc

❖ MATTHEW 4:18-22 ❖

❖ Power in the Word ❖

Are you aware of the power that may be in a word you may speak, for good or for bad and often when least aware of it happening?

We were invited to Spirit of Joy Lutheran Church, Clarkdale, Arizona, for the joyous dedication of their new sanctuary. Pastor Mari Larson, their much-loved and faithful pastor, reminded us that years before we had come to her Minnesota home when she was only ten. She remembered how Bishop Chilstrom, looking at her, suggested she might become a pastor. It was a powerful word, she explained, stirring up early within her what was to become God's strong and persistent call to ministry.

Much greater than ours can ever be, God's word is powerful, packed with action. When the earth "was a formless void" (Gen. 1:1), God spoke, creating light and land and plants and animals and humankind! Humankind was created in relationship with God.

When and since Adam and Eve broke that relationship with God, Paul says, "All . . . are under the power of sin" (Rom. 3:9). Arland Hultgren in *Paul's Letter to the Romans* says, "For the love of humanity, God is not willing to cease relationship with his own (p. 116). . . . So it is God's activity, by which he justifies, or sets relationships right between humanity and himself . . . sets free from the power of sin . . . sheer gift (p. 149)." Hultgren quotes A. Nygren (footnote p. 75), "It is not man's faith that gives the gospel power; quite the contrary, it is the power of the gospel that makes it possible for one to believe."

Empowered to proclaim it, Paul professes, "I am not ashamed of the gospel, it is the power of God for salvation . . ." (Rom. 1:16). Will you claim this power of God for yourself today?

~ ecc

❖ ROMANS 1:16-17; 3:9-12 ❖

❖ Forget Not All His Benefits ❖

Winter mornings on our South Dakota farm were very cold. Even in the house it was cold by morning because the furnace fire had burned out. Our wood-burning furnace was in the basement. Last thing at night before going to bed, my father would go down to "bank the furnace." That was a process that kept heat in the house as long as possible by stacking logs a certain way so that when the fire was burned out, coals would be still alive to ignite new logs quickly. However, it is fire that heats, not coals. So by morning the house was cold.

On those winter mornings, first sounds we'd hear were the 5:30 a.m. clanging of the cast iron furnace door opening and closing. Signs of our ever-faithful dad putting in fresh logs to ignite a fire. Soon heat would be wafting through registers in our upstairs bedrooms so we could dress in comfort. Remembering those sounds still warms my heart as I think about my father's love and care. Although never given to much show of affection, his actions showed love for us. His actions gave us a deep sense of security. His faithfulness gave us trust.

In Psalm 103 we see God's action like a loving parent showing love and faithfulness. Notice the verbs: God forgives. Heals. Redeems. Crowns us with steadfast love and mercy. Satisfies. Renews. Works vindication. Removes our transgressions. Has compassion for his children. Knows how we were made. Is merciful and gracious. Is full of steadfast love. What gifts to claim!

My father is gone now. But whenever I recall the clanging of the furnace door on a cold morning, it still warms my heart with security from my father's love. May recalling God's actions warm our hearts on a wintry day. "Do not forget all his benefits."

~ ecc

❖ PSALM 103:1-22 ❖

❖ Born Again and Again and Again ❖

Youth of our LCA Minnesota Synod were gathered in assembly under the theme of baptism. In a group activity throughout the week, teenagers worked hard creating a cope—a finger length vestment a pastor wears over the alb while serving communion—for Herb, as bishop, to wear at the closing communion service. It was an object lesson that made an unforgettable impact of what they had learned in confirmation and now again at this conference, that in baptism, we are born again. But also, that we need daily to renew that covenant with God. In other words, we need to be born again every day. So on the bottom of the circular white cope, they attached words made of large red felt letters—BORN AGAIN AND AGAIN AND AGAIN AND AGAIN.

Shortly after that event, I was invited by women from a Baptist church to lead them in an all-day retreat. Their theme was "Daily Renewal." I brought the cope our youth had made and hung it front and center in the gathering space. They were surprised to learn that being born again is important for Lutherans, too. But once is not enough, I explained. For we believe we must be born again every new day.

Luther explains that baptism is important in our everyday living: Each new day we need to die to sin and self and be born again as a child of God.

> Daily the old person in us with all our sins and evil desires is to be drowned through sorrow for sin and repentance, and that daily a new person is to come forth and rise up to live before God in righteousness and purity forever.
> (*Luther's Small Catechism*, The Sacrament of Holy Baptism)

> Therefore we were buried with him by baptism into his death, so that, just as Christ was raised from the dead by the glory of the Father, we too might walk in newness of life (Rom. 6:4).

~ ecc

❖ JOHN 3:1-13 ❖

❖ Where to Get Good Advice ❖

I enjoy working on crossword puzzles. One soon learns that crossword puzzle creators use certain words on regular occasion because those words have common letters. For example, a frequent clue is the phrase, "Witch of ______." The answer is "Endor." The word works well because those five letters (e–n–d–o–r) are used often in many other words.

Who was this "Witch of Endor?" You will find her in 1 Samuel 28. King Saul is in trouble. He needs advice and would like to talk to Samuel. The problem is that Samuel is dead. Saul decides that he may be able to get in touch with Samuel through a medium, also commonly known as a "witch." It worked. The Witch of Endor was able to bring Samuel back from the dead. Unfortunately, Saul's hope that Samuel might bring him words of encouragement went bad. Instead of good news, Samuel utters words of judgment on Saul for his misdeeds and abandonment of God's way.

Regardless of what you think of this unusual story from the Bible, it carries some important lessons for life. First and foremost, be careful what you ask for. You may get something completely unexpected. More important than that, look into your own soul for the best counsel of all. Saul knew in his heart of hearts that he had abandoned the way of God. He knew his lust for power and authority were not what God had expected of him. He didn't need to summon Samuel through a witch to inform him that he needed to change his ways and return to the vision God had planned for his leadership of the people of Israel.

And we? Don't we all know in our heart of hearts how God wants us to live?

~ hwc

❖ JAMES 1:19-21 ❖

❖ Those Unexpected Saints ❖

Every now and then we are in for a surprise when someone we had judged to be a "sinner" turns out to be anything but that. We think of them as bad apples in the barrel. Then they say or do something that bowls us over. In that moment we realize that we have completely misjudged them.

"A tax collector?" some bystanders might have asked. "How can a scoundrel like Levi be a disciple of Jesus?"

And again, "A political radical? A fellow on the far left? How can Simon the Zealot be one of the chosen twelve?"

"A woman taken in adultery? How can Jesus forgive her so easily?"

"An enemy of the followers of Jesus, determined to put any of them to death when he finds them? How can we trust that this man Saul has really been converted?"

Hidden away in Hebrews 11 is another such character. In what is sometimes referred to as the "Hall of Faith" we meet memorable biblical stars like Abraham, Isaac, Jacob, Moses, Samuel, David, the prophets, and others. Then comes a shocker. Included in this list is "the prostitute Rahab" (v. 31). We read it again. Is this right? A prostitute numbered among the great saints of God? Indeed she is. The woman who sheltered and protected Joshua and Caleb when they scouted out the Promised Land is accorded the same high status as the others.

Hardly seems fair. But can God be held to our human standards of fairness? If so, who really measures up? Here's a reminder to be careful when we make judgments of others. Their circumstances of life may not have allowed for them to sit in the front pew. No, not even in the back pew. But by the grace of God they may rank ahead of most others.

~ hwc

❖ LUKE 18: 9-14 ❖

❖ Good Habits for Tough Times ❖

Habits may be good or bad. Developing good ones lends confidence to daily tasks.

A navy helicopter pilot learned this as he was about to make his first landing on an aircraft carrier. The ocean was rough that day. Gigantic waves beat against the carrier. The ship was tossing in heavy seas. But the inexperienced pilot remembered the advice of a seasoned senior officer: "Wiggle your toes." A simple act, yet the young pilot discovered it worked. As he descended to the deck he wiggled his toes. It helped him concentrate on the task at hand. He alit safely.

Isn't the Christian life a bit like this? We face challenges every day. Some require little concentration. Others, however, can throw us into a sweaty frenzy, testing even the most seasoned believer. It's at times like this that little habits, honed over years of experience, help us to meet the challenge. For Christians the best way to "wiggle our toes" is to pray. And to pray regularly means that when we suddenly come up against a seemingly impossible challenge we reach into the depth of our souls to connect with the Spirit of God, our Helper and Counselor and Advocate.

I think Jesus favored good habits. It's clear that he attended worship at the temple and prayer at the synagogue. When the disciples asked him for a suggestion on how to pray he gave them the Lord's Prayer, a prayer we all use with regularity, not only on Sundays but through the week as well. When Corinne and I pray the Lord's Prayer at the end of our morning devotions I feel that it incorporates everything I need to give us stability for another day, for challenges large and small. Then as the day unfolds we keep "wiggling our toes," finding needed confidence as we encounter whatever the day may bring.

~ hwc

❖ EPHESIANS 4:14-16 ❖

❖ BACKSIDE OF THE MOUNTAIN ❖

John Donne was one of England's greatest seventeenth century preachers. His greatness had to do both with walking among his people, knowing their struggles, and being vulnerable to his own. So his preaching was to himself as well as to his flock. Doubt came to him as to others. But he says, it means neither that it's wrong nor that we're going astray.

> Doubt wisely; in strange way
> To stand inquiring right is not to stray;
> To sleep or run, wrong is.
> On a huge hill
> Cragged and steep,
> Truth stands, and he that will
> Reach her, about must, and about must go;
> And what the hill's suddenness resist, win so.
>
> (*Daily Readings from Lutheran Classics*, edited by Paul Ofstedahl, Augsburg Fortress, 1990)

Our journey through life is often uncertain. Sometimes our path takes us to the backside of the mountain where we meet a beast, never before encountered—a situation where we're left with no coping skills. We may be desperate and angry. That happened to Job.

When his family and fortune were suddenly lost, he despaired. Disease racked his body. Those he thought were his friends betrayed him. When it seemed even God deserted him, Job cursed the day he was born and cried, "Oh that I knew where I might find him" (Job 23:3).

Truly he found himself on the backside of the mountain. Job had met the beast of doubt and bitterness. He was left with no coping skills. That was when God told Job, "Pour out the overflowings of your anger" (Job 40:11).

When we hit tight spots, God wants us to do the same: empty out our pain. Even though God seems too far away to hear, God does hear. God does care. God will answer. The emptying makes space for the filling. Then we, like Job, by the power of the Spirit, even from the backside of the mountain can proclaim: "I know that my redeemer lives" (Job 19:25).

~ ecc

❖ JOB 19:1-29 ❖

❖ Hidden Faults ❖

There is a procedure called "debridement," which is to surgically remove lacerated, macerated, or contaminated tissue from a wound. Because debris takes energy out of the body and can even cause harmful effects, it is important to remove it. Because the removing can be painful, topical or general anesthesia is used. Healing can happen once the wound is made clean.

Often as debris accumulates it is hardly noticed. One gradually gets accustomed to or perhaps denies its existence. So similar to the way our hidden faults accumulate. Others may see them. God knows they're there. But we get used to them and make excuses. In one way it's good we cannot see the depths of our faults and sin. Luther said that would crush us. So God is merciful in revealing them to us only in part.

Like removing debris, allowing God to reveal and remove our hidden faults can be painful. God's word is harsh, like a floodlight burning into the corners of our soul.

> The word of God is living and active, sharper than a two-edged sword, piercing until it divides soul from spirit, joints from marrow; it is able to judge the thoughts and intentions of the heart. And before him no creature is hidden, but all are naked and laid bare to the eyes of the one to whom we must render an account (Heb. 4:12).

We need the mirror of God's word to show us our sins. We need regular worship, confessing sins both known and unknown. We need to gather as a community of faith to confess personal, community, and national sin. We need together to hear God's word, the law to show us our sins, and the gospel that declares forgiveness. We need debridement of our souls—God to clear us of hidden faults. And the healing that brings new vitality with the Holy Spirit's power to proclaim this life-giving good news to others.

~ ecc

❖ PSALM 19:7-14 ❖

❖ On Being "Too Christian" ❖

At a meeting in Geneva, Switzerland a Danish friend told me over coffee that she had just returned from a pleasure trip to the United States. When she said she had been to California I asked if she had by chance visited Solvang. Solvang is a city that has been transformed over the years into a place that looks like it might have been lifted out of a corner of Denmark and set down in California. Wherever one turns one sees things "Danish"—shops, churches, public squares, and civic buildings.

It was natural for me to ask my friend, "How did you like Solvang?" Her reply set me back on my heels. With candor she said, "Too Danish!" She thought that the creators of Solvang had tried a bit too hard to duplicate a Danish village.

The same might be said of Lindsborg, Kansas. It's a delightful place. Each time I've been to this equally quaint place I imagine myself in Sweden. I've been to Sweden enough times, however, to know that a visitor from Sweden might well say the same of Lindsborg: "Too Swedish!"

Because I marvel at the creativity and imagination of those who remake places like Solvang and Lindsborg, I'll never tire of visiting these lovely places. But I must also say that I can't help but draw a comparison with some folks I've known of whom we might say: "Too Christian!" I have in mind those who give the impression that it's enough to carry the outer trappings of being a Christian, but whose life in Christ is only skin deep. Of them we sometimes observe that they are so "heavenly" that they are "no earthly good."

Yes, God wants us to bear the marks of being a believer. But God also wants it to be a life that penetrates to the core of our being.

~ hwc

❖ ROMANS 12:9-16 ❖

❖ SEEING IN THE DARK ❖

When my failing eyesight made it impossible for me to drive on the open road I felt a good deal of frustration. After so many decades of enjoying travel by car, including reading maps and then a GPS, I felt quite helpless in the passenger seat.

Then one day I made a discovery. I noted that I was able to read the GPS when we traveled at night. That gave me an idea: "Put a jacket over your head in the daytime and you may be able to read that screen." Sure enough—it worked. Folks passing us on the highway may have wondered who that strange character was in the next car, hunched over with his jacket over his head. I could care less. Those few moments in the dark made it possible for me to feel useful in giving Corinne some clues as to where we were and how far it would be to the next turn in the road.

It occurred to me, of course, that there was a lesson for life in this. We would all prefer to travel in sunshine. Unfortunately, that's not how it is. Inevitably, there will be obstacles, including times in the dark. Most of us have learned, however, that there are things to be seen in the dark that we never dreamed possible.

I'm reminded of childhood days on my Uncle Sig's farm. In the 1930s there were only lanterns and candles to illuminate the farm. After milking his cows on a dark winter night Sig made his way through the darkness with a milk pail in one hand and a lantern in the other as he walked from barn to house.

And so it was in ancient Israel. At night it was dark everywhere. The psalmist suggests that his "GPS" was "the word of God." By this light in the darkness he could walk with confidence.

~ hwc

❖ PSALM 119:105-112 ❖

❖ Know That the Lord Is God ❖

"An Opportunity to Practice not Being God," was the title of Peter Marty's article that caught our eye. Oh, but who would ever pretend to be God? One certainly doesn't set out to do that. And even if the fault is there, as Marty suggests, do we need weekly time for undoing it?

A mother tells of her serious talk with her daughter who was preparing to leave for college. Because it was known as a party college, the mother felt urgency to give some protective advice. But it was not met kindly. Her daughter whirled away on her fashion heels saying, "Mom, I can handle it!"

That's precisely the motion inherent in the soul of every human person in our relationship with God. Luther explains that this turning away motion is basic to our original sin. What also is inherent in this turning action is that we refuse to see our own action or acknowledge it. Perhaps even worse is that we cannot see or acknowledge the depth of our sin or our helplessness to make it right with God. It's a turning away from God who knows and understands us while we continue to stroke ego and self-determination to make it on our own. We, like daughter to parent, are telling God, "I can handle it!" And like the mother, God waits until parent help is finally sought and love is accepted.

Knowing this universal human need, the psalmist declares," Know that the Lord is God. It is he that has made us, and we are his; we are his people, and the sheep of his pasture" (Ps. 100:3).

So enter God's presence and courts with praise. You need regular worship. You need to remember and give thanks. Let's memorize Psalm 100 so we have daily help and encouragement to worship our God. Daily help in practicing not being God. Weekly may not be enough. Daily is better!

~ ecc

❖ PSALM 100 ❖

❖ Safe in Dad's Arms ❖

Once every summer we made the trek to grandparents still on their South Dakota farm. During those three fun-filled days, our young children explored and discovered so many adventures, new every visit. There were baby raccoons with white and black circling their eyes nesting in the abandoned threshing machine. Frogs to catch in a jar. Fireflies to chase after dark. Tiny garter snakes to put in a quart jar with holes pounded open in the cover for oxygen. And always a fresh batch of kittens to locate. Because the days were too few and none long enough, they stayed up way past their bedtime.

When heading home the third day, we had three tired children. Routine had us stopping in Windom to put on pajamas and have ice cream at the Dairy Queen. And they were asleep before we got out of the parking lot. Two hours later their dad would gather up limp arms and legs and lovingly carry each child safely up to bed. Next morning at breakfast when our son said he knew nothing after the Dairy Queen, I asked if he wasn't afraid we might forget him there. "No," he said confidently, "I knew I'd be safe in dad's arms and he would carry me safe to my bed."

After the funeral, a widow pressed the question, "Where is my husband now?" With a vague promise of heaven, this widow, still longing to care for her husband needed a clearer picture. To be sure he was safe.

Scripture is not helpful in defining the place. Words from John are the best help we have, as they draw us to God's heart of love. And to trust wherever it will be, we will be safe in the strong arms of God. And in the promise, "I . . . will take you to myself" (John 14:3). We need faith like the child, "I knew I'd be safe in Dad's arms."

~ ecc

❖ JOHN 14:1-6 ❖

❖ There's a Solo in There ❖

Nancy had sung in the church choir, as she said, "all my life." A new, young choir director came to their church and after several weeks of recognizing the unique quality of Nancy's voice took her aside and said seriously, "There's a solo in there." Always thinking her voice mediocre, she only knew that she loved singing. With the encouragement of her choir director and voice lessons, her singing grew ever more beautiful. Soon she was singing solos in church and beyond, so easy, so natural.

Robert Frost wrote in his poem "A Minor Bird": There must be something wrong, With trying to silence a song.

Silencing a God-given gift often leaves one frustrated and depressed. Ernest Becker, author of *The Denial of Death*, suggests that our greatest sin may be denying the use of our best gifts. When unlocked, those best gifts flow so easily. And we're surprised. There's such great satisfaction. We wonder why we didn't discover this sooner. Using our best gifts is satisfying and rewarding for us and becomes a great blessing to others.

It was said of journalist Gary Wills, "Behind impassive expression, ideas and words form and churn like storm clouds waiting to rush from his pen."

Studies prove that using one's best gifts in a career gives a high level of job satisfaction. So in choosing careers, young people do well to study aptitudes and areas of best achievement. After retirement, we need to remember what work gave us high satisfaction. The task is to imagine how those best gifts can be used, perhaps in volunteer work. Studies show this improves both health and longevity.

Nancy learned that the Spirit had apportioned to her the unique gift of a beautiful singing voice. Using it brought both great personal joy and a blessing to others. True, also for your best gifts and mine. So ask God to touch your best gift and bring it to usefulness today.

~ ecc

❖ I CORINTHIANS 12:1-11 ❖

❖ Amazing Good News ❖

What amazing good news! As a parish pastor, I was caught up in the turmoil of a young person who was overwhelmed about a terrible decision that turned into a nightmare. It included getting caught up in a scam and receiving illegal funds. When the scam broke there was a felony charge that brought sleepless nights and unrelenting fear and uncertainty.

Then came a glimmer of hope. After learning that because it had happened while under age, there was possibility of getting the felony erased from the record. No stone was left unturned. The work was hard but worth it. One day my phone rang bringing good news. How can I forget those words of relief: "It's expunged from the record! I'm free of all charges."

It is the same for all of us. Every day we stand guilty under God's law. Christ intercedes for us. He clears the record, removing our guilt and shame. What amazing good news there is for us:

> While we still were sinners Christ died for us. . . . we have been justified by his blood . . . reconciled to God (Rom. 8-10).
>
> Though your sins are like scarlet, they shall be like snow (Isa. 1:18).
>
> Just as I am without one plea,
> but that thy blood was shed for me,
> And that thou bidd'st me come to thee,
> O Lamb of God, I come, I come.
> Just as I am, and waiting not,
> to rid my soul of one dark blot,
> To thee, whose blood can cleanse each spot,
> O Lamb of God, I come, I come.
> Just as I am, thou wilt receive,
> wilt welcome, pardon, cleanse, relieve;
> Because thy promise I believe,
> O Lamb of God, I come, I come (*LBW* #296).

Amazing good news!

~ ecc

❖ ROMANS 5:6-11 ❖

❖ God Answers Prayer ❖

Betty was eight years old and serious about saying her evening prayers. She said her routine "God bless" prayers but added others of her own from time to time, assured that God would hear and answer.

The whole family had been invited with the dad on a certain day's business trip and would be entertained in the home of the chief executive. The children, especially, were included because of various connections. The invitation had come early in advance and the host family was planning special entertainment for the children.

Then came the blip in the family plans. Betty received an invitation to her good friend's birthday party on that day. And for an eight-year-old, that was the highest of social events, one that could not be turned down. Alternatives were considered but it was finally decided the family should stay intact and go with the dad.

Early on the morning of the family outing, Betty awoke with a high fever, very sick. Plans changed quickly and the dad went alone. Mother and the other children stayed home with Betty who did not get to the birthday party either.

A few days later, after Betty was well again, she confessed to her mother that she had prayed to God asking that someone in the family would get sick so plans would change and she'd still be able to go to the birthday party. God did answer her prayer. But not in the way she had hoped. Someone did get sick. But she never thought about that it might be herself.

God does answer prayer. But often it is not the answer we expect. We gradually learn to also pray "not my will but thy will be done." And we also begin gradually to learn that praying is not so much going to God to get what we want, but more just being in God's presence.

~ ecc

❖ MATTHEW 7:7 ❖

❖ The Heart of Luther's Teaching ❖

On this day in 1546 Martin Luther died in Eisleben, the same city where he had been born a little more than 63 years earlier. He had come to Eisleben to settle a family dispute, took ill, and died before he could return to Wittenberg.

Though he never wished for a church to be named after him, it happened. Why? Because of his name? No, surely not. I would prefer to believe that it was because of what he believed and taught—we can do nothing to merit God's grace and mercy. It is by grace alone through faith that we are saved.

This is no easy idea for us to comprehend. We admire those who pull themselves up by their own bootstraps, who work hard for each achievement in life, who never give up. Is there something wrong with these ideas? No, not so long as we are speaking only about life together in community. In that setting, even an avowed atheist may do more good for the community than a church-going neighbor.

Luther's idea is more radical than that. He forces us to think, first and foremost, not about our relationship with our neighbor, but our relationship with God. When we stand in this place we must look inward, weighing our motivations for doing things and asking the question: "Have I done all that is expected of me?"

In the awesome presence of God we soon realize that even our best, most sincere deeds fall far short of the perfection God expects of us. In this place we have but one way to find peace. That is to cast ourselves entirely on the mercy of God. Once we have done so, we are ready to move back into everyday life, broken and humbled, but ready to serve our neighbor in love.

~ hwc

❖ EPHESIANS 2:1-10 ❖

❖ Dah! Why Don't We Get It? ❖

Malachi is one of the Old Testament prophets we hear from during the season of Epiphany. He lived at a time when Israel had abandoned its enthusiasm for God. They were drifting.

But they were also puzzled. Why, they wondered, weren't they being blessed by God?

Along comes Malachi and says, in effect, "Dah! Don't you see the connection between how you are living and your relationship with God?" Malachi pointed specifically to their paltry giving. He speaks plainly for God, "You are robbing me . . . Bring the full tithe into the storehouse, that there may be food in my house, and thus put me to the test . . . see if I will not throw open the windows of heaven and pour down for you an overflowing blessing" (Duet. 3:8-10).

This is a biblical text that would be easy to misunderstand. It appears that all we need to do is be more generous and God will bless us with whatever we want. That would be a faulty conclusion. Malachi is speaking of something much deeper. The core of the issue is that they have moved away from God. Malachi begins his prophecy with this word from God: "I have loved you" (1:2). That is the starting point—God's love for us. God always makes the first move. Because they had lost sight of this, they had also lost sight of their responsibility to respond to that grace. They were stingy because they had forgotten how generous God is.

We don't think much about stewardship in the church until the fall season when congregations stress the need to pay the bills for the current year and set the budget for the next. How much better if we could keep before us in all seasons of the year the need to respond to grace with generosity. It's so simple. Dah—why don't we get it?

~ hwc

❖ DEUTERONOMY 8:6-14 ❖

❖ GIVING THANKS FOR OUR PASTORS ❖

This is a good day to remember the earliest Lutheran pastors in North America. The very first was Rasmus Jensen, a Danish pastor who sailed in 1619 with sixty-four explorers to Hudson Bay. Jensen died on this day in 1620. Most of the crew on the ill-fated expedition were dead by the next spring.

The Danes learned their lesson. When they returned to the West nearly fifty years later to plant colonies in the West Indies, Pastor Slagelse established Frederick Lutheran Church on St. Thomas in the Virgin Islands. This oldest of all ELCA congregations continues to have a strong witness and ministry. I have had the privilege of preaching at this vibrant congregation on occasion.

Other early pioneer pastors included Reorus Torkillus and John Campanius from Sweden. Their churches at Wilmington and below Philadelphia eventually became Episcopal when the Swedish church failed to send successor pastors.

Germans like to trace their initial roots in the West to Justus Falckner who was ordained by the Swedes at Gloria Dei Church in Philadelphia. He went on to establish German-speaking congregations from Albany down through New Jersey. He also gave pastoral care to the Dutch Lutherans who settled in present day New York City.

All this may seem like ancient, even rather dull and uninteresting history to some readers. But where would we be today were it not for pioneer pastors who were willing to leave a more comfortable parish in Europe and venture to the unknown world with the good news of the gospel?

This may be a day to think about the congregation where you are a member and to give thanks for faithful pastors who founded it. In those dusty old anniversary books you will find the stories of those who sacrificed to give life to your church. Give thanks for solid foundations of faith.

~ hwc

❖ MATTHEW 16:13-18 ❖

❖ Parent Pain ❖

How did the father even dare to take his son out, never knowing when or where it *may* happen. First the foaming at the mouth and then grinding the teeth. Can't you imagine everyone staring and how the parent would feel helpless and embarrassed? Not only would onlookers stare, but they would be also blaming the parents. That's what onlookers did, asking parents of the blind man, "Who sinned, this man or his parents?" (John 9:2). In our culture, we sympathize in the face of a child's physical illness. But when a child displays mental or behavioral disorders, parents often feel implications of fingers pointing their way.

After the Jan. 8, 2011, shooting spree in Tucson, AZ, when six were killed and several were wounded, including Congresswoman Giffords, many reported having seen signs of mental illness in the 22-year-old who was responsible. And some blamed the parents who could only cry out their pain. Imagine all they'd been through, like the father who came pleading to Jesus, "Have mercy on us and help us."

Just as there was healing in the hands of Jesus then, help can come now through psychiatric research, counseling, medication, and treatment. But parents still suffer the reproach and judgment of those who have simple answers. Often times it comes from parents who have not suffered hard times, whose journey has been without difficult challenge—parents who still believe good parenting always produces ideal children.

For parents of all ages who face difficulty and sometimes impossible challenges, Jesus is still listening when we come pleading, "Have pity on us and help us." Whether there is quick and complete healing or a lifetime of continued pain, we can be sure of one thing. God's presence will give sturdiness and strength to endure. You who have grown strong through struggle may be God's best answer then, to help other parents who plead for pity and help.

~ ecc

❖ MARK 9:14-29 ❖

❖ Surely It Is God Who Saves Us ❖

Jesus used parables or stories in his teaching to help his followers understand the Scriptures. Stories are effective today as well, such as this one to help us understand God's saving help.

Innocently playing one day near his master, a small pet dog was suddenly accosted by a large angry dog. Too small to defend himself and too afraid to fight back, he instinctively did the opposite, cowering on the ground. Like a beast, the big dog leaped fiercely upon him, ready to tear him apart. Defenseless, the little dog knew that all hope depended solely on the action of his master. So he cried out with a desperate yelp, knowing his master would come to rescue him. It was his only hope.

The storyteller likened the beast to the devil: "Cast all your anxiety on [God], because he cares for you. Discipline yourselves, keep alert. Like a roaring lion, your adversary the devil prowls around, looking for someone to devour" (1 Peter 5:8). He then concludes by likening us to the situation of the little dog and the compassion of the master to Jesus, who alone through his death and resurrection can save us who are members of his flock. The yelp of the little dog is our cry for Jesus' help, our only hope.

If we put our trust in him, he will not allow the enemy to do us violence. He will send his angels to save us from the devil. Throwing ourselves before God when we cannot trust our own strength, we know Christ will rescue us. For that is why he came.

> Surely it is God who saves me; I shall trust and have no fear.
> For the Lord defends and shields me and his saving help is near.
> So rejoice as you draw water from salvation's healing spring;
> In the day of your deliv'rance, thank the lord, his mercies sing
> (WOV #635).

~ ecc

❖ 1 PETER 5:6-11 ❖

❖ Caring for the Whole Person ❖

Try getting your tongue around this name: Bartholomaes Ziegenbalg. Indeed, a mouthful! Born into a pious German home in Saxony, Ziegenbalg grew up to become a pioneer missionary in India. If you want a hero who accomplished a great deal in his short life—he was just thirty-six when he died on this day in 1719—this man would be a good candidate.

When he arrived as the first Lutheran missionary in India he was met with strong opposition from local Indian authorities. And though he had been commissioned by the king of Denmark to go to India, local Danish officials frustrated his work at every turn.

Ziegenbalg persisted in spite of this opposition. His translation of the New Testament into the local Tamil language is still in use after all these years. Contrary to some missionary groups who believed that it was sufficient to preach the gospel to native peoples, Ziegenbalg believed that we are called to minister to the whole person, spirit and body as well.

I have had the privilege of visiting mission settings around the world. Among many, I can never forget the colony of people with leprosy near Delhi, outcasts from society, who have found shelter and meaningful work because our Lutheran church in the United States is in partnership with the churches in India. The exquisitely colorful cloths that adorn table tops in our home, woven on looms by those misshapen hands, are constant reminders that Christ has called us to minister to the whole person and to find ways for those with maimed arms and missing legs to lead a productive life.

This is as it should be. When Jesus commissioned those first disciples to go with the gospel to new places, he did not simply command them to preach. No, healing the sick and lifting up the downhearted was as important as anything else they did.

~ hwc

❖ MATTHEW 10:1-8 ❖

❖ They All Walked Out ❖

When the searchlight of God's word starts piercing the corners of our hearts, God's law can certainly hit just where it hurts. And it can hit like a club. That is exactly what happened the morning our preacher used the Sermon on the Mount text: You are liable to judgment, says our Lord, if you break even one of these commandments. If angry with a sister or brother. If you insult a brother or sister. If you call someone a fool. On and on. Yes, and remember, God knows the thoughts and intents of the heart. If. If. If.

Stopping there, the pastor looked from the pulpit across the congregation, like watching the law of God stinging our souls. We thought for a minute he was going to call for a show of hands, whoever felt guilty. But instead, he suggested that maybe the guilty should just get up and walk out now.

Who among us hasn't had an altercation that may not completely be settled. Anger. Doing gossip. Insulting others. My mind went on a reverie imagining that if one of us who felt guilty got up to leave, so would another. And another. And another. I imagined the preacher finally into the gospel part of the sermon, speaking only to empty pews. Or maybe he himself would have walked out by then too. Anyway, none of that happened.

Instead we waited out the uncomfortable pounding of the law until the sweet good news of the gospel arrived. It saved us once again. Hear it.

> All of us . . . [are] by nature children of wrath. . . . But God, who is rich in mercy, out of the great love with which he loved us, even when we were dead through our trespasses, made us alive together with Christ (Eph. 2:3-5).

No one walked out. Instead we received the gospel. And so can you.

~ ecc

❖ MATTHEW 5:21-37 ❖

❖ THOSE WONDERFUL WOMEN ❖

Do you know a deaconess? Chances are most members of our churches do not. That's unfortunate. Deaconesses have always been an important part of the church's leadership. Orphanages, congregations, nursing homes, hospitals, and many other key ministries of the church were often started by these self-effacing servants of Christ. Though smaller in number now, they continue to play key roles in many aspects of church life.

Today is a good day to honor these servants. On our calendar of commemorations is a Norwegian deaconess who died on this day in 1921. Elizabeth Fedde was born on one of Norway's fjords. She was called to cross the Atlantic and work with Norwegian seamen on ships and in the harbor at New York City. Out of her early efforts grew one of the largest medical centers in the country's most populous city.

Later Fedde answered the call to move on to the Midwest where she established the Lutheran Deaconess Hospital in Minneapolis. Eventually this was folded into the broader ministry of the Fairview Hospital system, a leading medical center in the Twin Cities today. Who could have believed that the young girl born in far away Norway would play such a huge role in founding what are today such important health care missions in two of America's metropolitan centers?

A quick walk through the New Testament introduces us to women whose partnership with the apostles was crucial for the early church—Mary, Dorcas, Lydia, Priscilla, Junius, the daughters of Philip, Eunice, Lois—the list goes on and on.

Annie Okeson, Mildred and Myrtle Oslund, Luella Nelson, Margaret Wilson. These names may ring no bells for many others. But for me they were shapers of my early walk with Christ. Take some moments to name women who were important in shaping your life as a child of God.

~ hwc

❖ ACTS 16:12-15 ❖

❖ Who Am I? ❖

Madeline Albright had a brilliant career, first as a UN General Assembly delegate and in 1996 being named U.S. Secretary of State. No one knew that as she sat close to the president giving the Inaugural Address on January 1996 that it was also for her, a time of fresh sadness. She had just received documents revealing her hidden personal history. Raised Roman Catholic, she'd just learned that she was Jewish. What she and others would soon know is that there were thousands of adults in Europe, Russia, and the United States who, fifty years after World War II, were discovering roots different than what they'd been told. For her, it was an overwhelming identity confusion.

Her father, a brilliant diplomat with the Czechoslovakian government, saw trouble coming and fled with his family to London where he broadcast for the BBC. To protect the family from holocaust horrors, each was baptized Roman Catholic and a fictional past was created. Three of Madeline's grandparents and a dozen relatives died in the holocaust.

Identity confusion happens in various situations. Parents aren't whom you thought. Adopted, one has no history and wonders where he or she belongs. With such confusion, one feels stripped and bare. We need the surety of known family and friends. But one day that will be stripped away. When we come to die, we must go alone except for the One who promises to never leave or forsake us. It will be then that we do need to know the answer to our question of "Who am I?"

"I have been crucified with Christ . . . And the life I now live in the flesh, I live by faith in the Son of God who loved me and gave himself for me" (Gal. 2:20). We need to memorize and hold this treasured assurance in our hearts.

> When all supports are washed away, he then is all my hope and stay.
> On Christ the solid rock, I stand; all other ground is sinking sand (*ELW* #597).

~ ecc

❖ GALATIANS 2:20 ❖

❖ FINDING FREEDOM IN CHRIST ❖

It was my privilege to be Paul Granlund's pastor at St. Peter, Minnesota in the early 1970s. Artist in residence at Gustavus Adolphus College, Granlund fashioned hundreds of sculptures that may be found across the country and around the world in public squares and parks, corporate plazas, churches, and many other places.

One of my favorite Granlund pieces is "Birth of Freedom." Commissioned by Westminster Presbyterian Church in downtown Minneapolis, it brings many passersby to a standstill as they view the eighteen-foot-high work against the rose window of the church in the background.

Buried at the base of the sculpture is a figure that represents what the pastor of the congregation called "a state of spiritual lethargy, indifference, unawareness." Granlund referred to it as "a sleeping figure." On each side are two more images, male and female, who are reaching up as if in a quest for a better life. One appears to be just awakening. The other seems to be more alert, more in tune with the world around it. Finally, at the top is a figure with arms reaching for the heavens, giving the impression of one in free flight, like a bird winging its way to new horizons. Surrounding all four figures is a cube that resembles a box out of which the figures have emerged. I like to see it as a cross.

The inspiration for this work of art comes from Galatians 5:1: "For freedom Christ has set us free. Stand firm, therefore, and do submit again to the yoke of slavery."

When we left the parish at St. Peter we were given a smaller scale model of this spectacular work. It occupies a prominent place in our home. It reminds us—as well as our guests—that it is only in Christ's death and resurrection we find true freedom.

~ hwc

❖ GALATIANS 5:1, 13-14 ❖

❖ Focused on Cross and Resurrection ❖

Yesterday I wrote about one of my favorite Paul Granlund works of art. Today I want to focus on another.

When I was pastor at First Lutheran Church in St. Peter, Minnesota one of our families wanted to give a gift in memory of their son. Paul Granlund was commissioned to do the work.

Granlund liked to talk out his ideas. One morning just he and I sat in the empty sanctuary. He talked; I listened. He looked at the lines in the brick-work at the front of the sanctuary. He ruminated about the other elements that made up the space. He kept talking; I kept listening. Suddenly he said, "I think I have it. This space needs a cross that follows those diagonal lines. It needs something out of the ordinary. It also needs a cross that has more than one dimension."

The end result was a spectacular piece of artistry. A stationary eight-foot cross has a reverse image of the crucified Christ. But in front of it is a processional piece that bears a double image of Christ. In it one sees both the crucified Christ as well as the risen Lord. The fact that he was able to incorporate two elements in one—both crucifixion and resurrection—amazed me.

When the mobile part of the sculpture is carried in at the beginning of a service one can imagine Christ going to his death on the cross, bearing our sins and the sins of the world. At the end of the service, after we have heard the gospel and received the sacraments, the recessional gives one the feeling that the resurrected Christ is leading us, the Body of Christ, out into the world.

The final word at every service at First Lutheran Church in St. Peter is exactly right for this moment: "Renewed by Christ in word, water, bread and wine, we go into the world to witness and to serve."

~ hwc

❖ GALATIANS 2:20-21 ❖

❖ KINDNESS ❖

Riding the shuttle from the parking lot to the airport, we stopped to pick up a passenger—a good-looking, middle-aged muscular man who looked like he had a destination in mind. He was dressed in jeans and a neat loose shirt, comfortable for travel. With elbows on knees, he relaxed with head in his hands, as though seeking just a moment of needed rest before rushing off to catch his flight. When the van stopped he stood and grabbed his bag, ready to step down and out the door. Then I spied a whole ring of keys where he'd been sitting. Calling after him, I asked, "Sir, are these your keys?" As he recognized and reached for them, I said, "I prayed this morning, asking God to help me show special kindness to someone today." Stepping back to look into my eyes, he said, "God certainly answered your prayer today. Thank you!"

If you were to think over and list all the kindnesses shown to you today—big or small—how many would there be? Someone showed you his or her appreciation. Gave you a lift. Helped you. Encouraged you. Loved you. And what about God? What kindness has God shown you today? Love and care. Protection and forgiveness. Accepted you because of Jesus Christ. Called you precious. Royal priesthood status. Indeed, we have received much from the Lord and from many others.

Gratitude is the key that opens us to become channels of God's kindness to others. There's a song, "Count your blessings, name them one by one; and it will surprise you what the Lord has done." Let's make this a habit. Gratitude comes with counting our blessings.

Enumerating God's kindnesses opens us to proclaim to others great things God has done. Enumerating kindnesses from others makes us want to pass it on. With God's help, it will happen almost without our knowing.

You have tasted the kindness of the Lord (1 Peter 2:3 *RSV*).

~ ecc

❖ 1 PETER 2:1-10 ❖

❖ BREAKING WALLS OF SEPARATION ❖

Lutherans and Methodists have not always been agreeable bedfellows. Many emigrants from northern Europe—the famous St. Olaf choir conductor F. Melius Christiansen being one of them—were forewarned before they left for America to "watch out for the Methodists." And for good reason. Methodists often met the immigrant ships in New York Harbor and tried to persuade Lutherans to "convert" to Methodism.

That was most unfortunate, given the fact that John Wesley, whose death in 1791 we commemorate today, was profoundly influenced by the writings of Martin Luther. John and Charles (the sixteenth and eighteenth children of Susanna and Samuel Wesley!) made a mark on Christianity that is equal to that of any other person since the Reformation.

We can be thankful that the rift between Lutherans and Methodists healed over the years as we came to know one another more directly. Surely a milestone on that journey was the decision of our ELCA and the Methodist church to establish "full communion" with each other a few years ago. Now we affirm the validity of the gospel and the sacraments in our respective churches.

Possibly the greatest gifts Lutherans have received form Methodists are the hymns of Charles Wesley. No less than a dozen are found in our worship book, including such familiar ones as: "Come, Thou Long-Expected Jesus," "Hark! The Herald Angels Sing," "Jesus Christ Is Risen Today," "You Servants of God," "Love Divine, All Loves Excelling," "Oh, for a Thousand Tongues to Sing," and many more.

Some have suggested that the twentieth century be named "The Ecumenical Century." The idea is an apt one. In the lifetime of many of us there has been a remarkable movement to bring believers of like mind together in worship and service. Today we give thanks for the Methodists.

~ hwc

❖ JOHN 17:20-23 ❖

❖ THE MOST IMPORTANT MISSION ❖

What do Hot Springs, Arkansas; Rochester, Minnesota; Canistota, South Dakota; and Guadeloupe, Mexico, have in common? All are places for healing. Whether it be mineral waters, the latest in medical technology, a chiropractic treatment, or the touch of a priest, the aim is the same—healing. When we do battle with a major illness we long for any kind of help that might bring wholeness.

Jesus understood this human need. At the very beginning of his ministry Mark writes; "[Jesus] cured many who were sick with various diseases" (1:34). He could easily have devoted his entire ministry to this alone—healing the sick and distressed in body and mind.

In Mark's Gospel we read that after he had spent much time with the sick, Jesus retreated. Early the next morning he rose and went off to pray. When the disciples found him they urged him to return and continue his healing ministry. It seemed the natural thing to do. Indeed, Jesus could have spent his entire ministry in one place doing nothing but this. He would have been hailed far and wide for his ministry of healing. Instead, Jesus said to the disciples, "Let us go on to the neighboring towns, so that I may proclaim the message there also" (v. 38). Important as it was to heal, Jesus knew that he had an even more important mission—to proclaim the kingdom of God.

There is surely nothing wrong with our own search for the best medical care we can afford. Nor is there anything wrong with seeking it for all who are in need. It is part of the mission of the church.

We must not lose sight, however, of what is even more important for the church. Eventually, no matter how effective a treatment may be, we will all die. For that ultimate experience we will need something more—the good news that God loves all.

~ hwc

❖ MARK 1:32-39 ❖

❖ That I Could See ❖

Christina Green was only nine-years-old but already interested in how our government worked. That's why she wanted to go with a neighbor to hear the speech given by Congresswoman Gabrielle Giffords, her role model. It was there at the mall that the gunman appeared. Innocent Christina was caught in the line of fire and was hit by his bullet. The death of this precious, gifted child tore at our heartstrings. When her face later flashed on the TV screen, showing her beautiful smile and sparkling eyes, the reporter said her parents had donated Christina's eyes for cornea transplants.

Hearing that was emotional for me. Emotional, because I am a recipient of cornea transplants. They have saved me from going blind. The first transplant was done during Holy Week. During those quiet days of recovery I thought thankfully about Jesus giving his life that I might live. And also about the person who died willing their eyes to me that I might see.

Recovering after the second operation, my surgeon was exceptionally pleased with the outcome and called in other cornea specialists. Looking into my eye, both said, "Wow!" Chrystal clear. It must have come from a young eye. Given so that I could see.

Jesus laid hands on the blind man's eyes and his sight was restored. He saw everything clearly. But an even greater gift is to be given eyes of faith. When his disciples told Jesus who folks thought he was, he directed the question at them asking, "But who do you say that I am?" Peter knew, exclaiming with eyes of faith, "You are the Messiah" (Mark 8:29).

How smudged our seeing gets, weighed down with cares of this world. Jesus meets us again today on our road, ready and waiting to touch and heal us. Waiting to give again the miracle of sight so we can see. "Ask and it will be given you" (Matt. 7:7).

~ ecc

❖ MARK 8:22-30 ❖

MARCH 5

❖ BE STILL ❖

Americans are known for being workaholics. A Minneapolis *Star Tribune* article that caught my attention some years ago stated, "The ancient ideal of leisure is a lost art in America. . . it is a disgrace to just do nothing." Even vacation is packed with productivity. We manage it like work, indicating our importance. Our many gadgets keep us wired to work. The article continued, that for ancient Athenians, leisure meant "absence of the necessity of being occupied." Can we even imagine leisure of this kind? Is it possible for us to relax fully? Know how to be still? Meditate and spend time in contemplation?

Scripture says, "Be still before the Lord, and wait patiently for him" (Ps 37:7). Not to fret. "Take delight in the Lord and he will give you the desires of your heart" (v. 4).

If only for our physical health and well-being, it would help to relax and be still. It would relieve stress, lower blood pressure, and renew us in body, mind, and spirit. We need periodically to quiet mind, body, and spirit.

The psalmist shows us added benefits of being in God's presence. Fretting can turn to trust in God's guidance. Then we can be opened to understand God's will and find grace to commit our ways to the Lord, leading us to new trust that God will act for us.

Elijah was all stressed out in the Lord's work. He had searched everywhere for answers. The Lord was not in the wind. Not in the earthquake. And not in the fire. But "after the fire a still, small voice" (I Kings 19:12 *RSV*). It was God's answer and he had peace.

It is hard to be quiet in God's presence. Let us pray for the Holy Spirit to help us be still. To wait patiently. New joy and blessing comes in patient waiting. When we learn to be still, God has surprises waiting.

~ ecc

❖ PSALM 37:1-9 ❖

❖ Have No Fear of Learning ❖

I have at least two things in common with Thomas Aquinas, who died in 1274 AD and whose life we commemorate tomorrow. First, his handwriting, like mine, was all but impossible to read. I once had a secretary who was so good at deciphering my scribbling that I would bring my notes to her for interpretation! Second, he was tall and a bit shy. Beyond that, I make no claim to any likeness.

Thomas Aquinas was an intellectual giant, one of the high towers of Christian history. He had an insatiable appetite for learning. "The pursuit of wisdom," he wrote, "is more perfect than all human pursuits, more noble, more useful, more full of joy."

One of the finest lessons we can learn from him is that we need not fear the pursuit of wisdom, no matter where it may lead us. God is always higher than our loftiest thoughts and deeper than our most profound ideas.

This is a good day to give thanks for our church's liberal arts colleges. When they do their best work, these centers of learning are not ashamed to identify freely with the Christian faith. One of my favorite places is Gustavus Adolphus College at St. Peter, Minnesota. There one finds Christ Chapel towering over the campus. Wherever one walks on those grounds one can see the steeple of the chapel looming over everything else. Sidewalks from other buildings—science, music, social studies, business, psychology, philosophy, biology, fine arts, recreation—all lead to Christ Chapel. One cannot walk the campus without a sense that all intellectual pursuits are centered in Christ. And the Christ who is proclaimed in these places is not One who limits those pursuits, but enhances them. With our feet firmly anchored in Christ, we are free to follow wisdom wherever she leads us.

~ hwc

❖ PROVERBS 2:1-6 ❖

❖ A GOOD WAY TO RESOLVE DIFFERENCES ❖

During my nearly twenty years as a bishop I presided over many disputes. Sometimes they were between members of a congregation, sometimes between a pastor and a congregation, and sometimes between one congregation and another. At times the issues were serious. More often, however, they were of no great consequence. In time both sides saw the folly of their disagreement and the issue melted away.

There were times, especially when the disagreement was inconsequential, that I wondered how the disputants might act if the issues really were a matter of life and death. Suppose their very lives were at stake?

Today we commemorate the martyrdom of several courageous women who lived in North Africa way back in the third century. The Roman emperor had declared that anyone who converted to the Christian faith must be killed. Several women, led by twenty-two-year-old Perpetua, declared that they would not deny Christ, that they would be faithful to death. Perpetua's father, a nobleman in Carthage, pleaded with his daughter to renounce Christianity. His father's heart did not want to see his dear daughter slaughtered by wild animals. But she and her sisters in the faith held strong to their convictions. After beatings by guards they were led into the public amphitheater to be torn by beasts. When they survived that ordeal all of the women were beheaded.

Next time we find ourselves embroiled in a dispute or disagreement of some kind, might it not be well to stop for a moment and ask a few questions: "How important is this issue? Is this something I am willing to die for? And if not, what can I do to resolve it in a peaceful way? What can I do to go the second mile, to turn the other cheek, to do something that will help my enemy become my friend?"

~ hwc

❖ MATTHEW 5:43-48 ❖

❖ Those Good Old Days ❖

I have visited the ruins of the ancient city of Corinth twice. Archaeologists have dubbed it "the cesspool of the Roman Empire." As they have dug through the remains of the city they have unearthed evidence that these people deserved such an epithet.

In his two letters to the believers in Corinth the apostle Paul addresses one problem after another. The congregation reflected its surroundings.

> They argued about whether Paul or Peter or others were the best "pastors."
> Members took one another to court rather than settle their differences peacefully.
> They winked at immorality in the congregation.
> They made gluttons of themselves at the Lord's Supper.
> Some thought their intellectual acumen was above that of others.
> A few prided themselves in their ability to speak in tongues.

What about the church where you are a member? Any problems? It would be an unusual congregation if there were not some issues that threatened to divide you. This is why I smile whenever I hear someone wax nostalgic about "the good old days" in the church, and especially if they suggest how wonderful it would be if we could just live like the believers in the early Christian church. Those who make such comments show that they have never studied their Bible very carefully.

There never has been, nor will there ever be a time, when the church, whether it be the local congregation or the church at large, is not threatened with division. What is the antidote for these threats? What can hold us together when our fellowship is about to be broken?

Paul's answer is in that most familiar chapter we have all treasured as one of our favorites: 1 Corinthians 13. In the end, only love can overcome division:

> Love is patient; love is kind; love is not envious, or boastful or arrogant or rude (v. 4).

~ hwc

❖ 1 CORINTHIANS 13 ❖

❖ EVERY MORNING ❖

At Augustana Academy, our high school Latin teacher was Viola Scot, who started class each morning with a special thought for the day. Some were real keepers especially this one: "Every morning lean thine arm awhile upon the windowsill of heaven, and gaze upon thy God. Then with the vision in thy heart, turn strong to meet thy day."

A young woman told me how she needed to start her day alone with God. Her routine was to arrive at her office early, close the door, and spend quiet time reading from her devotional book and the assigned Bible reading for the day. Meditation and prayer, she said, helped make her day start right. She must have learned from Jesus who needed that too: "While it was still very dark, he got up and went out to a deserted place, and there he prayed."

It's wonderful to have hymns stored in our memory bank. One wonders how so long ago someone was inspired to write this hymn of prayer or praise that is exactly what we need just now. You may have found, as I have, that morning hymns are a great help as we lean our arm on the windowsill of heaven. They open us to fresh vision and hope for the day. Like this one:

> Awake, my soul, and with the sun
> thy daily stage of duty run;
> Shake off dull sloth, and joyful rise
> to pay thy morning sacrifice.
> All praise to thee, who safe hast kept
> and hast refreshed me while I slept.
> Grant, Lord, when I from death shall wake,
> I may of endless light partake.
> Lord, I my vows to thee renew.
> Disperse my sins as morning dew;
> Guard my first springs of thought and will;
> and with thyself my spirit fill.
> Direct, control, suggest, this day,
> all I design, or do, or say,
> That all my pow'rs, with all their might,
> in thy sole glory may unite (*ELW* #557).

~ ecc

❖ MARK 1:35 ❖

❖ Love Endures ❖

Henry Melchior Muhlenberg told the story of a hen that made her nest in the rough near his house. After laying several eggs, she instinctively stayed on her nest, faithfully keeping them covered with her body heat. She grew scrawny because rarely did she leave her eggs to get food and drink. After her chicks were hatched, she brought her brood day after day up close to the house, asking for food. Her mothering was amazing. Fiercely, she protected her offspring from soaring hawks and gathering storms. In each of those frightening times, she hurried to rescue the strays, bidding them under her protective wings whenever danger threatened. But when the chicks were able to fend for themselves, they went independently on their own way. None showed gratitude. Or brought food to their mother. Or protected her. She was quietly alone. Hers was love that endured.

Endure means to last. Stay firm under suffering. To bear up patiently in difficult times. The word from Latin means "to harden." Other derivatives explain it even further. *Dura mater* is a tough, fibrous, protective membrane lining the brain and spinal cord. Botanists know about dura mater, which is the hard, tough heartwood of a deciduous tree. Think protection and steadfastness.

Love endures all things. Is patient and kind. Not jealous or rude, irritable or resentful. Not boastful. Does not pass on juicy gossip. Love keeps hoping. Love lasts—endures no matter what.

How wonderful if such a love could honestly describe you and me. Instead, perhaps for you as they are for me, these words are like a searchlight, finding us so needy that we can only run to the cross of Jesus, confessing our lack. So let us run to the one, the only one, who does have enduring love, asking to be emptied of all sin so that we can be an open channel of God's enduring love flowing to others.

~ ecc

❖ I CORINTHIANS 13 ❖

❖ Stay in Tune ❖

It was a great privilege while a student at Augustana Academy to sing in the a cappella choir directed by Clifton Madson. Even at times when our singing seemed to sound good, he might stop us and reach in his pocket for the pitch pipe. Hearing again the pitch, we would discover how much we'd slipped.

In our confirmation classes we learned about our need for God's word, both law and gospel. Memorizing the Catechism helped us know why we need the law. Because it is our schoolmaster to bring us to (show us our need for) Christ. The gospel, on the other hand, is God's good news of Jesus who has done for us what we cannot do in keeping God's law. So we do need both. That is why Jesus warns us, "Continue in my word . . . and you will know the truth, and the truth will make you free" (John 8:31-32).

God's word is like the choirmaster's pitch pipe bringing us back in tune. In tune again with God's grace. With what God has done for us in Jesus Christ. In tune with God's will from which we so easily stray. In tune so that we can receive strength to persevere. In tune with God is the only way to peace and joy.

Let us continue in God's word telling us the price Jesus paid so that we can live in tune. And praying hymns that help us stay in tune.

> How art thou pale with anguish, with sore abuse and scorn;
> How does thy face now languish, which once was bright as morn!
> Thy grief and bitter passion were all for sinners' gain;
> Mine, mine was the transgression, but thine the deadly pain.
> What language shall I borrow to thank thee, dearest friend,
> For this thy dying sorrow, thy pity without end?
> Oh, make me thine forever, and should I fainting be,
> Lord, let me never, never, outlive my love for thee (*ELW* #352).

~ ecc

❖ COLOSSIANS 1:11-23 ❖

❖ Do As I Say, Do As I Do ❖

Woops. I think I got that wrong didn't I? I should have written, "Do as I say, not as I do," right?

Well, it seems that Paul got it all wrong. He said to the believers in Corinth, "I urge you to imitate me" (1 Cor. 4:16). Is this the same Paul who says in another place that "Christ Jesus came into the world to save sinners—of whom I am the worst"? (1 Tim. 1:15).

To understand how Paul can say both of these things—that they should imitate him and that he is the worst sinner of all—calls for some explanation.

No, Paul is not speaking of perfection when he suggests that others should imitate him. He believes that in baptism he has been crucified with Christ (Rom. 6:4). But through baptism and faith he now walks as a new person, a believer whose daily life has been transformed by the power of the Holy Spirit.

All of us can think of people who have set a good example for us. Maybe it was a parent or grandparent. Or possibly a pastor, Sunday school teacher, a youth leader, a coworker, a friend. We strive to follow their example, not because they were perfect but because they believed in Jesus and that faith made a difference in the way they walked in their daily life.

That is the sense in which any of us might say as Paul did, "Imitate me." If we have been reborn in baptism and love God we need not be apologetic about the way we live. Like Paul, we can be honest about our failure to live up to God's expectations. But at the same time we can confidently invite others to follow our lead, whether it be in regular worship, generous giving, visiting those in need, caring for the environment—in countless ways we can say, "Imitate me."

~ hwc

❖ 1 TIMOTHY 4:11-16 ❖

❖ NO MASTER CHRISTIANS ❖

It was exactly what I had hoped for. We had just retired when I noticed an announcement in the area newspaper that the master gardener course would be offered in our community. Sponsored by the University of Minnesota, it called for fifty hours of class taught by faculty from the university. I signed up the next morning.

It was one of the most satisfying educational experiences I have ever had. Perennials, annuals, trees, shrubs, grasses, landscape design, plant and tree diseases, and much more. Our study guide was four inches thick, with enough material for us to digest for years to come.

There were, of course, requirements. Each year we had to commit ourselves to at least twenty hours of volunteer service in our community and five hours of continuing education. What sticks in my memory most vividly is the warning we heard in almost every class: "Being a master gardener does not make you an expert. When gardeners start asking questions you will probably be able to answer only two of ten. For the rest you will have to dig."

How right they were! The world of gardening is so vast, the number of species of plants and trees so broad, that even those who have spent a lifetime at it freely admit that they have only taken a few steps.

The parallel to the Christian life is obvious. How quickly we get turned off by those who parade about as "experts" in the Christian experience. In my ministry of visitation I was always impressed by the humility of the most seasoned saints. The longer they lived the fewer answers they claimed to have. But, like an avid gardener who loves trees and flowers, these mature believers love the Lord and are ready to share their faith. There are no "master Christians." We are always on the way.

~ hwc

❖ PHILIPPIANS 3:12-16 ❖

❖ Christ Had to Become Human ❖

A chaplain in World War I, W.E. Sangster tells the story of how the military dealt with soldiers who faked illness. The medical tent was placed on the highest hill in the area. If a soldier could make it to that place the medics assumed he was healthy enough to return to the battle.

Christ, wrote Sangster, did not remove himself from the scene of human suffering and death. He descended into the world of misery and pain and identified completely with us.

Isaiah prophesied about "the suffering servant of the Lord." He had only a dim vision of who that one might be. But he knew one thing—that his people could only be set free by one who would be entirely one with them.

We give thanks that God did not remain aloof from us. In Christ God comes into the human condition. "For God so loved the world that he gave his only Son" (John 3: 16). We may ask, "Did it really have to be that way? Couldn't God have solved the human dilemma some other way? Can't we make up for our failure, our sin, and our brokenness simply by pulling ourselves up by our bootstraps?" The answer is "no." Only by becoming completely human and then suffering the most despicable death—only in this way could we be sure that Christ really understands the depth of our need.

During my ministry as a synod and presiding bishop I preached mostly in places where I recognized only a handful of the listeners. How could I know what to say to strangers? How could I know their heartaches, their problems, and their need for God? I always took courage in being certain that in each congregation were those whose hearts were like my own, hearts that needed to hear over and over again that Christ lived and died for each of us.

~ hwc

❖ JOHN 3:16-21 ❖

❖ Lay Up These Words ❖

Our ninth grade general science teacher was unique in many ways, especially in using the teaching tool of repetition. Certain principles of science, he insisted, could be fixed in one's mind if repeated often. His favorite line was, "If water drips on a rock long enough, it finally wears a hole." Early on, his repeated sentences were our dismay, but we came to appreciate his method because important principles became for us building blocks for future learning.

God gave his law and made a covenant with Abraham for him and for his descendants to be a light to the nations. To remain faithful, they were to remember the covenant: "Put these words of mine in your heart and soul" (Deut. 11:18). Repeat them in worship and teach the children. With temptation to worship other gods, they needed continually to remember the covenant in worship, using repetition as the tool.

Use every opportunity to teach your children—when sitting, walking, at bedtime, and in the morning. Write God's words. Talk about them. Repeat them so you and your children never forget that you are God's and God loves you.

Luther used this principle in writing and teaching the Catechism. Memorize and repeat it. Older generations of Lutherans benefitted from this practice. We were required to memorize not only the Catechism, but also Bible passages and hymns, laying it up in our hearts. God's word, bound in heart and soul becomes readily available, night or day. Available, it comes bringing God's presence to renew us with his grace.

> The word of God is source and seed;
> it comes to die, and sprout and grow.
> So make your dark earth welcome warm;
> root deep the grain God bent to sow.
> The word of God is breath and life;
> it comes to heal and wake and save.
> So let the Spirit touch and mend
> and rouse your dry bones from the grave (*ELW* #506).

~ ecc

❖ DEUTERONOMY 10:12-14; 11:18-21 ❖

❖ How Can I Keep from Singing? ❖

Ben Larson and his wife, both students at Luther Seminary, were serving a term in Haiti when the earthquake struck. Together with a cousin they were working in a downtown building when with no warning, their whole world began shaking and they found themselves inside of a collapsing building. His wife and cousin, who were working in a different part of the building, were able to escape. But Ben, working in a vulnerable part, was trapped under debris, beyond rescue. His wife was unable to get to him but could hear him singing as he was dying under rubble.

How good to know that God is able to give us a song even in the midst of such pain. May God give you today, a confident and sturdy song.

> My life flows on in endless song;
> above earth's lamentation.
> I catch the sweet, though far-off hymn
> that hails a new creation.
> No storm can shake my inmost calm
> while to that Rock I'm clinging.
> Since Christ is Lord of heaven and earth,
> how can I keep from singing?
> Through all the tumult and the strife,
> I hear that music ringing.
> It finds an echo in my soul.
> How can I keep from singing?
> No storm can shake my inmost calm
> while to that Rock I'm clinging.
> Since Christ is Lord of heaven and earth,
> how can I keep from singing? (*ELW* #763).

For you today, God's grace is real beyond our knowing!

~ ecc

❖ PHILIPPIANS 4:4-7 ❖

❖ God Uses All Kinds ❖

"It takes all kinds," we often say. And so it seems that God does indeed use all kinds. A few days ago we remembered Thomas Aquinas, an intellectual giant in church history. Today we recall St. Patrick, who brought the gospel to the people of Ireland. No one ever suggested in his lifetime that Patrick was unusually bright. He was more of a doer than a thinker. After his own conversion to Christianity, Patrick's passion was for the conversion of the Irish. He threw caution to the winds, risking persecution in order to teach and preach the faith.

We are reminded of the twelve disciples. Patrick was more like Simon the zealot; Thomas Aquinas more like John. Patrick was also more like impetuous Peter, whose enthusiasm outran his better common sense; Aquinas, on the other hand, had a closer likeness to Andrew.

During my years as a synod bishop I oversaw more than 500 pastors. I often marveled at how God could use men and women of such entirely different personality types. There were the quiet, reserved, scholarly types; the ebullient, bombastic, energetic types; those who were good at starting and building up a new congregation; those whose best gifts were to shepherd a church that needed administrative skill to keep its mission alive. As each kind of pastor found her or his best setting the church as a whole was blessed. How sad if all were identical.

The apostle Paul understood this need for variety. Using the human body as an example, he pointed out that each part of the body, though very different in shape and function, has a common purpose—to give unity to the body of Christ.

So there is room for Patrick and Aquinas—and for you and me as well.

~ hwc

❖ 1 CORINTHIANS 12:14-20 ❖

❖ THOSE LOVELY CROSSES ❖

It was only a hole in the ground. Yet for more than twenty years Anna, a student of mine, had visions that wakened her at night, forcing her to sit straight up in a cold sweat.

Anna worked for the World Health Organization (WHO) in Greece after World War II. It was a tumultuous time. Civil war raged everywhere. Terrorism was common in cities and villages.

Anna's young friend taught school in one of the smaller outlaying places. One day she got the terrifying news that he had not only been murdered, but actually crucified, just as the Romans had done in the time of Jesus.

Anna rushed out to the scene of the atrocity. By then the body had been buried and the cross carried away. All that remained was that hole—that hole in the ground. She stood there for a long time, contemplating what had happened, what kind of agonizing death her young friend had suffered. Now Anna suffered, year after year, as the new meaning of the cross settled into her memory forever.

Like you who read these words, I have many crosses. Some are exquisitely designed. One is a gift from Pope John Paul II. Another is from Dimitrios, ecumenical patriarch of the Orthodox Church. For eight years as presiding bishop of the ELCA I wore the beautiful one given by St. Luke's Lutheran Church in Silver Spring, Maryland. Our home has crosses here and there as part of lovely artwork.

All of us treasure our crosses. But are we ever able to comprehend the horror, the anguish, the suffering, and the despair of a rugged cross and of those who were hung on them? If we had witnessed such a cruel death, the kind Jesus suffered, would we not also waken in the night with terror, unable to ever comprehend how humans could be so cruel?

It was for us that he suffered and died.

~ hwc

❖ MATTHEW 27:45-50 ❖

❖ FOUR GOSPELS, ONE STORY ❖

Why are there four gospels: Matthew, Mark, Luke, and John? Don't they all tell the same story? Could we not do well with just one of them?

The answer is both yes and no. Each gospel is complete. But those who have studied these books know that each author has his own unique way of telling the story of Jesus' life and ministry. Though many of the accounts are the same, each gospel has stories that the other three do not include.

What is fascinating, however, is that when they come to the place where they relate the account of Jesus' death the four gospels are very similar. Up to this point each gospel tends to focus on where Jesus was—his geographical location. Now all four concentrate on what he did.

In the earlier part of each gospel the time stretches over most of three years. Now all four concentrate on what happened in the course of a week, and much focuses on a single day. As one reads one can feel the intensity of what is happening to Jesus. Now the account is not just told, but told in such a way that the reader must pay close attention to what is unfolding. In Mark this intensity reaches its climax when Christ utters the words, "My God, my God, why have you forsaken me?" (15:34).

These movements in the four gospels can be a guide for us during the season of Lent. Over the rest of the church year we look at the life of Christ from a broader perspective. We pay more attention to how we should live as followers of Christ. But with each step through Lent the intensity of our journey increases. Now we find ourselves saying, "This is what is unique about Christianity. This is when we move to the center. This is the point of it all—that Christ died for us.

~ hwc

❖ PHILIPPIANS 2:5-11 ❖

❖ Those Quiet Men of Faith ❖

There is an old tradition that suggests March 20 as a day to give some respect to Joseph, the husband of Mary. This is no easy task. Joseph is that quiet, almost invisible character in the biblical account of the birth of Jesus. His name doesn't even appear in the Gospel of Mark, and John only mentions him in passing.

In the other gospels, Matthew and Luke, Joseph has a somewhat more visible role, but even there the primary focus is on Mary, the mother of Jesus.

So what do we do with this seemingly minor figure in the life of Jesus? I think there is a good clue in what Matthew writes: "Her husband was a righteous man." Matthew says that Joseph responded positively when an angel told him not to fear taking Mary as his wife. Furthermore, it is Joseph who gives Mary's son the name "Jesus."

These seemingly meager references to Joseph are enough to give us reason to honor this man. He might have dismissed the dream and the appearance of the angel as an illusion, a meaningless, foolish idea. But he didn't. He acted in faith, believing that this child was no ordinary little boy.

As a parish pastor I often marveled at the quiet faith of some of the men in the congregation. They made no waves, seldom spoke at meetings of the congregation. They were simply there, worshipping with regularity, giving generously, witnessing quietly in their daily work by the way they spoke and acted. I came to know them as the backbones of the congregation. When I needed a word of encouragement in tough times they were there at the right moment to say quietly, "You have my support, pastor. I'm remembering you in my prayers."

Thank God today for all the "Josephs" in your congregation.

~ hwc

❖ MATTHEW 1:18-25 ❖

❖ Before You Call I Will Answer ❖

It was a beautiful summer day filled with excitement. And Michael loved excitement. His best friend had invited him to go swimming. His mother was bringing a picnic lunch, and they would pick him up at 11 a.m. But before that, he had an early game at the park. He worried how everything would fit together because he didn't want to miss a beat. Hoping it would work out, he was off happily for his first event of the day.

But there was a delay and he came rushing in the door just after the car pulled into the drive. Breathless, he wondered where were his swim trunks. And a towel. Bursting into tears, he saw his mother come with everything he needed neatly folded in a swim bag. A quick smile and hug and he was out the door happy and thankful.

How many times are you and I like young Michael, rushing breathlessly to God in prayer, worried and anxious? Feeling there's no way this difficult situation can work out. Desperate because we are not able of ourselves to change what seems impossible. And then to stop and realize that like a good and loving mother, God has been quietly working behind the scene. Preparing everything. Working in ways we could not have imagined or even thought to ask.

In Isaiah, God's people have despaired. But God assures them that even as he first created heaven and earth, God says even now, "I . . . create new heavens and a new earth" (Isa. 65:17). Right now, if you're trapped in a dilemma, God may be creating something new. Preparing the way. Answering, even before you ask. The promise is for you, "Before they call, I will answer" (v. 24).

> He is my Lord, my friend, my loving Brother,
> And Jesus Christ is His most blessed name.
> He loves more tenderly than any mother:
> To rest in Him is more than wealth and fame
> (*The Hymnal*, #468).

~ ecc

❖ ISAIAH 65:17-25 ❖

❖ Reaching for Higher Standards ❖

Jonathan Edwards, who died on this day in 1758, is one of America's most controversial religious figures. So strong-willed and demanding that he was finally dismissed by his own New England congregation, Edwards nevertheless was a key figure in the Great Awakening that swept through this young country from 1740–1742.

Edwards' message was a stern one. He was convinced that too many preachers had watered down the demands of discipleship to the point where members of Christian churches paid little attention to the call to a life of discipline. Little wonder that he was so unpopular. Yet one cannot help but ask if we do not need a good dose of his theology and preaching in every age, including our own.

Just prior to and during World War II a German pastor by the name of Dietrich Bonhoeffer issued the same call. He saw the churches around him cowering before satanic political forces and failing to call for a life of sacrifice and resistance. Like Edwards, Bonhoeffer paid a price for his criticism of those in high places, both in the church and in the political realm. He was executed for attempting to resist Hitler.

We often speak of "giving up something" for Lent. That may be well and good. But does not Jesus call for something far more demanding than losing a few pounds or foregoing a favorite activity?

When he called those first disciples Jesus did not set a low standard. He spoke of sacrifice and hardship, of self-denial and unselfish giving. As each of us examines our own lives in this season of Lent, how does our pattern conform to what Jesus expects of us? Do we not need a good dose of the kind of preaching that came from giants like Edwards and Bonhoeffer?

~ hwc

❖ LUKE 9:23-27 ❖

❖ PEARLS ❖

Would you be able to tell the difference between pearls—genuine, cultured, or fake? The difference in value is enormous.

An expensive genuine pearl grows for many years in the mouth of an oyster in response to an irritating grain of sand and takes on the color of the oyster's lip—black, gray, pink, purple, green. Secretions form layer after layer around the irritant, thus making a pearl. Pearl farming off the coast of China has human industry placing irritants into the mouths of oysters. These are harvested after only three or four years. They are quite inexpensive. Fake pearls are manufactured, layering ground mother of pearl or plastic. If offered as a gift and without knowing worth, one might choose the cultured or fake pearl over the genuine because they are shinier and more symmetrically round. Perhaps only a gemologist could know its worth, and that only with high-powered magnification.

In telling these twin parables—someone selling all that he had to buy either fine pearls or a field containing a treasure—Jesus invites us to think seriously about the treasure we have in being part of the kingdom of heaven and following Jesus Christ. To love the Lord your God with all your heart, all your soul, all your strength, and your neighbor as yourself.

Choosing to follow Jesus may mean selling fake values. Choosing such fine pearls will be costly. The choice will affect our actions, our thoughts, the way we live. But the treasure will fill the heart's longing. What treasure and what joy.

> In the morning when I rise, . . . give me Jesus.
> Dark midnight was my cry, . . . give me Jesus.
> Oh, when I come to die, . . . give me Jesus.
> And when I want to sing, . . . give me Jesus.
> You may have all the rest, give me Jesus (WOV #777).

~ ecc

❖ MATTHEW 13:44-45 ❖

❖ Sealed ❖

With jars sealed tight, our vegetables were preserved safe for good winter meals. The vegetable garden was a mainstay of food for our family of seven during years following the great depression. Our parents helped plant the garden, but we children were assigned the tending and harvesting. It was lots of work, weeding and picking those long rows of string beans. We carried in pails full of beans and succulent, sun-ripened tomatoes. Quart jars were washed, scalded, filled with vegetables, and sealed with metal lids lined with white glass interiors and screwed tightly over a red, rubber ring. Jars were placed into the copper boiler and cooked for ninety minutes. These vegetables were made secure and safe for our family. Safe because the jars were sealed.

God, too, set his seal. On Jesus, "God the Father has set his seal" (John 6:27). So that he is our food for eternal life. The seal was already set at creation:

> He is the image of the invisible God, the firstborn of all creation. . . . All things have been created through him and for him. He himself is before all things, and in him all things hold together. . . . In him all the fullness of God was pleased to dwell, and through him God was pleased to reconcile to himself all things, whether in earth or heaven, by making peace through the blood of the cross (Col. 1:15, ff).

God has also set his seal on us in baptism. Like jars sealed in the water bath, in the waters of baptism we were sealed by the Holy Spirit. Sealed for life eternal as children of God. "It is God who establishes us . . . and has anointed us, by putting his seal on us and giving us his Spirit in our hearts as a first installment" (2 Cor. 1:21-22). We have been sealed and called to be food for the world.

~ ecc

❖ JOHN 6:25-35 ❖

❖ The Day Jesus Was Conceived ❖

If Jesus was born on December 25 it only makes sense that he was conceived nine months earlier—about March 25. The problem, of course, is that we have no idea on what day of the year he actually was born. The church wanted to celebrate that important event and simply chose December 25 because it was convenient. Little wonder it took the early Christian church more than six centuries to settle on the day of his conception. They called it "The Annunciation of Our Lord."

Because this day falls in the season of Lent—and often during Holy Week—it goes unnoticed and unobserved in most of our churches. That's unfortunate. If the incarnation of Jesus—the act of taking on human flesh—is central to our Christian message, then this day is as much a part of the story of the passion as is Good Friday. The moment the angel announces to Mary that "You will conceive in your womb and bear a son, and you will name him Jesus" (Luke 1:31), the story begins to unfold. This conceived One, who will go to the cross for the sins of the world, is already on a destiny that cannot be reversed. Little wonder that devout old Simeon felt moved to tell Mary after the birth of Jesus that "a sword will pierce your own soul too" (Luke 2:35).

We cannot even begin to plumb the mystery of the conception and birth of Jesus. We can no more understand it than we can comprehend our own conception. Why, of all the possibilities, did that particular sperm and egg come together at the moment we first were given life? The best we can do is say, "I believe; help my unbelief."

Today let us give thanks that in Christ God took on human life, and that he lived and died for us.

~ hwc

❖ LUKE 1:26-34 ❖

❖ Make Your Voice Sound Like Mine ❖

After Harry's accident, he was hospitalized. But this was a bad day because it was his son's big game, and he couldn't be there to cheer him on. So important for him as a father, and he never missed a game. Important for the son too. Having his dad there gave him confidence. It was a special father-son thing. In the midst of Harry's discouragement, his brother walked in. After hearing him out, his brother said, "Harry, I'll go there for you and yell like everything." As his brother was leaving, Harry said, "Be sure you make your voice sound just like mine."

What is there about a familiar voice? The door opens or the phone rings and it's the voice of your loved one. What happens to you? In a moment, the whole history of a close relationship comes together in hearing that voice. And it fills you with joy.

John uses the image of shepherd and sheep to picture Jesus' relationship with us. When the sheep hear the voice of the shepherd, they become responsive, alert, and excited. When he calls them by name, they come, eager to follow because they know his voice, which summons trust and goodness. They have reinforced memories of the shepherd's protection and loving care. Hearing his voice is promise of more goodness.

The word *know* is full of meaning—much more than understanding facts. "They know his voice" (John 10:4) indicates a relationship with one who also knows them. Like Jesus, who has revealed himself to us. And there's a history, like shepherd with sheep, of Jesus rescuing, protecting, healing wounds, leading to green pastures, always loving us.

Jesus said, "I have other sheep that do not belong to this fold" (v. 16). So with hearts full of thanks for Jesus as *our* shepherd, we are called to the sidelines today with Jesus saying, "Be sure you make your voice sound like mine."

~ ecc

❖ JOHN 10:1-6 ❖

❖ DOING OUR DUTY ❖

I seldom look at old sermons. It can be embarrassing. But one day I stumbled on to one that caught my attention. I was in my first call, a two-point parish at Pelican Rapids and Elizabeth, Minnesota. The date on the sermon reads March 14, 1960. Here's an excerpt:

"If God gives me the strength to spend fifty years in the ministry, and if I could lead thousands of souls to faith in Christ during that time, I would still have to stand before God one day and say, "I have only done my duty."

Well, now more than those fifty years have elapsed. I have preached to more people in more places than I could ever have imagined on that day long ago.

I have taught many hundreds of students in a college setting.

In one congregation the service was broadcast to a wide radio audience.

As a synod bishop I preached in a different congregation every Sunday, totaling many thousands of listeners in a year.

As the presiding bishop of the ELCA I roved the country and the world, again preaching to countless thousands. On one occasion there were 10,000 in an arena when I preached.

And there have been books and articles and videotapes that have reached the eyes and ears of more thousands.

And I'm not done yet! As God gives strength and opportunity I want to keep sharing the good news. How many have come to know Christ through all these efforts? How many have seen the need to go into the world to heal and clothe and give more generously because of something I have said?

I have no idea. Nor do I have a need to know. When all is said and done, all that I—or you—will have to say is this, "I have only done my duty."

~ hwc

❖ LUKE 17:7-10 ❖

❖ Many Texts, One Theme ❖

Carl Anderson, our Old Testament professor at Augustana Seminary, said it very plainly one day: "After you have preached for many years you will discover that every sermon is a variation on one basic theme."

Anderson was right. In the course of a year a pastor may preach on many different subjects. But central to all must be one theme—that Christ was crucified for us and that he rose from the dead for us.

The apostle Paul kept Christ at the center of his preaching. When he wrote to the believers in Corinth he said that some want a stage show when they worship. Others yearn for intellectual stimulation. Paul said his aim was to "preach Christ crucified."

Times have changed, but the human condition has not. On those rare occasions when I watch a religious telecast I am appalled by what I hear. Some unabashedly promise prosperity to those who live in a certain way. Others appeal to the intellectual desires of the listeners. Still others remind us more of a style show than a worship experience.

In recent years it has been popular in some settings for pastors to preach "How to" sermons. How to be a better parent. How to be a better spouse. How to manage your life more effectively. And on and on.

There may be some value in these kinds of sermons. But if they are to walk in the footsteps of the apostles and prophets and great proclaimers of the faith down through the years, pastors must keep one theme always in the forefront—that Christ came to give his life for us and that he rose again to give us hope.

The message of the cross is a radical word that most would rather not hear. We would like to think that we can make it on our own. Over and over we need to hear that one basic theme: "Christ crucified."

~ hwc

❖ 1 CORINTHIANS 1:20-25 ❖

❖ HANS NIELSEN HAUGE ❖

Hans Nielsen Hauge (1771–1824), a farmer with only a sixth-grade education, began the greatest revival Norway has ever known. The Thirty Years War had left Europe in chaos and the State Church of Norway had become cold and sterile. Class distinction separated a controlling "Herr Pastor" from people.

Into that milieu, Hauge was raised up by God to revive the church. At twenty-five, while plowing his field, praying the memorized hymn "Jesus, for Thee and They Blessed Communion," he describes an ecstatic experience: [I was] "lifted out of myself into union with God." That inspired him to preach and write more than thirty books. He emphasized conversion, downplayed the sacraments, harshly criticized clergy, encouraged lay preaching, and adopted rigorous discipline. Grieving over pastors giving false assurance instead of calling for conversion, he gathered folks in private homes to hear the word, pray, and give testimonies of their experiences with God. "The Conventicle Act of 1741" forbade such meetings (called conventicles), unless the local pastor was both informed and gave his blessing. "Hauge sows seed of distrust against pastors," wrote the bishop and for it Hauge was imprisoned seven years.

Positive results of Hauge's work include widespread Bible reading and family devotions, small group fellowship gatherings, lay people witnessing in word and deed, and growth in stewardship and social action for the poor and oppressed. Hauge championed businesses to keep the old and disabled on their payroll. He died at fifty-three, but his influence lived on.

His work was the impetus for many voluntary religious organizations independent of the State Church: Inner Mission Society; Norwegian Foreign Mission Society, which sent missionaries to many countries like Africa and India; and a university where pastors could be trained at home instead of in Denmark. We can thank God for Hauge's work that accented the importance of separation of church and state.

On his commemoration day, we thank God for Hauge, even as we share with others our faith in Jesus Christ.

~ ecc

❖ EPHESIANS 5:15-20 ❖

❖ I Just Want to Fly ❖

Already as a child, Emily wanted to fly. That fascination kept growing. But when she and her twin sister dreamed about what they would do after high school, flying hardly seemed a possibility to Emily in the early 1950s. So she joined her sister studying for a career in nursing. For her sister, it was a good fit. But, not for quiet Emily who abandoned nursing school and went back home. She told her parents, "I just want to fly."

She began hanging out at the nearby flying school and was paid for doing menial jobs. Soon she was taking flying lessons and earned her private pilot's license while only eighteen. From there, she began advancing—first to flight instructor, then flight school manager, and finally an FAA pilot examiner. Before women were ever considered to fly with major airlines, Emily began making applications. During this process, she experienced many put-downs because she was a woman. But she persisted until she aced with Frontier Airlines and in 1973 became the first woman to be hired by a major U.S. carrier. Three years later, she became the first US woman to earn captain wings. In honor of Captain Emily Howell's achievement and other awards, her Frontier pilot uniform was installed in 1976 at the Smithsonian National Air and Space Museum. All because she just wanted to fly.

Are we surprised that an early fascination for flying led her to accomplish such great things? The psalmist describes God forming us in our mother's womb, knitting us together. Like with knitting, sometimes we need to rip back when a mistake is made. So, with life. The knitting went well in Emily's life when she began doing what God created her to do.

At each stage of your life and mine, God has a plan. Can we allow some ripping until we get placed right and doing what we were born to do?

~ ecc

❖ PSALM 139:13-18 ❖

❖ For Whom Does the Bell Toll? ❖

During my growing up years my parents were the custodians of our local congregation. It was a family enterprise, with all eight of us children getting involved in one way or another.

My favorite duty was ringing the big bell that hung in the highest steeple in town—first, on Saturday evening at six o'clock to remind members to come to worship the next day and, second, to signal the beginning of the worship service on Sunday morning.

It was more sobering to ring the bell at funeral services. This was done with a separate rope attached to a clapper that struck the bell whenever I pulled on it. I would lean out the window above the church entrance to watch carefully as the casket emerged. That was the signal to strike the first toll of the bell. Then, after counting slowly to ten, I would pull again. And then again and again until the cortege was out of sight.

Even as a young lad I could feel the solemnity. I was sending a sobering message to the entire city, reminding everyone that our time would also come, that one and all would die.

Only later would I learn those familiar lines from John Donne, whom the Christian church commemorates today: "Never send to know for whom the bell tolls; it tolls for thee" and "Now, this bell tolling softly for another, says to me: Thou must die."

Again and again Jesus warned his listeners to beware of taking any day for granted. He called for us to "Keep awake" (Matt. 24:42) to be alert, to stand ready for the unexpected, including our own death.

Whether this day—March 31—falls in the season of Lent or just after Easter, is it not a good time to stop and listen for the bell that tolls for each of us?

~ hwc

❖ MATTHEW 24:42-44 ❖

❖ Those Real Fools ❖

As my family and friends will tell you, I've enjoyed pulling April fool jokes on them for years. Much as we may enjoy our lighthearted tricks to fool someone on this day, the Bible is deadly serious about fools. Not once, but twice the Psalms declare that "Fools say in their hearts, 'There is no God'" (14:1; 53:1). These writers think that anyone who looks around at the world of creation must be convinced that there is One who has made all things.

But is it really so easy to believe? Paul doesn't seem to think so, especially when one is talking about Jesus Christ and his life, death, and resurrection. That Christ became human, died for the sins of the whole world, and conquered death by his resurrection—this seems foolish to many rational persons. It takes a gigantic leap of faith to believe such an unbelievable message.

Luther spoke in that same vein. In fact, he taught that this is such an affront to any reasonable person that we must say, "I believe that by my own understanding or strength I cannot believe in Jesus Christ my Lord or come to him." It is so impossible that we must have the help of the Holy Spirit who "has called me through the gospel . . . and makes holy the whole Christian church on earth" (*Luther's Small Catechism*, The Third Article).

That is why Paul speaks of the gospel as "foolishness." The wise of the world often cannot accept these ideas that are at the heart of the gospel. In fact, these words that are such good news to believers are, according to Paul, "a stumbling block" to many.

Bringing new members into our churches is never a matter of welcoming them into another nice club in the community. It is calling them to embrace a radical way of life that the world around regards as foolish. Be a fool today—a fool for Christ.

~ hwc

❖ 1 CORINTHIANS 1:20-26 ❖

❖ AROMA ❖

How can we describe a wonderful aroma except with a memory? Maybe it's from the rose garden. Or perhaps from the kitchen on Thanksgiving Day, connected to a memory of our mother's loving hands. When you think of a wonderful aroma, what memory comes first to your mind? My memory is of freshly baked bread.

As children, the long afternoon since lunch plus walking home from school always made us hungry. Almost a mile we walked, first down a gravel road, then along the fence line of our neighbor's field. Finally, we'd squeeze through the barbed wire fence and hike down the hill through our pasture, toward home. It was there, walking down that last hill on a spring afternoon when the windows of our house were open, that we could first smell the fresh bread. Just out of the oven, the bread's aroma would always quicken our step. I can't think of a better aroma. And with it the anticipation of home-churned butter on a thick warm slice of whole wheat bread in the presence of mother's love. What an after school snack!

Scripture tells us that "God, who in Christ always leads us in triumphal procession, and through us spreads in every place the fragrance that comes from knowing him. For we are the aroma of Christ to God among those who are being saved and among those who are perishing" (2 Cor. 2:14-15). The "aroma of Christ!" Commissioned by God. Every day we meet someone who longs, even hungers to have some empty hole in their souls filled. Is it possible that we can be used as an aroma leading that someone hungry to receive God's grace and love today? Only by the grace and working of God's Holy Spirit can this happen. So let us ask boldly that today, we will be an aroma God can use to lead someone to eat and drink of God's love until they are satisfied.

~ ecc

❖ 2 CORINTHIANS 2:14-17 ❖

❖ Blessings ❖

An older couple came to visit in our home. We wanted to share hospitality because they had come to make a presentation at our church. Not knowing them well, we were eager to get acquainted, yet hardly expected that their presence would be such a gift.

We learned several things about these new friends, but were surprised by their genuine interest in both of us and in each of our children. More than interest, they brought to our home warmth that was palpable. Coming as strangers, they were fast becoming friends in such a short time. When leaving after lunch, they stood in our doorway and simply said, "The Lord bless you." More than words, a quiet benediction descended upon our home. After they had left, everything seemed different because of their presence in our lives. It had happened so quietly. Clearly their benediction was not from the surface but had come through often-cleansed-channels in their souls. We. knew that the blessing left in our home started with the One "from whom all blessings flow" (*LBW* #564).

Is it possible that your life and mine can also be channels of such blessings? We need to begin by being open and honest in God's presence, allowing our sin to be exposed, confessed, forgiven, which allows us to rejoice in the peace that only God can give. Then, in thanksgiving, as we regularly spend time blessing God, God's blessings will flow through us. "Bless the Lord, O my soul, and all that is within me, bless his holy name" (Ps. 103:1).

Blessings happen in miraculous ways and come in a variety of packages—simple kindness, a caring phone call, a knock on the door, a gesture, a letter, intercessory prayer. May such blessings come to you and flow through you, today.

> The Lord bless you and keep you; the Lord make his face to shine upon you, and be gracious to you; the Lord lift up his countenance upon you, and give you peace (Num. 6:22-26).

~ ecc

❖ NUMBERS 6:22-27 ❖

APRIL 4

❖ For You ❖

One day flying home to Chicago, I was delighted to have an engaging seatmate. Even more delighted when I learned that he was one of our ELCA pastors. He spoke with animation about his pastoral ministry. So I asked, "What is the most exciting thing that has happened in your parish lately?" Without a moment's hesitation, he answered, "The new member instruction class for our Vietnamese refugee folks."

In their study of Holy Communion, Luther's catechism had come alive in his teaching about the benefits we receive from this sacrament—forgiveness of sin, life, and salvation—and the words "given for you" and "shed for you" for the forgiveness of sins.

Speaking pointedly, the pastor stressed that the gift is *for you* and *you* and *you*. Timidly, one man raised his hand asking, "For me?" He was assured by the pastor, "Yes, it is for you." Again with observable disbelief he asked, "For me?" And the pastor, a second time said, "Yes, it is for you," as he watched the miracle of faith take hold. He witnessed the young man literally grasping on to the words of Jesus and then saw the joy that filled his face when faith was born. What a powerful gift of the Holy Spirit to translate the hearing of the ear to believing with the heart.

That is the work of the Holy Spirit as Luther explains, "I believe that by my own understanding or strength I cannot believe in Jesus Christ my Lord or come to him, but instead the Holy Spirit has called me through the gospel" (*Luther's Small Catechism*, The Third Article).

With eyes of faith, this man was then eager to receive the sacrament. For "a person who has faith in these words, 'given for you' and 'shed for you . . . for the forgiveness of sin,' is really worthy and well prepared. . . . because the words, 'for you' require truly believing hearts" (*Luther's Small Catechism*, The Sacrament of Holy Communion).

~ ecc

❖ 1 CORINTHIANS 11:23-26 ❖

❖ Inadequate ❖

Do you sometimes feel inadequate for the task God calls you to do? In our occupations and in daily life, we have all faced this feeling, especially when new challenges arise. It can almost overwhelm us. It certainly happens to church workers.

In writing a sermon or a devotional, I'm tempted to feel so inadequate that I get writer's block. Not enough knowledge. Or experience. Or wisdom. Or skills. How does one quash those voices and get on with the task?

Since Sunday School teachers struggle with this, we invited Dr. Gerhard Frost to speak to them. Along with other important things, he talked about feeling inadequate. He knew from his own experience that the evil one always works to prevent us from doing God's will, often tempting us with the feeling of being too inadequate for the task. It still was happening to him, he confessed. We wondered, after his many years of teaching and preaching, after his many years of experience, and with his superior education and particular giftedness, could this even be possible.

He explained how he handled it. Whenever he stepped into a pulpit or to a teaching podium his prayer would be the same, saying to God, "This is the best I can do right now. Will you fill in the missing pieces and bless it anyway?"

The story is told of Ignacy Paderewski, the famous musician who always arrived ahead of his concert to practice. Usually folks were already gathered to hear those notes as well. Once a small boy sat innocently at the piano playing "Chopsticks." A man gestured to move the child away, but Paderewski intervened and sat down beside the child encouraging him to continue. Each time through, he accompanied the simple tune ever more elaborately until it became a great rendition. And so our gifts can be magnified and blessed when the Holy Spirit accompanies us. "Sustain in me a willing spirit" (Ps. 51:12).

~ ecc

❖ PSALM 51:10-12 ❖

THE ONLY WAY TO ESCAPE JUDGMENT

Visiting a grave can evoke deep feelings of gratitude for the person whose body lies there. That was my sense as I looked at the marker that read "Albrecht Dürer" in the cemetery at Johanniskirche in Nuremberg, Germany. His grave site is only a few steps from the wall of the church.

Dürer was a contemporary of Martin Luther. Though he remained a devout Roman Catholic for all of his life, he was an ardent admirer of Luther. He mourned when he heard that Luther's books were burned. He thought that Luther had explained the Christian faith more clearly than anyone else had done for centuries.

When Dürer died on this day in 1528, Luther later described him as "the best of men."

We remember Dürer, of course, for his artistic talent. Artists often say that the most difficult object for them to recreate is the human hand. But who of us has not been moved to pray as we have looked on Duerer's most lasting legacy—the praying hands?

After visiting the cemetery I entered the sanctuary of the church. Again, my heart was moved. They followed the old custom of hanging a liturgical piece over the front of the pulpit. That day I read in German the words from 1 John 3:22—"God is greater than our hearts." Given his appreciation for the teachings of Luther, I would like to believe that Dürer understood the essence of this text from 1 John. Our hearts do condemn us because as we examine them carefully we cannot help but see that we have sinned and come far short of what God expects of us. Where is our refuge? It is only in bringing our hands together in prayer, looking to God and being reassured again and again that "God is greater than our hearts."

~ hwc

❖ 1 JOHN 3:16-20 ❖

❖ In the Awesome Presence of God ❖

Yesterday, in addition to Dürer, was the commemoration day for another renowned artist—Michaelangelo. Among his famous works are the Pietà in Rome and the statue of David in Florence. But possibly the most noted is the Sistine Chapel.

I have visited the Sistine Chapel several times, both before and after its restoration. The earlier visits were by far the more satisfying. How can that be? Certainly the restored colors of those scenes from creation to the last judgment should be appreciated more fully when seen in something closer to their original condition.

The truth is that my differing reactions had nothing to do with Michaelangelo. It had to do with the people in the chapel on each occasion. On the earlier visits I was with friends who not only appreciated fine art, but who also shared my awe at the thought of what Michaelangelo had done. It was a worship experience. On the last visit the space was jammed with tourists, many of whom seemed to have no appreciation for the artist or the place of the chapel in Christian history. Loud talking, whispering on cell phones, and shuffling feet brought a stern reprimand from the priest monitor, "Quiet! Quiet!"

Unfortunately, it is not only in Rome where reverence has been lost. In my memory from childhood and youth I can see a congregation gathering in hushed silence for worship. Heads were bowed as members prayed and listened to the organ prelude with appreciation. When the pastor went to the altar all eyes were on him. As he intoned the opening phrases of the liturgy we felt we stood in the presence of God: "Holy, holy, holy is the Lord of hosts!" (Isa. 6:3).

These words from the prophet Isaiah remind us of the need to find a time and a place to be silent before our God.

~ hwc

❖ ISAIAH 6:1-8 ❖

❖ One Day at a Time ❖

Red Skelton was one of my all-time favorite comedians. His humor could be enjoyed by all ages. Just looking at him made me laugh.

Skelton had an unusual habit. After every performance he would walk quietly from his dressing room back on to the stage in the empty auditorium. He would look at all of the vacant seats and say to himself, "An hour ago I was a star; tomorrow I'll have to start all over again." He knew he always had to be on the lookout for fresh material, for a clever line, and for a new way to tell an old joke. And he knew that whatever a new day might bring, he had an obligation to entertain his audience.

What a wholesome way to live. And what an appropriate way to look at life—including our Christian life. Oh yes, we do build on each day's record. We surely carry much of what we did today into tomorrow's endeavors. Yet, we all know that the glories and satisfactions of today will not last long. Tomorrow we'll have to start all over again. If we don't, life will soon stagnate; the fresh stream that flows so easily today will turn into putrid algae in a short time; the happiness we thought would never leave us will disintegrate quickly into depression and boredom.

The Letter to the Hebrews depicts the Christian life as a race. We are urged to "run with perseverance the race that is set before us" (Heb.12:1). Like Skelton, we may bomb now and then, messing up a good day with less than our best effort. But each time we step into a new morning we have one more opportunity to begin again, to set our feet in the starter blocks, to run "with perseverance" one more day.

~ hwc

❖ HEBREWS 12:1-3 ❖

❖ GUARANTEE ❖

Parents told us the very moving story of losing their small child after a long hospitalization. It happened many years ago, before there was good treatment for leukemia. From the outset, the child's mother developed a routine of daily hospital visits. As she was leaving that first day, the child cried uncontrollably. An experienced and understanding nurse suggested that the mother leave something for the boy to hug in his crib—something that had the comforting smell of his mother. So that day and every day after until his death, the mother always left her sweater with her son. It became her habit, and it worked. A guarantee that she would return.

Even though Jesus promised to come again, his disciples were sad when he announced that he was going away. He promised he would not leave them desolate, and to guarantee his return he assured them he would send an "Advocate, to be with you forever. This is the Spirit of truth . . . and he will be in you" (John 14:15-17).

In 2 Corinthians 5:2, a tent is the image of our earthly place of existence. Such a flimsy dwelling, and so easily destroyed. So vulnerable we are in this life, pictured in the text as being stripped bare and naked. Indeed, in this life we are often anxious and afraid. Like a little child might feel when left alone in a hospital crib. But God promises security and gives us the Holy Spirit as a guarantee. Like a mother leaving her sweater to be a comfort and an assurance of her return, the Holy Spirit dwells with us and in us. To be our comfort.

> Oh, let me nestle near thee, within thy downy breast,
> Where I will find sweet comfort and peace within thy nest.
> Oh, close thy wings around me and keep me safely there,
> For I am but a newborn and need thy tender care (*WOV* #741).

~ ecc

❖ 2 CORINTHIANS 5:1-5 ❖

❖ Those Tough Finns ❖

Although the Swedish Lutheran heritage was my childhood experience, I was blessed in high school to learn to know a number of Finns. Over the rest of my life I have had a growing appreciation for this important stream in the Lutheran family of faith.

Finland was profoundly affected by the Reformation. A key leader among them was Mikael Agricola (AH-gricola), a bright young man who rose quickly to become the bishop of Turku, the center of that church's life. Like the Petri brothers in Sweden, Agricola went to Germany to study at the feet of Luther. When he returned to Finland he expended his energy in bringing the gospel of grace by faith to his people. To do that meant translating the New Testament and other important books into the native tongue of his people. In the spirit of Luther, Agricola worked hard to keep the finest of the old religious traditions, while promoting the best of the new understanding of the gospel.

With all of the mergers across ethnic lines over the past half century, it is easy to forget how much we owe to the contributions of various churches that formed the foundation of faith for the millions who came to America between the mid-1800s and the early 1900s. Finns were in that latter group and, because they were latecomers, tended to remain somewhat isolated from other Lutherans. Today we give thanks for the gift they shared with all of us.

A favorite Finnish word is *sisu*. Its meaning is somewhat mystical. Sometimes it is translated, "fortitude" or "endurance" or simply "guts." No single word can adequately carry its meaning into English. For believers it stands as a call to be strong and courageous because of the strength God promises to those who walk in the Christian way.

~ hwc

❖ EPHESIANS 6:10-18 ❖

❖ DRAGON ❖

Instructing his catechumens, St. Cyril of Jerusalem gave this warning about adversaries along life's journey: "The dragon sits by the side of the road, watching those who pass. Beware lest he devour you. We go to the Father of Souls, but it is necessary to pass by the dragon."

Being snatched by the dragon is what the psalmist experiences, crying, "My God, my God, why have you forsaken me?" (Ps. 22:1). It may be physical pain, but the greater suffering is his anguish of mind, doubting God will hear or even come to him. God is now silent. So he has both fear and loneliness. He's terrified with nowhere to go for help. In desperation and no longer feeling human he cries, "I am a worm" (v.6).

But he does find an island of comfort in the middle of his ocean of despair, remembering that God has been there for him in the past and for his ancestors. That is when the brightness of hope begins to break through.

We all have our stories of passing the dragon. Flannery O'Conner writes, "No matter what form the dragon may take, it is of this mysterious passage past him, or into his jaws, that stories of any depths will always be concerned to tell" (*Daily Readings from Spiritual Classics* edited by Paul Ofstedal). Is there any other way that trust in God is born, except through times in the dragon's jaw? When God who is our only help seems silent. When we feel lonely and desperate. But somehow in the dragon's jaw, a light of hope glimmers. God touches us through Scripture or a hymn. We too remember what God has done in the past and can do again. "O Lord, do not be far away! O my help, come quickly to my aid" (Ps. 22:19).

It happens. We have a story to tell and a song to sing. And hope to share with others. Thanks be to God!

~ ecc

❖ PSALM 22:1-11; 19-26 ❖

❖ Grief Is Physical ❖

It was a beautiful spring day several weeks after our son had died so suddenly and unexpectedly. I was in his room making up the bed for an arriving overnight guest when without warning, like many times before, an overwhelming sadness overcame me. It felt like a heavy ball in my stomach. All I could do was fall into the chair and call out to God, "I am so full of sadness, and it's too heavy to carry. Jesus, will you carry it from me to the cross?"

Whatever else it is, grief is also physical. Describing how physical it is, the psalmist says, "I am poured out like water, and all my bones are out of joint; my heart is like wax, it is melted within my breast" (Ps. 22:14). Certainly there is emotional and spiritual pain, but it is also physical.

Scientific research documents several adverse effects from grieving that are physical. These include increased incidents of cancer, heart attacks, doctor visits, and hospitalizations.

Physical healing ordinarily comes to us through medicine. The psalmist helps us find it also in God's presence, saying, "O my help, come quickly to my aid" (v.19). Surely for emotional and spiritual healing, but also for physical healing, the psalmist gives us words to cry out in our pain alone with God. We experience Jesus' presence; it's so real as he lifts our burden from us, carrying it to the cross. We go away free again.

One never asks for such times of deep sorrow. And yet, it is precisely because of being so needy that we draw close, and often, to the cross of Jesus, the "man of suffering and acquainted with infirmity" (Isaiah 53:3). And there, waiting in his presence there is joy—and also physical healing. Joy beyond anything we'd ever known before.

> Come to me, all you that are weary and are carrying heavy burdens, and I will give you rest (Matt. 11:28).

~ ecc

❖ PSALM 22:14-19 ❖

❖ You Are with Me ❖

Nine years old and it was the day I was to have my tonsils removed—a common procedure in those days to prevent illness. My father took me to our small town hospital that was quite casual then. So informal that he was able to walk alongside the gurney that took me to the operating room and wait there in the doorway. The pea green walls are vivid to me still as I remember sliding over onto the operating table. It was all a big adventure up to that point. Until a mask was placed over my mouth and nose and then the horrible smell of ether! I shouted in fear and panic. In that instant, I heard my father's comforting voice, "It's okay, Corinne." I knew he was right there in the doorway with me, and all fear was gone.

Psalm 23 takes us to the desert setting of shepherds tending their sheep. Getting them to water and pasture sometimes necessitated going through dangerous passes and ravines where robbers hid. But sheep trusted their shepherd because of many rescues and much tender care. No fear when he was with them.

Israel's ancient worship centered in the context of the whole people of God, not in individual spirituality. However, out of that community worship, an important individual relationship with God was kindled.

Our journey in life sometimes takes us through harrowing passes in order to arrive at green pastures. An accident. Frightening diagnosis. Loss of job. Worsening relationship that leads to divorce. There's fear and panic. We then begin to understand "the darkest valley." The dangerous passes can truly be little deaths along the way. How comforting then, in our panic and fear, to hear God's voice in the doorway. We know God is right beside us and we need no longer fear. For each has the promise, "You are with me."

~ ecc

❖ PSALM 23:4 ❖

APRIL 14

❖ THE BELLY OF LIFE ❖

Over my lifetime of angling I've hooked thousands of fish. That's no fish tale. And cleaned just as many! When I catch an unusually large fish my surgeon instinct comes out, and I cut open and examine the contents of the belly. I can tell you that it's not very appetizing.

Whatever one makes of the story of Jonah in the Old Testament, at least one lesson is that the idea of being in the belly of a huge sea creature is not very pleasant. If Jonah were ever to think that he was somewhat special, he would soon learn that he was just another piece of meat. Fish are not discriminating. Food is food.

Another lesson to be learned is that life has a way of bringing each of us to places where we would rather not be, places that are messy and foul, places we want to escape as quickly as possible. This is why texts from Jonah are appropriate for the Easter season in the church year. As God lifted Jonah out of the belly of evil, so we are given the promise that God will be with us in our most dire place—the jaws of death. That is the Easter message.

But the Easter promise is not easy to believe. In every account of the resurrection of Jesus there is doubt. If anyone should have believed that Jesus would rise from the dead it was the chief priest, the scribes, and the Pharisees. They knew the Holy Scriptures. They should have recognized him as Messiah. Even the disciples, who had been his intimate companions, missed it.

Would we have missed it, too, had we been there? Yes, I'm afraid so. I confess that the thought of the resurrection is just too incredible. You and I can only pray, "Lord, I believe; help my unbelief!" (Mark 9:24).

~ hwc

❖ JONAH 2:2-10 ❖

APRIL 15

Paying Tax and Loving Our Neighbor

April 15—a day we tend to think only about how much tax we are paying to state and federal budgets. But shouldn't this also be a day when we reflect on the income on which we pay those taxes?

We share in common with our Jewish friends what is called the "Judeo-Christian tradition." Among other things, this tradition teaches us something about money and the values and ideals of the Jewish and Christian faiths as they are spelled out in the Old and New Testaments.

There are two principles that are especially relevant to our views on money.

First, the Bible urges each of us to resist the temptations of wealth. "Give me neither poverty nor riches," says the writer of Proverbs (30:8). In the New Testament the watchword is "Keep your lives free from the love of money, and be content with what you have" (Hebrews 13:5). Many of us grew up with the idea that we should live within our means. That's not easy to do in a consumer-driven society. We are constantly tempted to buy more than we need or can afford.

The second apt lesson to be learned from our common roots is that we are given life and possessions so that we can serve our neighbor. Both Old and New Testaments summarize this requirement in the words: "You shall love your neighbor as yourself" (Leviticus 19:18, Mark 12:31).

Some, inevitably, will accumulate wealth. Hard work, good fortune, or inheritance will move some to the top. Others, often through no fault of their own, will fall through the cracks.

We pay taxes to close that gap. Can we have better education, health care, roads and bridges, and law enforcement without raising taxes? Isn't it time for many of us to stop looking at taxes as a burden and start seeing them as our opportunity to serve our neighbor?

~ hwc

MATTHEW 22:15-22

❖ Straight Paths ❖

Looking forward to retirement feels so good. Imagine at last having perennial leisure and peace away from the rat race. Just hunker down and sleep late—every day a Saturday. However, there are wise ones warning us that good retirement requires one to cull out things in work that brought the greatest rewards and find the same good feelings in other ways, perhaps in the volunteer world. A Harvard study was done to find the greatest fears of folks in the 60–70 age range, and they discovered this surprising order:

Meaninglessness
Being alone and not loved
Not belonging, feeling lost
Dying

Are you surprised as I was when I learned that *meaningless*, not dying, was the #1 fear for this age group? Meaninglessness will happen at any stage of life if we choose the wrong path and for the wrong reason—for riches or prestige or to avoid hard work and conflict. But God who formed us and the Holy Spirit who apportioned gifts to each of us, knows us. We're created for a purpose and for doing God's will. Created for walking a right path, a straight path for each and every stage of our life. Doing what we have been gifted to do brings rewards and deep meaning in our lives. So, as we enter each new stage of life, we must rediscover what is now intended for us by God who promises, "In all your ways acknowledge him, and he will make straight your paths" (Prov. 3:6).

Oh, that the Lord would guide my ways to keep his statutes still!
Oh that my God would grant me grace to know and do his will!
Order my footsteps by your word, and make my heart sincere;
Let sin have no dominion, Lord, but keep my conscience clear.
Assist my soul, too apt to stray, a stricter watch to keep;
And should I e'er forget your way, restore your wand'ring sheep
(*ELW* #772).

~ ecc

❖ PROVERBS 3:5-6 ❖

❖ TEST YOURSELVES ❖

"Take out a half sheet of paper," our English teacher would say as class began. The Latin teacher did the same. And in seminary, Greek class often started that way too. Surprise quizzes are great to make sure students are keeping up with daily homework. Frequent testing keeps us on our toes. It is important not to fall behind in any language study because each day's learning becomes the building block for what comes next. It readies us for new learning.

Being ready for a test is important also in our walk with God. Paul, as teacher of the faith and mentor for the Christians of Corinth, challenges them to examine themselves, in effect saying, "Take out a half sheet of paper." Take account of your faith, of your walk with Jesus Christ. Today, each of us is asked to do the same.

After the Day of Pentecost (Acts 2) we have a remarkable account of Christians worshipping "day by day" (v. 46) in the temple and praising God. Like faithfully doing daily homework, they were getting ready for whatever test may come.

Part of the quiz for the Corinthians and for us today is this: Don't you realize that Jesus Christ *is in you*? Jesus assures us (John 14) that the Holy Spirit dwells with us, and that Jesus and the Father will make their home with us. Ask yourself, could they be any closer? Yes, in you, even at times when God seems distant.

After a Greek "quickie test" one morning, a young man looked worried saying, "I think I failed." How do you and I come out on our test question today, "Do you realize Jesus Christ is in you?"

If we pass this test, it will make a difference in our day—our hope and joy, our attitude toward others, our mission, our victory and peace, our praise and thanksgiving. And it prepares us for the next test of faith that life may bring.

~ ecc

❖ 2 CORINTHIANS 13:5-10 ❖

It's All about the Resurrection

We were traveling across Nebraska on I-80, an endless stretch of interstate highway. Over three hours together this corporate attorney and I covered a number of subjects. But there was one question more than any other that he wanted to ask: "Is the resurrection of Jesus," he wondered, "the only evidence we have of life after death?" "Yes," I replied, "it all hangs on the resurrection of Jesus. If that's not true, the whole case for Christianity falls."

Christianity shares a good deal with other religions. Most religions call for a distinct way of life, including strict obedience to a leader, concern for the welfare of others, self-sacrifice that may call for giving one's life for the cause, and in most cases, belief in life beyond this one. But none other, no other religion, can point to the resurrection of its leader from the dead. That alone makes Christianity unique.

Religions also depend on symbols to accent their belief system. Among Christians we often point to symbols like trees that seem to spring to life with the warming sun, of butterflies that emerge from their cocoons, and of tulips that rise from the frozen ground to bless us with a blaze of color. But these are mere symbols. Even an elementary school student knows that if a tree or butterfly or tulip really dies it does not come back to life.

The attorney was right. It is solely on the resurrection of Jesus Christ from the dead that we stake our claim for eternal life.

Paul understood this. He does not make his case on the basis of symbols. Rather, it is because of the testimony of those who actually saw Jesus after the resurrection—Peter, the disciples, and "more than five hundred brothers and sisters at one time, most of whom are still alive" (1 Cor. 15:6).

It's a gigantic leap, isn't it? A leap of faith.

~ hwc

1 CORINTHIANS 15:12-20

❖ The Gift of Good Liturgy and Strong Preaching ❖

Revival and awakening in the church come in different ways. Sometimes from the bottom, led by lay persons and in opposition to the clergy. And sometimes from the top, with pastors and bishops leading the way.

In Sweden the Reformation came from the top. Two brothers, Olavus and Laurentius Petri, whom we commemorate today, were the prime movers. As young priests, both studied in Germany and came under the influence of Luther and other reformers. Convinced that this was the way the gospel should be preached and taught, they returned to Sweden and did exactly that.

Their efforts were not always greeted with warm acceptance. At one point the king of Sweden, Gustavus Vasa, condemned Olavus to death when he resisted the king's desire to have complete control of the church. He was later pardoned.

Key to the work of the Petri brothers was that they translated the Bible into the language of the people and preserved the best of the liturgy from the past.

Those of us who are heirs of the Swedish Lutheran tradition are debtors to these two brothers. We grew up taking for granted that our pattern of formal liturgy and strong proclamation of the gospel were the norm for most churches. Then as we moved into new patterns of church life we discovered that it was not necessarily the case in other churches. It made us more thankful than ever that we had received, free and unmerited, such a profound heritage.

The Augustana Lutheran Church ceased to exist in 1963 due to mergers, but its heritage has been a gift to the other Lutherans in this country.

Though ways of worship will inevitably continue to evolve as the church moves into new times and changed cultures, the combination of strong liturgy and powerful preaching will always be important.

~ hwc

❖ COLOSSIANS 3:15-17 ❖

EVIL IS EVERYWHERE; HOPE IS NEAR

April 19, 1995, is "a day in infamy" in my mind. I was in New York City for a meeting. Someone interrupted us with the sobering message that there had been a bombing of a federal building in Oklahoma City. We were stunned, but I more so. The next day, April 20, I was scheduled to fly to Oklahoma for the Arkansas-Oklahoma synod assembly.

Over the next hours speculation about the perpetrators ran wild. Many, including me to my shame, assumed it had to be rooted in some Middle Eastern terrorist group.

As we flew from Chicago to Oklahoma City the next day, the cabin grew eerily silent when the captain announced our descent. By chance I happened to be sitting in a window seat on the side of the plane where I had a clear view of the smoldering hulk of the Federal Building below. By then we knew that hundreds of innocent persons, including many children, had perished.

At the synod assembly I was scheduled to preach that day. I knew that in the congregation were many who had lost friends in the bombing. What can one say?

Thank God it was the season of Easter. If the Easter message is not for times like this, then the message is worthless. I told the assembly about my recent meeting with youth from across the church. At a Q & A session one young man asked for my favorite Bible verse. I welcomed the question because for years it has been Romans 6:4—"We have been buried with [Christ] by baptism into death, so that, just as Christ was raised from the dead by the glory of God the Father, so we too might walk in newness of life."

I concluded with these words: "Only Christ, crucified and risen, can set us free from despair and death. He is risen! He is risen indeed!"

~ hwc

JOHN 11:17-25

A Table in the Presence of Enemies

A word can have different levels of meaning. What that word means in one era can mean something different in another. Its meaning may vary from one culture to another. So we wonder what special meaning came to those who sang in the Jerusalem temple so long ago, these words, "You prepare a table before me in the presence of my enemies" (Ps. 23:5).

Maybe they thought of God's eternal table beyond death. Or of their own sheep guided through harrowing dangers until they arrived at green pastures and calm smooth waters, only to be surrounded by predators lurking around them there—venomous snakes, preying wolves, and robbers waiting to snatch sheep from their shepherd. Maybe they thought of God's protecting hand leading them through the wilderness to the table of the Promised Land.

But for "after Easter" people who are united by baptism into the death and resurrection of Jesus Christ, the table means the Sacrament of Holy Communion where we celebrate the new covenant of Jesus' blood, shed for us and all people for the forgiveness of sins.

At the table we too eat and drink *in the presence of our enemies.* Personal enemies of envy, pride, anger, bitterness, or worry. Feelings of inferiority, put-downs, anxiety, or lost relationships. Like snake venom, they snatch us away from peace and a trusting, loving relationship with God. If we could name these enemies to Jesus, he will carry them to his cross. It is for these he died to gain victory for us.

We come to the table as Jesus' guest. Bread and wine are his real presence. Enemies may look askance as we come, but they cannot spoil our time enjoying God. And they cower when they see us receiving grace at God's hand. Jesus Christ is there at the table to protect and help us overcome them. Right there in the presence of our enemies.

~ ecc

❖ PSALM 23:5 ❖

❖ Remember the Poor ❖

Ce'sar Chavez (1927–1993) lived a humble life, yet made himself known for his compassionate advocacy for exploited workers. Because he was the child of an itinerant migrant family, he attended more than thirty elementary schools, learning deeply the plight of those living in poverty. With growing abilities and deep desire to help needy people surrounding him, he studied to learn community organizing and later organized the United Farm Workers (UFW). Through national boycotts of farm products, such as lettuce, wine, and grapes, California growers were pressured into making contracts with their agricultural workers. By the time of the death of Chavez, the UFW had grown to more than fifty thousand active members. The UFW brought a new face of justice for many.

But there are many others to care about. For example, in winter of 2011, we read of Mexican workers rising at 1:00 a.m. for travel to the U.S. border where they then waited sometimes two hours for a bus leaving for the Arizona lettuce fields of Yuma. After a long day of work in the hot sun they returned on the difficult journey home to Mexico, arriving after 8:00 p.m., leaving little time for family or rest. And they worked for minimal wages at jobs few would choose.

Throughout Scripture, we are reminded of the poor. With scathing realism, Isaiah uses harsh words that make us cringe. The Lord God of hosts says, "What do you mean by crushing my people, by grinding the face of the poor?" (Isa. 3:15). We're called to care for the poor by learning about and advocating for their justice, following the example of a Ce'sar Chavez.

It's too easy to isolate ourselves, ignoring the poor, when we are the privileged. Some worship services end the benediction with, "Remember the poor." Let us make it our daily prayer so we're moved to act on behalf of those who "never live before they die" (*ELW* #729).

~ ecc

❖ ISAIAH 3:13-15 ❖

❖ That Little Giant ❖

From my 6 foot 3 inch perspective, he looked like one of the shortest and thinnest persons I had ever seen. President Christensen introduced him at the Augsburg College chapel service, telling us that his name was Kagawa—Toyohiko Kagawa. I had never heard of him. But before the chapel service concluded I knew I had met a giant.

Born out of wedlock to a geisha girl, Toyohiko's father was a prominent member of the Japanese Cabinet. When Toyohiko became a Christian while a teenager, his father disinherited him. Christian missionaries took him under their wings and helped him through college.

For the next fourteen years he devoted himself to the poor slum dwellers in Kobe, living in a six-by-six foot hut. He was arrested for his work in organizing labor unions among farmers and shipbuilders. He kept persisting until the government finally gave voting rights to Japanese males.

Refusing to give up his ideals, Kagawa went on to organize credit unions, schools, hospitals, and churches, always making certain that the good news of the gospel was linked to the needs of everyday people.

Is it any wonder that on this day the church commemorates his life? He exemplified what Jesus taught over his entire ministry on earth. It is not enough to go to church on Sunday, confess our sins, receive the sacraments, and then go our way for the rest of the week, oblivious to the aches and deprivations at our doorstep.

In the most disturbing words of the New Testament, Jesus forces us to look about and ask, "Do I care for the sick, the hungry, the naked, those in prison, the aliens, and all others whom the world passes by so easily?"

Yes, I learned that day in chapel that the measure of a person has nothing to do with their physical stature. I met a little man who was a giant.

~ hwc

❖ MATTHEW 25:41-46 ❖

❖ Use Gifts Given ❖

Nearing the Christmas shopping season, a woman told me it was a time of sadness for her. Sadness because she knew that whatever she gave to one of her children it would be returned for cash, given away, or never used. Her disappointment was real. Perhaps it is the same when we disregard God's gifts to us.

In a morning devotional from *For All the Saints: A Prayer Book For and By the Church*, we prayed, "Not our thought of thee, O God—let thy thought for us hold our eyes and keep us steadfast. We do not ask so much for the strength which thou hast promised as for the grace to use what thou hast already supplied in Jesus Christ, our Lord." Like the woman, might God's carefully chosen gifts cause disappointment? Gifts that we undervalue. Or cast aside. Exchange for things of far lesser value. Don't bother to use.

Think of God's gifts. In baptism we are made children of God—given value and love, saved by grace through faith. While being formed in the womb, we were thought about and knit together by almighty God's workmanship—made for witness and service, given significant abilities, "prepared beforehand to be our way of life" (Eph. 2:10). We have been made to be salt of the earth and light for the world. Thank you, O God, for these carefully chosen gifts!

For us, thanks are ever more real when we see our gift appreciated and used. There is joy also for God, seeing gifts to us being used. So, we pray with St. Francis of Assisi:

> Grant that we may not so much seek to be consoled as to console;
> To be understood as to understand;
> to be loved, as to love.
> For it is in giving that we receive;
> it is in pardoning that we are pardoned;
> And it is in dying that we are born to eternal life (*LBW*, p. 48).

~ ecc

❖ MATTHEW 5:13-16 ❖

❖ Those Thorns in the Flesh ❖

Glaucoma has been robbing me of vision for the past fifteen years. I've done everything medical science suggests to do battle with it. But nothing can stop it completely. It is like dust that gathers on a window screen. If you asked if I noticed any more dust today compared to yesterday, I'd say I had not. But if you asked if there was a difference from a year ago, I'd say, yes, definitely. The disease is relentless. I must use a desktop enlarger to read normal print. And as I type this meditation on my computer the font size is set at more than three times what is normal for others.

This is my issue. But most everyone, especially as they age, has something they must deal with that diminishes their quality of life.

What do we do about these "thorns in the flesh?" The apostle Paul gives us a clue. In his letter to the church at Corinth he writes about experiences of ecstasy, times when he felt unusually close to God. But to keep life in perspective, Paul says that God gave him a "thorn in the flesh" so that he might learn humility. This limitation, this weakness, taught him to trust in God rather than in his achievements. "When I am weak," he writes, "then I am strong."

We have a choice to make. When these "thorns" inevitably come into our lives we can grow bitter. We can complain that life has dealt us a rotten hand, that it's not fair that we should have to endure this limitation while others we know seem to sail through untroubled waters.

But we can also stop long enough to look about and see how much we have been blessed. Above all, we can bring our weakness to God, as Paul did, and discover through it the strength that only God can give.

~ hwc

❖ 2 CORINTHIANS 12:7-10 ❖

❖ VINDICATION ❖

Worst of all false accusations is when a person experiences dehumanization, suffering, and agony of imprisonment for many years for a crime he or she never committed. Now, in recent years with DNA testing, we hear of acquittal for innocent victims. But often this takes place after many lost years in prison. Even the joy of being set free does not make up for those lost years.

Although we may know nothing of such extreme false accusation, most of us have been the brunt of it by slander, gossip, or hurtful rumors. Perpetuated sometimes by one who feels guilt and projects it onto another. Although not so extreme, it is still painful.

Being an age-old problem, Scripture gives us help. Ancients had a refuge in fleeing to the Temple—to the horns of the altar where animals were sacrificed. When holding on to the horns of the altar, no evildoer could do them harm (1 Kings 1:49-53).

We too, when falsely accused and suffering inward pain, can flee to the presence of God, equivalent to their horns of the altar. Flee to God who knows us, where we can cry out with the psalmist, "I wash my hands in innocence" (Ps. 26:6). Washing one's hands has become a figure of speech for innocence going way back to Pilate who washed his hands of Jesus' innocence before the people falsely accusing him (Matt. 27:24).

We, like the psalmist, in times of such testing can ask, "Search me, O God, and know my heart; test me and know my thoughts. See if there is any wicked way in me" (Ps. 139:23-24). And God who knows us promises to work vindication for all who are oppressed. It happened for Job when he asked God to vindicate and clear him of false charges (Job 13:18). It can happen for us too, even though the waiting may be trying. But we can be at peace, knowing God can vindicate us.

~ ecc

❖ PSALM 26:1-12 ❖

APRIL 27

❖ Light Shines in Darkness ❖

Henry Soso (1295–1366) became one of Germany's most famous mystics. He was mentored by two of Germany's other well-known mystics, Tauler and Eckert. His greatness as a writer and preacher grew out of struggle, being falsely accused of terrible things, such as theft and adultery. Because of these accusations, Soso suffered long periods of darkness, holding always to his innocence until finally acquitted publicly. It was his patient endurance in the darkness that became the doorway for his greatness as a mystic. This deep struggle drew him into the loving arms of God—into the very presence of Jesus who became his light in darkness.

Early Christians have much to teach us of darkness. Especially those who observed prayers of vigils, the night watch hour where they learned to trust the darkness and its mystery.

We too know times when the Holy Spirit comes to us in powerful ways in our darkness. The Spirit comes unseen and often unexpectedly, like wind blowing open our veiled sight so we can see clearly the light of Jesus who is our light. What creative energy in the darkness, like at that first creation. "He was in the beginning with God. All things came into being through him. . . in him was life, and the life was the light of all people. The light shines in the darkness, and the darkness did not overcome it" (John 1:2-5).

Think of the vast darkness that embraces the limits of our everyday reality. And the darkness from the beginning of time that holds mystery. It can be frightening to us. But when we meet Jesus shining in the darkness, we find him embracing us as frightened children. Right there, giving us amazing courage as he touches our gifts. He touches us as he touched Soso to give him greatness as a writer and a preacher. Jesus touches our gifts too, sending us in mission bringing his light to others.

~ ecc

❖ JOHN 1:1-14 ❖

❖ Tough Bible Texts ❖

Many denominations use what is called "The Lectionary." This consists of assigned texts for each Sunday. Every pastor knows the temptation to avoid a difficult text. We read it and say, "That looks too tough. I think I'll choose one of the other lessons."

A good example is Acts 4:32-35. It describes how the first Christians lived: "No one claimed private ownership of any possessions, but everything they owned was held in common. . . . for as many as owned lands or houses sold them and brought the proceeds of what was sold. They laid it at the apostles' feet, and it was distributed to each as any had need" (vv. 33-35).

"Whoa!" we recoil. "Is this the model for Christians for all time? And if so, just how are we to do it?"

As we all know, from time to time religious groups spring up that try to emulate these early Christians. They do so with varying success. In colonial America some tried it. Even as late as the nineteenth century, Scandinavians attempted various forms of it in Wisconsin, Illinois, and Kansas. In most cases they eventually fell on hard times and the vision disintegrated.

Given the general failure of these ventures, we can dismiss this model from Acts 3, right?

I suggest we slow down a bit before we draw that conclusion. It may be possible to make a strong case against communal living as a standard for all times and all places. But we must not miss a very basic principle that lies at the heart of this text. It is found in the phrase: "it was distributed to each as anyone had need" (v. 35).

The great deficiency of most economic systems is that greed and selfishness flourish at the expense of the poor. Christians in every generation are called to stand against greed and selfishness and to spend every effort, in church and community, to see that the poor are not forgotten.

~ hwc

❖ JAMES 2:14-17 ❖

❖ Those Remarkable Single Women ❖

Today we honor Catherine of Sienna, that noble woman from Tuscany in northern Italy. She died on this day in 1380 at the age of thirty-three. In that short life she shaped the culture of her church, her country, and far beyond.

Catherine had her first vision when she was only six years of age. Through her short life she continued to have these kinds of mystical experiences. When we hear about persons like Catherine we tend to assume they are rather odd and out of touch with reality. Catherine proves how wrong that is. She knew what was going on in her world and had no hesitation to give advice to those in religious and civil authority. While many dismissed her as irrelevant, others had the good sense to listen to her.

Unlike those who joined orders of nuns and withdrew to convents and cloisters, Catherine lived life in the public square. When her family urged her to marry, she declared that her mission was to be single. Even though we in the Lutheran tradition give little attention to celibacy, we should make a careful distinction between requiring celibacy and freely choosing it. It is an honorable choice.

Among the references to single women in the New Testament I've always been fascinated by a verse in Acts 21. We know a good deal about Philip, a prominent evangelist in the early chapters of the Book of Acts. But in chapter 21 there is a reference to a visit by Paul to Caesarea, a Roman city along the coast of the Mediterranean Sea in Palestine. There Paul visits Philip. All the text says is that Philip had "four unmarried daughters who had the gift of prophecy" (v. 9).

Though I wish we knew more about those four women, I think today is a good time to remember all those single women whose life and witness has made an impact on us.

~ hwc

❖ ACTS 21:7-9 ❖

❖ Who Is My Neighbor? ❖

On March 3, 1991, forty-five-year-old African American Rodney King was brutally beaten with batons by four Los Angeles police officers. Bystanders watched and no one did anything to stop it. But then, who would you call but the police, and they were the ones doing the beating. However, there was one person, George Holliday, who from his apartment not only witnessed the beating, but videotaped it. He took it to the news media and it was aired around the world. Riots started, leaving over fifty dead and 2,300 injured. Fires were started damaging over 3,000 businesses. Because of evidence on the video, the four officers were prosecuted, found guilty, and punished for civil rights violations. All because of the neighbor who helped.

Jesus tells a similar story of someone just looking the other way and doing nothing for a man that was beaten. But because another man who was a true neighbor stopped and did all he could do to help, a life was saved. He did not know if robbers were still around. It could have been dangerous. He put his life on the line for a man who desperately needed what he could do to help.

God's concern is always for those who are voiceless, poor, beaten down, and cannot help themselves. Some of those may be right in our pathway today—someone crying out to God for help. Might God be waiting for us to look their way? Dare we ask God for eyes of compassion to see them? And for grace to be a true neighbor?

> Neighbors are wealthy and poor, varied in color and race,
> Neighbors are nearby and far away.
> These are the ones we will serve; these are the ones we will love;
> All these are neighbors to us and you.
> Jesu, Jesu, fill us with your love, show us how to serve
> The neighbors we have from you (*WOV* #765).

~ ecc

❖ LUKE 10:29-37 ❖

❖ Hope for Creation ❖

About this time of year we observe Arbor Day. For Christians it is a time to affirm our concern for the preservation of the earth.

Is there something unique about our Christian view of nature? I believe there is. We begin by asking, "Is God intermingled in every aspect of the natural order?" It's easy to think so on a summer evening as we view a golden sunset over the quiet waters of a lake or when the soft snow nestles gently on a pine bough on a crisp January morning or when a bed of tulips treats us to every hue of the rainbow.

But what about when a raging tornado destroys everything in its path, leaving hundreds dead? Where is God in all of this?

As Christians we never identify God with nature. Instead, we link nature with us, with humans. As Augustine observed, we see glimpses of God in people, and we see glimpses of God in nature. But only glimpses. We do not see God and nature as one and the same. As Paul writes to the Romans, nature, like us, is groaning like a woman in childbirth, longing to be delivered.

This is why celebrating Arbor Day takes on a different, very radical perspective. We Christians have this revolutionary idea that both we and nature are eventually destined for destruction and death.

And what do we radical believers say in the face of all of this? The Easter answer is clear. We stand in the face of decay and death and say, "Neither death nor life . . . nor anything else in all creation, will be able to separate us from the love of God that is in Christ Jesus our Lord" (Rom. 8:38).

That love extends to more than the human family. It is for all of creation. What better news for Arbor Day!

~ hwc

❖ ROMANS 8:18-25 ❖

❖ Do We Have to Use *That* Creed? ❖

When the pastor announces, "Let us confess our faith in the words of the Nicene Creed," one can almost hear a sigh sweeping over the congregation. "Why do we have to use *that* one? The Apostles' Creed says it all, doesn't it? All those repetitious words and phrases seem completely unnecessary."

Indeed, it does seem that way: "begotten, not made, of one Being with the Father."

There is a good reason for all these seemingly excessive words and phrases. It all goes back to the early church in the fourth century. Believe it or not, they, too, had strong differences of opinion. In fact, their disputes make our current ones seem like a Sunday school picnic.

One of the most intense was the debate over the nature of Christ. There was a faction known as the Arians who insisted that Jesus was not divine. Yes, a good and honorable man, but not "one with the Father."

The principal voice in favor of holding to the idea that Jesus Christ was one with the Father was the man we commemorate today—Athanasius, bishop of Alexandria in Egypt. He battled for a trinitarian faith, a belief that Jesus Christ was eternally one with the Father.

For his strong stance Athanasius paid a price. He had to go into exile five times and was almost constantly under threat from those who opposed him.

It would be a mistake to think that the battles Athanasius fought back in the fourth century were forever settled. In every age, including our own, there are those who prefer to see Jesus Christ primarily as a good man or as one who gradually became divine in the course of his life.

As Lutherans we stand firm on the biblical confession that "all things have been created through him and for him. He himself is before all things, and in him all things hold together" (Col. 1:16-17).

~ hwc

❖ COLOSSIANS 1:15-20 ❖

❖ I HAVE HEARD THEIR CRY ❖

Pictures can speak louder than words. Especially where words are not allowed. Such was the case with the photos of young Earnest Cole, a black native of South Africa. Before leaving his homeland, Cole captured with his camera the plight and desperation of blacks living under apartheid. After emigrating to the United States, his work was published in a book, *Hour of Bondage*. Neither he nor his works were allowed back in South Africa.

In New York he became homeless and died young, shortly after Nelson Mandela was freed from a long prison term. Now, Cole's photographs, displayed at the Johannesburg Art Gallery, have power to shock and enrage white people's prejudice as it reveals demeaning of black folks. Oh, the pictures: a black boy with sweat running down his face in a crowded class, eager to learn and holding only a slate; a black maid holding her little white charge saying, "I love this child though she'll grow up to treat me just like her mother does" (*New York Times*, 11-10-10).

God loves all creation. Notice God's concern for people in bondage: "I have observed the misery . . . I have heard their cry . . . I know their sufferings, and I have come down to deliver them" (Exod. 3:7-8). Then there was the burning bush. God got Moses' attention and he heard the call, "I will send you" (v. 10). Is God trying to get your attention because someone you know is crying to God, someone who needs help that you can give?

> I the Lord of earth and sky,
> I have heard my people cry. . . .
> I, who made the stars of night,
> I will make their darkness bright.
> Who will bear my light to them?
> Whom shall I send?
> Here I am, Lord. Is it I, Lord?
> I have heard you calling in the night.
> I will go, Lord if you lead me.
> I will hold your people in my heart (*WOV* #752).

Amen

~ ecc

❖ EXODUS 3:1-12 ❖

❖ A LETTER ❖

Unlike the twenty-first century of emails, text messages, and other electronic communication, in our earlier life it was common to receive and send letters. Every Sunday evening, like clockwork, my mother faithfully placed three pieces of carbon paper between four sheets of typing paper and rolled them into her Smith Corona, readying herself to type her weekly letter to her four daughters. On Wednesday each week it would arrive in our mailboxes.

A letter can be held in your hand, savored, and be re-read. It conveys a fresh image of the sender, and tightens the bond between the sender and the receiver. A letter can inform, encourage, inspire, motivate, build one's confidence, open new possibilities, reassure love, and enliven hope. Most of all, a letter can strengthen and solidify a relationship. Love letters are like that. How eagerly lovers, when separated by miles, await another letter—just to see the handwriting, to be reassured that love continues, to know both of you are counting the days until you can be together again.

In the ancient world it was common that before leaving for a new location people would take with them letters of recommendation from others who knew them. This would assure the new community that they were good people.

Plato, the philosopher, said that a good teacher did not write his message in ink that would fade and in words that could not speak, but in the heart of a disciple who understood. Paul says Jesus has written his message in our hearts so we are a letter from him (2 Cor. 3:1-3). So whether we like it or not, we advertise for Christ. Like an open letter.

It's overwhelming, but take heart. It is Christ who wrote the letter we are to deliver, "not with ink but with the Spirit of the living God" (v. 3). We are neither confident or competent of ourselves but "Our competence is from God, who has made us competent to be ministers" (vv. 5-6).

~ ecc

❖ 2 CORINTHIANS 3:1-6 ❖

❖ The Importance of Letting Go ❖

Our favorite walking path with our dog Jonah is in a meadow two blocks from our home. Along the path we pass a number of young oak trees. One distinguishing characteristic of an oak is that it holds on to its leaves in the fall while neighboring varieties shed theirs. In fact, it holds on all winter, even in a raging snowstorm.

I asked Jim Gilbert, Minnesota's most well-known naturalist, why this happens. Jim said it's a mystery. No one knows.

What we do know is that as spring advances the leaves begin to fall. No matter how fiercely they cling to the branch, new growth forces them to let go and finally fall to the ground.

These oaks remind me of our tendency as Christians to cling to old habits and familiar ways of doing things long after we should have shed them. Change is challenging. It means adopting new habits, learning new procedures, getting used to change. It's never easy, of course, but new growth demands that we accept change.

To illustrate this point Jesus took an example from everyday Palestinian life. His listeners knew about wine making. They understood that wine expands when it ferments. Everyone knows, Jesus observed, that new wine must be preserved in fresh, new, elastic wineskins. Putting it into a dry, rigid skin would burst the skin and the precious wine would be lost.

Today may be a good day to make an assessment of our lives. What old habits need to be dropped so that new life can grow? What familiar and comfortable ways of doing things are keeping us from experiencing an exciting new aspect of the Christian life? What "dry leaves" are keeping us from knowing God's grace in a new way? Are we so anchored in the winter of our past that we miss some of the springtime excitement of God's grace?

~ hwc

❖ MATTHEW 9:16-17 ❖

❖ Set upon a Rock ❖

There are no words to describe a sudden and unexpected tragic loss. It feels like falling, falling, falling, with nothing to stop you. Everything in your life goes topsy-turvy. Your world is no longer what you have known. It is when falling that one probably realizes for the first time an utter helplessness.

That is how I felt the morning we found our eighteen-year-old, Andrew, dead. But that was the day I began for the first time to understand God's promise through the psalmist, "He will set me high on a rock" (Ps. 27:5). Because after falling, the place where I landed was in the arms of God. And that was a solid rock of comfort and hope. It was not I who found the rock. It was God there waiting who set me on the rock.

There are so many things we can do to protect ourselves from calamity—health care, good investments and wise saving, good diet and exercise, health insurance, life insurance, car insurance, crop insurance, intellectual insurance. But ultimately, nothing can assure us of complete protection against calamity. We need to be assured often of our only real protection. And how do we believe the assurance of the psalmist?

> The Lord is my light and my salvation; whom shall I fear?
> The Lord is the stronghold of my life; of whom shall I be afraid?
> (Ps. 27:1).

It is in regular worship with the body of believers where we hear the word, sing the hymns, speak words of the Creed, pray together, and grow in believing. As we grow in faith with the whole family of God, we grow in faith in our personal lives. As we wait for the Lord, we grow strong and our hearts take courage. Then when we fall helpless, it is God who "will set me high on a rock." A rock during this lifetime and for all eternity. Thanks be to God.

~ ecc

❖ Praying about the Small Stuff ❖

You couldn't have a better neighbor than Jim. A devout Roman Catholic, he was often at early mass before going to work or other activities. If I needed help for anything I couldn't do alone, he was right there to lend a hand.

Over coffee one morning we were discussing prayer. I suggested that some things might be so inconsequential that we should not bother God with them. Jim thought for a moment and then said quietly, "Maybe we should let God decide about that."

He was right. I was embarrassed to have been so cavalier in my attitude. I knew better.

One day a friend asked me to write about my prayer life. It was then that I realized that I was nearly always in prayer. When I hear a siren I pray for those in distress. When I get into my car I pray for safety. When I see those who are developmentally challenged in some way I pray that life will be as good as possible. When I'm awake at night I pray for family, friends, my pastors, and leaders of the church. Often on an early Sunday morning I let my spirit rove across the country, asking the Spirit to fill those who preach and teach in our churches. When I lose something of value I pray for help to find it. And much more.

Jim was right. It's never inappropriate to say a prayer, to ask for God's help, to intercede for someone in need, to pray for God's guidance in even the smallest and seemingly inconsequential corners of our lives.

As you move through another day, try to fill your moments with prayer. And yes, even praying about those things you think are too small for God's time and attention. As Jim said so wisely, let God decide about that.

~ hwc

❖ EPHESIANS 6:18-20 ❖

Stronger When Broken and Bound

After being at a Kenyan retreat with missionaries, we stopped in Egypt on our way home and enjoyed a sunset sail on the Nile River. How peaceful and still gliding over smooth water as we viewed the red horizon and verdant lush green river valley bordered by sandy desert. With eight passengers, the rustic sailboat was sturdy enough. The captain was sturdy too. He was ruddy, weather worn, and seasoned. Herb asked about the mast that held the sail and looked broken and bound with heavy ropes. The captain, wise after plenty of experience braving the river winds, explained, "A single mast could never withstand the heavy winds. So the mast has been broken into three pieces and bound together. It's much stronger," he said, "when broken and bound together."

No one likes trials and suffering. When they come, we sometimes wonder why. We even cry out to God with anger feeling life is unfair. Sometimes feeling we've been cheated out of bliss we had expected. Suffering can lead to bitterness. We've all seen it, and maybe even experienced it ourselves. But bitterness is very harmful, and it's like walking dead. Instead of bitterness, we're called to endure, even to rejoice in suffering. How can we? There is only one way to go—to the cross of Jesus, the man who knew sorrow and was acquainted with grief. He is able to bind us when we are broken, making us strong enough to withstand the winds of suffering. Strength that gives endurance and hope is ours.

Suffering then opens us to deep longing for the presence of Jesus who was broken for us. Jesus pours God's love into our hearts, brings the body of Christ to help bind us, and gives us the Holy Spirit to dwell within us and to intercede for us. Without having been broken and bound, we could never know such joy. Or could we be channels of God's love to others who suffer.

~ ecc

❖ ROMANS 5:1-5 ❖

❖ THIS LAND IS OUR LAND? ❖

When my great grandparents settled north of Willmar, Minnesota, in the summer of 1861, they were certain they had found their utopia. Having left behind the stony province of Småland in Sweden, this was what they had longed for—fertile land where they could turn the soil and raise cattle and fields of grain.

In doing so, of course, they would push away those who roamed these lands—the Sioux natives.

How differently these two peoples looked at land.

> For Indians the land's value lay in its grass, which supplied food for deer, elk, bison, and horses as well as prairie turnips, wild fruits, and other plants for people to harvest. European settlers, however, believed the land's greatest potential could be released only by breaking it open with plow and planting in it the seeds of domesticated grains.
>
> (from *Women of the Northern Plains*, Minnesota Historical Society Press)

My ancestors only lived there for a year until the Great Sioux Uprising drove them away, leaving in its wake hundreds of dead Native Americans and European settlers.

I know we can't turn the clock back. What then can we do?

I'm reminded that at this time of year it was once customary to celebrate "Rogation Sunday." It was a day to stop and pray for God's blessing on the land, to remember that we are responsible stewards of the gift of the earth, and that the harvest of the fields is for all of God's children.

At the Linnaeus Arboretum at St. Peter, Minnesota, a large acreage has been restored to native prairie, reminding visitors of what the land looked like before that soil was turned. From its highest point I can look out and see both the waving prairie grass as well as nearby fields of corn and beans. From there I can see what was and what is and thank God for both.

~ hwc

❖ PSALM 24 ❖

❖ THIRSTY ❖

With each reading of this story, I'm drawn to like the Samaritan woman so much that I've given her a name–Samantha. I like her for how ably she's handled hard times. And for her openness in this encounter with Jesus. For her daring to see how thirsty she really was.

Busy about her household chores, she's off to the town well for water. And by chance, Jesus is there, tired from his journey, and resting. He asks her for a drink. How alarming, a Jewish man looks at and speaks to a Samaritan who is only a woman. She should not look at him or talk to him. When Jesus asks about her husband, she's honest to say she has none. But somehow he knows she's had five and the present "live in" is not a husband. Divorced five times already?

Divorce was easy then. A wife was property. If a husband got annoyed with his wife, even for burned toast, all he needed to do was stand up saying three times, "I divorce you," and she was out of there. Now Jesus is exposing all of this baggage she's carrying. But I envision Samantha figuring out how, at each new painful juncture of new hurt, to balance it until again she could gracefully walk tall.

Then Jesus said, if she only knew who he was, she'd ask him for something far greater than water from this well—for living water, water springing out of a boundless source. It would fill her thirst forever. That's when Samantha's eyes are opened. This Jewish man, Jesus, knows her through and through. Knows her with all the baggage she's carrying. She feels his care and knows she can trust him. Daring now to look at him, she realizes her thirst, for living water. We, too, are in Jesus' presence.

> As a deer longs for flowing steams, so my soul longs for you,
> O God. My soul thirsts for God, for the living God (Ps. 42:1-2).

~ ecc

❖ JOHN 4:3-19; 25-30 ❖

❖ Help for the Thirsty ❖

We're blessed this day to read again John 4 and meet thirsty Samantha. Think of someone you've seen, really thirsty—runners in a marathon or victims of an earthquake reaching desperately when the water truck arrives.

The greatest thirst I've seen has been during the years in my nursing career, caring for patients in the end stage of dying when the kidneys fail. With tongue parched and beefy red, one becomes feverish and restless. No amount of water by mouth or fed intravenously can quench the thirst because the kidneys are unable to process water.

Perhaps there is no greater miracle in the entire universe than the work of a healthy kidney, working within us twenty-four hours a day without any effort on our part. Within its miles of hair like tubules, blood circulates to interface with intricate microscopic structures on those tubules. By osmosis, poisons from the blood are pulled into the kidney and cast off as waste. Only with this continual cleansing can the body circulate fresh blood to every cell of the body. Without this action, one would become weak, desperately thirsty, and would die.

Samantha's eyes were opened that day meeting Jesus, not only to know how desperately thirsty she was, but also to know that her only help was the living water he offered. Like a dying person reaching for a cure, she said to Jesus, "Sir, give me this water, so that I may never be thirsty" (John 4:15). Even more miraculous than what kidneys do for the human body is what Jesus offers. First, through the word, he helps us know how needy and thirsty we are, just like Jesus helped Samantha that day. And secondly, he offers us "a spring of water gushing up to eternal life" (v.14). It's free again today. Let's drink deeply.

> I came to Jesus as I was, so weary, worn, and sad. . . .
> My thirst was quenched, my soul revived, and now I live in him
> (*ELW* #611)

~ ecc

❖ JOHN 4:3-19; 25-30 ❖

❖ Surprise ❖

Today, our third day reading from John 4, we learn again from Samantha who acknowledges her needs, her excessive baggage that's she's been carrying, and her desperate thirst. Furthermore, we watch Samantha open her life in receiving living water that only Jesus can give. How good if you and I, even in this moment, could have such a conversation with Jesus. Jesus, who is looking into our souls right now. And there in his presence we can name each need, each anxiety, and each burden, giving them one by one to Jesus. We're invited, "Cast all your anxiety on him, because he cares for you" (1 Pet. 5:7).

Sometimes even though we pray repeatedly for God to help in a certain situation, it doesn't seem to help. Could it be that we come away from prayer still carrying our burden? Like Samantha, are we are learning more and more to balance our ever-increasing burdens, never allowing Jesus to lift and carry them for us? Not really believing that the invitation is "for you"? The invitation is for you; Jesus says, "Come to me, all you that are weary and are carrying heavy burdens, and I will give you rest" (Matt. 11:28).

I like watching Samantha as she drank the living water, allowing Jesus to take her burden from her. Can you see her leaving it with him at the well? She even forgot why she'd come there. She left her water jug and went away free. All she could think of was running to tell others about Jesus, saying, "Come and see a man who told me everything I have ever done! He cannot be the Messiah, can he?" (John 4:29). After what he'd done for her, no one needed to encourage her to tell others about Jesus.

Then came the surprise! Because of what she had told them, her hearers hurried to meet Jesus. May our witness be so powerful. And that can happen after being with Jesus.

~ ecc

❖ JOHN 4:3-19; 25-30 ❖

❖ Those Little Words ❖

I was blessed with a good mother. She was a strong woman with seemingly endless energy to care for her family of eight children, to tend to a huge garden, and to help my father with his custodian duties at our church. Very often on a summer morning she would be up with the sun to enjoy her gardens before coming into the house to prepare breakfast for her family.

Most of all, I'm thankful for the mark she made on my young Christian life. Inside the cover of my confirmation Bible she wrote: *Be careful how you live; you may be the only Bible some people ever read.*

At a time when I was making important choices about the future, this was sound advice. This was her way of impressing on my formative heart that the Christian life is more than words—it is actions as well.

Parents may be inclined to think that they have very little influence on their children, especially during their teenage years. We think our words are falling on deaf ears. School, their friends, television, cell phones, computers—we think that everything else except us must surely be having a more lasting impact on them.

But one never knows. A simple word of encouragement, a note left on their desk, a word written in their Bible, a phone call at a critical time—who knows what it may mean to them. A single sentence may last for a lifetime.

Paul had a number of companions. None, however, was as close to his heart as young Timothy. In his first letter to his inexperienced friend, Paul gave this good word of counsel, "Set the believers an example in speech and conduct, in love, in faith, in purity" (1 Tim. 4:12).

Who knows what a simple word from you may mean to a younger pilgrim on the way of faith?

~ hwc

❖ 1 TIMOTHY 4:11-14 ❖

❖ THANKS, GRANDMA! ❖

We honor our mothers at this time of the year. But why not grandmothers as well?

At a retreat in northwestern Minnesota some years ago I was sitting in a circle with about twenty-five women of various ages. I suggested at one point that we each share a brief statement about the person who had influenced us most in our Christian journey. Pastors and parents were named. But I wasn't surprised when a majority said it was a grandmother who left the deepest imprint on them.

That's how it was for me. In the heart of the Great Depression our family lived with my grandparents for several months. Though she lived in this country for nearly a half-century, my grandmother Hedda never conquered the English language. She would gather us for devotions after the evening meal. Though her body was wracked with pain from rheumatism, she would rise from the table, reach for her books, and be our chaplain for the day. She read from her Swedish Bible and its companion, the "Psalm Bok," a collection of psalms and other religious writings. The readings were followed by a quiet prayer.

Even when I was a restless 4-year-old lad and understood nothing of what she read, this hushed moment in a hectic day left an indelible impression that lingers even now. Through her I learned the importance of stopping for a moment every day and giving attention to the Bible and prayer.

In his words of encouragement and instruction to Timothy, the apostle Paul reminded his young companion that the faith did not start with their generation. It could be traced back to their Jewish roots where godly mothers and grandmothers had embraced that faith and passed it on to their children.

It's fine for someone to say they've been "born again." But nothing ever starts strictly with us. Most everything we have, including the gift of grace, comes from others. And more often than not, it's from a grandmother.

~ hwc

❖ 2 TIMOTHY 1:3-7 ❖

MAY 15

❖ Wrapping Up the Day with Prayer ❖

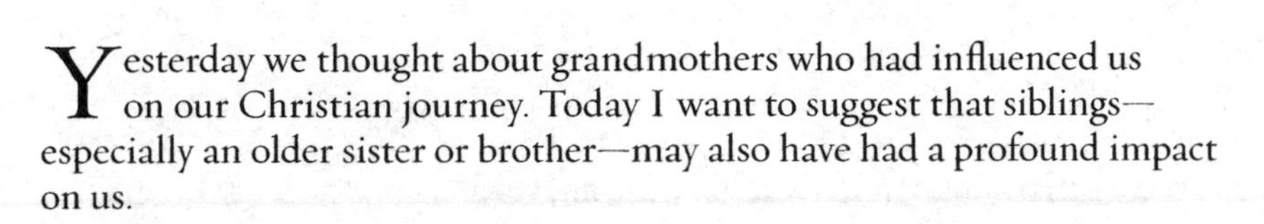

Yesterday we thought about grandmothers who had influenced us on our Christian journey. Today I want to suggest that siblings—especially an older sister or brother—may also have had a profound impact on us.

That was surely the case for me. Because our home was so small, most of us children slept in the same bedroom. I often refer to my oldest sister Addie as our "bedroom chaplain." As the oldest of eight, she took all of her responsibilities very seriously. That included leading us in our bedtime prayers. It wasn't always easy to get my brother Dave and me to settle down for the night. But her firm word usually did the trick. "All right everyone. It's time for our prayers," she would announce. "Fold your hands and close your eyes." In the pitch darkness of our small home on the edge of town I never understood why we had to close our eyes, but I followed her instructions dutifully.

We joined in one chorus, first with the Lord's Prayer, followed by, "Now I lay me down to sleep. . . ." The litany closed with "God bless Mama and Daddy, my sisters and my brothers, and all the children of the world. Amen."

When Addie left home the next in line took over the "chaplaincy" duties. That small exercise in prayer left a lifelong mark on each of us children.

In Old Testament times the people of God were taught that the first place to give attention to God was in the home. Every moment of the day was to be thought of as a time that belonged to God, a moment to bring God into whatever one was doing.

Surely no time is more important than the final moments when we entrust our sleeping hours into the hands of a loving God. If you haven't done so, there is no better time to begin this important practice than today.

~ hwc

❖ DEUTERONOMY 6:4-9 ❖

❖ He Restores My Soul ❖

After moving into a house with a vaulted ceiling, I called my father, who enjoyed going to estate sales, and asked him to be on the lookout for an antique piece that would fit a high wall. One day he called with urgency saying he had not only found, but bought an antique hutch. As he described it, I knew it was perfect. But what happened was that immediately after his bid had purchased it for sixty dollars, antique dealers arrived eager to buy it from him for a much greater price. And he wanted to know, "Do you want it?" With no hesitation, I said, "Yes, it's a prize!"

Sturdy, but it had had hard use. Smudged. Upper door singed from a candle burning on the flipped open door that became a desk. But what possibilities. We set about restoring it. Removed old cracked varnish. Bleached, sanded, and stained it. Applied coats of varnish with fine sanding between coats. How beautiful now the grain of old butternut wood setting off lovely, old carvings on drawer fronts with their freshly polished brass handles. Restored and now useful.

What does God see looking in your soul and mine? Perhaps it looks like a piece of old furniture with smudges, stains, burns, and scars. Hurts varnished over, maybe cracking by this time. God who sees it all sees each of us so precious, and wants to restore us if only we'll allow it. *Restore* means to bring back to a former condition; or to compensate for, producing equilibrium and balance, even making up for lack of ability.

For each of us, God is ready to start right now taking off the cracked layers we're hiding behind, getting down to the stain of sin. Jesus is waiting to bleach sin away at the cross, compensate for what we lack, and restore us back to our baptism—cleansed, forgiven, and set free.

He restores my soul (Ps. 23:3).

~ ecc

❖ First, Fast, Last Friend ❖

Reminiscing as we drove to Omaha for Rueben's memorial service, it was hard realizing that he was gone. This sturdy, stalwart, humble, and efficient statesman of the church. Respecting him as mentor, colleague, advisor, and friend, it was always comforting to know he was only a phone call away. Even as we were celebrating the gift of his servant life, we felt his loss so deeply, both personally as well as for the church where his name has been written large. Now these few years later, when his name is mentioned, some ask, "Who was he?" It's sobering to know that one day we, too, will not only be gone from this life but also forgotten. But never forgotten by Jesus.

In Old Testament times many priests were needed because death kept taking them away. But Jesus who is our high priest, as recorded in Hebrews 7:24-25, "continues forever. Consequently he is able for all time to save those who approach God through him, since he always lives to make intercession for them."

Our Triune God (Father, Son, and Holy Spirit) was, is, and always will be our friend. God formed us in the womb and is with us throughout our earthly life, even to old age. And forever. Hear the promises:

> You [God] knit me together in my mother's womb (Ps. 139:13).
>
> [You] have been borne by me from your birth, carried from the womb; even to your old age I am he, even when you turn gray I will carry you (Isa. 46:3-4).
>
> Neither death nor life . . . will be able to separate us from the love of God in Christ Jesus our Lord (Rom. 8:38-39).

It is hard imagining no longer living in this world. And it is sad thinking of not even being remembered here. But when Gerald Manley Hopkins writes about Jesus being our truest friend, he names him our "first, fast, last friend." Thanks be to God.

~ ecc

❖ ROMANS 8:38-39 ❖

Good Leaders Are an Exception

I may be a bit prejudiced, but I believe there is no cathedral in the world more beautiful than the one at Uppsala, Sweden. In fact, when Corinne and I visited that splendid architectural gem for the first time she broke into tears. It is that beautiful.

Among those buried at the cathedral is Eric, king of Sweden from 1151–1161.

We don't ordinarily think of political leaders as exemplary Christians. There are, however, some notable exceptions. Eric was one. His passion was to bring Christianity to all of Sweden and Finland. He became known for instituting fair laws for all of the people and for his concern for those who were poor, sick, and handicapped. These were noble characteristics in an age when such persons were pushed aside and ignored. Rivals murdered Eric on this day as he was leaving a worship service in old Uppsala.

I suggested to the pastors of our local congregation some time ago that three persons should be in our Sunday intercessions on a regular basis, if not weekly: the president of the United States, the presiding bishop of the ELCA, and the bishop of our synod. Are they more important than others we pray for? No and yes. No, because they are human like the rest of us. Like all of us, they are sinners in need of daily forgiveness and divine guidance. But, yes, because they are subject to greater temptation than most of us. The subtle allure of power, sex, and wealth are more intense for them. The sexual dalliances of some presidents and congresspersons in recent times are well known in this age of Twitter transparency. But as information about former times comes to light we know that these kinds of misdeeds are not new.

And the church? Yes, I can tell you that bishops and pastors are not immune from these temptations.

~ hwc

❖ 1 KINGS 3:6-9 ❖

❖ Danger of an Empty Soul ❖

It's dangerous to let the soul go on empty. It happened to a young person. Two professional counselors learned of a troubled young child who needed a foster home and decided to take him in to be raised alongside their own children. Things went well until as a teenager his soul went on empty. The demons of drugs knocked on his door and came in uninvited because his soul was swept empty. With a twisted mind, he began rewriting the history of his foster family until it was unrecognizable. Good memories were now darkened, leaving him sad and angry. Addicted to drugs, he became as one possessed by demons. One day with parents in the therapist's office, he announced that his parents were abusing him. Patience ran out. The parents stood saying, "That is enough." He was no longer allowed to stay in their home, fabricating lies and blaming others for the torture in his soul.

Jesus told the parable of a man whose soul was swept clean and empty. The evil spirit gathered seven more spirits, more evil than itself, to fill up the poor empty soul. The soul will be filled with something. Like a house, the soul needs continual regular cleaning. But after the cleaning, it needs filling.

Scripture warns, "Do not get drunk with wine, for that is debauchery; but be filled with the Spirit" (Eph. 5:18). Fill up the soul with psalms and hymns and thanks to God. Yes, the soul needs a daily sweeping clean, and after that the filling as we're told in Philippians 4:4-9. Fill up with rejoicing in the Lord and share that joy with others. Think not about negative things, but about what is honorable, just, pure, lovely, and things excellent and worthy of praise. Fill up the soul with memorized Bible verses and hymns. The Holy Spirit waits to do the filling if we ask. May your joy be full.

~ ecc

❖ LUKE 11:24-26 ❖

Dashing toward the Finish Line

In preparation for Memorial Day, many of us go to a cemetery to beautify the gravesite of a relative or friend. It's an important time to remember what these persons meant to us while they lived. And we also take time to think about the qualities of those persons we want to emulate in our lives.

Corinne and I go to prepare the site where our son is buried. Having lived in the community off and on for more than forty years, we usually wander through the other grave markers as well, noting names and telling stories about our connection with each name—Dennis, Evelyn, Paul, Edna, Ted, Ebba, Harold, Signe, Edgar, Clarice . . . and many others.

It was only recently that someone called my attention to the "dash" on each grave marker. She said that the dash represents one's life:

1918 – 1975
1955 – 1982

There are also markers placed in anticipation of one's death:

1931 –
1940 –

This—the "dash"—was a new insight for me. No matter how short or long one's life, everyone has that dash, that fleeting movement between birth and death.

Take a moment today to reflect on the dash in your lifespan. If you enjoy robust health the dash may not mean much. You assume it will be a long dash, no matter what your age may be. But if you face the prospect of a life that is shorter than you expected, that dash takes on an entirely different meaning. Whatever our situation, we know that life hangs by a very tenuous and flimsy thread. Believers in Christ and his resurrection live in the hope and expectation that no matter when that day comes, no matter how long or short the dash, we have a promise:

> Those who believe in me, even though they die, will live (John 11:25).

~ hwc

JAMES 4:13-17

❖ Praying for Peace ❖

This is the time of the year when we honor those who have sacrificed their lives for our country and for the freedoms we all too often take for granted.

Over the years I've traveled to many countries and have learned that each land takes unique pride in being an important member of the family of nations. Yet, I've never landed again on American soil without breathing a prayer of thanksgiving that I happened to be born in the United States. And over and over again I have felt gratitude for those who sacrificed so much to protect our freedoms.

I also reflect, however, on the words of a veteran of the invasion of France in World War II: Anyone who has fought in combat doesn't want war. There is a message in this man's words. We would do well on Memorial Day to not only honor heroes of our wars, but to also redouble our efforts to find ways to resolve conflict in peaceful, non-violent ways.

Men like Mahatma Gandhi and Martin Luther King, Jr. were impelled by the teachings of Jesus to resist oppression by confronting evil with the force of love and forgiveness. We may not think we wield much authority in the world. Yet, each of us in our smaller circles of life encounter events that could easily flame up into unnecessary conflict. In our walk with Christ today may we look for ways to use the power of love and grace.

Better yet, this may be a good day to sit down and write that letter or email to those who move in those larger places of authority—the president and our representatives in Washington—urging them to keep doors of communication open to all nations and to use military force only as a last and tragic alternative.

We may be tempted to think that the words of Jesus only work in person-to-person situations. Yet, history is replete with examples of leaders who kept open doors of conversation and avoided unnecessary bloodshed.

~ hwc

❖ MATTHEW 5:38-48 ❖

❖ An Oasis ❖

One Sunday morning in Arizona, Herb got up finding me on my knees in the bathroom blowing my hair dry, and he quickly asked why! It was because I was feeling faint. Later in the Emergency Room with an IV running, I was feeling better because my body was satisfied. I had become dehydrated. In a place of low humidity one must tend to keeping the body hydrated and therefore satisfied with sufficient fluids.

Like a person faint in an arid climate because the body is low on fluids, so also if lacking a close relationship with Christ we can become faint. Faint in peace and joy, unsatisfied because we lack the presence of Jesus Christ.

At mealtime when the disciples were ready to send people away, Jesus said no, that isn't a good idea. Jesus had compassion on them because he feared they would become faint on the way. Jesus cares for us too when we become faint because of our need for his presence. He has provided for us an oasis. These words from Carl Rosenius say it so beautifully:

"Christ has planted his Table like an oasis along our pathway, in order that when we become weary with travel, weak and hungry in our souls, discouraged and wounded because of our false steps, stumbling, and falling, we may then enter there and be refreshed with the living Bread of life" (from "On the Eucharist as the Viaticum, the Pilgrim's Food").

Luther teaches that our benefits at the Lord's Supper, along with the eating and drinking, are the words, "Given for you" and "shed for you . . . for the forgiveness of sin." For whoever "believes these very words has what they declare and state, namely, forgiveness of sin" (*Luther's Small Catechism*, The Sacrament of Holy Baptism).

Jesus invites us with compassion, as he invited the crowd long ago, to come to the table and be satisfied, at his oasis.

~ ecc

❖ MARK 8:1-10 ❖

❖ Paying the Ultimate Price ❖

I've traveled millions of miles by air and have known a few harrowing moments when thoughts about death crossed my mind. But I've never felt as close to my demise as I did while traveling by automobile on the island of Sumatra in Indonesia. Cows, goats, sheep, chickens, and, yes, humans ambled across the roadway at their leisure as we barreled along at breakneck speed. When I inquired of missionary Warner Luoma if this was a bit risky he replied, "The attitude here is that if your time has come, you may die; if not, you will live."

Though I contemplated the possibility of death by accident, I reflected on what life was like for the Christian missionaries who first evangelized this part of the world.

Today we honor Ludwig Nommensen, the Dane who became known as "The Apostle to the Bataks." Nommensen began his work there in June 1862, just as the Civil War was breaking out in the United States. He died there on this date in 1918.

Trained in Germany, Nommensen spent his entire life in Sumatra among the Batak tribe, a people who until then had not been reached either by Islam or Christianity. After difficult work in the first years, Nommensen and others succeeded in leading several tribal chiefs to faith in Christ. From this beachhead they were able to reach thousands more. The church flourished until it became one of the largest churches in the global Lutheran family.

But Nommensen paid a price. His first wife and all four of their children died in that tropical climate. Then his second wife died, leaving him with three children. Who can imagine such sorrow?

This is a good day to enfold in our prayers all who serve Christ and our church in countries around the globe, many of them in settings where they are in danger from accident and disease.

~ hwc

❖ MARK 16:19-20 ❖

❖ MAKE TIME FOR GOD ❖

Our morning farm routine was well established. Each person in the family had definite responsibilities that needed to be done on time. From my parents, I learned the cardinal principle that you make time for what is important.

The routine began every morning with my mother's voice calling out from the hallway below, "Time to get up." My job was to help milk cows at 6:00 a.m. Then there was a piping hot breakfast for all seven together around the kitchen table. And afterwards, family devotions. We took turns reading a chapter from the Bible and leading in a free prayer of thanksgiving and intercession. Next was doing dishes, making lunches, and walking across the field to school. You make time for what is important.

Jesus tells us that he is the vine and we are the branches, and to be healthy branches we must abide in him. That means taking time for God. We need to carve out a regular time so that it becomes a routine. To abide means more than a quick stop. It means a staying, like sitting down for a good meal. It means taking time each day to stay in God's presence. It's time for growing into the vine in order to bear healthy fruit. It means quiet listening to God's word. Hearing God speak to reassure us of his promises. Waiting while Jesus cleanses our hearts and God's love pours in. Listening for God to guide us into service. God waits to give us these gifts so that, "my joy may be in you, and that your joy may be complete" (John 15:11).

A young woman tells me of her need for this. Each morning she arrives early at work, closes her office door and has time alone with God. "I need it," she says, "to make my day go right." We can abide in God only if we make time for God.

~ ecc

❖ JOHN 15:1-11 ❖

❖ The Peace of God ❖

Ethel was a good friend and like a grandmother to our children. As a faithful Christian and church volunteer, she shared her faith through word and action. As a widow, she had learned through adversity that folks need a friend, and she was that for many, using her gifts of generosity and hospitality. Her goal each day was to do a good deed for someone. Earrings were her signature that she put on every day to bring joy to others.

But Ethel in her elder years, when health began to fail, was confined to a nursing home. And she became depressed. Even though she still wore her earrings that brought cheer to others, she did not feel happy or joyful herself. Such inner turmoil. Old losses loomed large and feelings of guilt overcame her. God seemed distant from her and angry. She longed for peace. One day in our visit, we found her pleading for some kind of help. So we wrote a promise from God in large letters. She kept this at her bedside and began repeating the words many times a day. This was the promise: "The peace of God, which passes all understanding, will keep your heart and mind in Christ Jesus" (Phil. 4:7).

Peace in the New Testament means *well-being.* It means to be secure in the goodness of God where a believer is protected from sin, death, and the power of evil. God's peace is the assurance of forgiveness, mercy, and love.

She memorized the promise and repeated it out loud, each word spoken slowly and with great emphasis: The peace—of God—will keep—your heart and mind, (and with even more emphasis) in Christ Jesus.

Luther said, "In adversity, we think God is angry, so comfort can never be offered enough." For Ethel, repeating this promise seemed to drive the devil away so that fresh faith could come into her heart. And it will for you.

~ ecc

❖ PHILIPPIANS 4:4-7 ❖

❖ Being the Church ❖

I've always been grateful for the privilege of growing up in the traditions of the Augustana Lutheran Church, the church founded by Swedish Lutherans in 1860. Though it had many faults, one of its accents was what I would call "churchmanship," for want of a better term. This is that quality that carries the church through times of dissention, times when there is disagreement, often bitter, over a particular issue.

Those who embrace churchmanship do not try to organize a new church body. They don't withdraw or reduce their support for the mission of the church. They don't change their wills or estate plans to cripple the seminaries, global missions, or other ministries of the church.

These believers are committed to respecting the "conscience-bound" stance of those who differ with them on a particular issue. This is part of their churchmanship. They even defend those who disagree with them. They make a covenant to live in one church with those holding other views, recognizing that in many areas we have differences that do not separate us at the heart of the gospel.

Those of us who have studied the long history of the Lutheran church realize that there were numerous times when vicious wounds and costly disruption could have been averted if responsible persons had taken time to think about the consequences of their actions.

Disagreement was no stranger to the early Christian church. Nearly every letter in the New Testament is addressed to a group of believers who were having some kind of disagreement. Paul always pointed to what holds us together in the midst of conflict—our common allegiance to Jesus Christ.

In one of the great hymns of the church we admit that at times we are "by schisms rent asunder" but we hold together because "the Church's one foundation is Jesus Christ her Lord" (*LBW* #369).

~ hwc

❖ EPHESIANS 2:14-22 ❖

❖ THE ROAD TO FULL COMMUNION ❖

While in seminary in the late 1950s I decided to write a paper on the different ways Martin Luther and John Calvin understood the meaning of the Lord's Supper. After plumbing first one source and then another I came to the conclusion that there were no substantial differences.

"They came by different roads to the same place," I wrote. I assumed I was dead wrong, given the fact that Lutherans, the faith descendants of Martin Luther, and Presbyterians and Reformed churches, the heirs of John Calvin, had little to do with each other at the time. I expected my professor to give me a low grade and suggest that I dig deeper. To my surprise and delight I got a good grade with a note at the end of the paper suggesting I was correct.

It is one of the few occasions I have been ahead of my time. Since then our churches, divided since the time of the Reformation, have engaged in serious dialogue, searching diligently for our likenesses rather than only our differences.

Today we commemorate two of the giants of the Reformed church movement—John Calvin and John Knox. Contemporaries of Martin Luther, they tended to be more rigid in their expectations of how Christians were to live out their faith in daily life. Calvin, in particular, outlined in quite specific rules and regulations how members of his church were to conduct themselves.

It is sometimes said that the twentieth century will go down in church history as the "Century of Ecumenism." In the course of our inter-church dialogues we have not only come to understand each other more fully, but have even advanced to the place where Christians, separated and misunderstood for centuries, now walk the same aisle together to the same altar to receive the body and blood of our Lord Jesus Christ. Give thanks today that walls have come down.

~ hwc

❖ JOHN 17:6-11 ❖

❖ Many People, One Purpose ❖

When I had gallbladder surgery some time ago I decided to get acquainted the hospital staff. It was a "pentecost" experience. The anesthetist grew up in Russia; the surgeon had family roots in the Ukraine; the assisting nurse was of Norwegian descent; the physician in charge of the floor on which I stayed was a native of Pakistan; the chief of staff came from Greece; on a follow-up visit my doctor was from India. The only thing they had in common was that they were committed to helping a full-blooded, Swedish-American get well!

As I recovered I couldn't help but think of the vision God had for the church on the Day of Pentecost. Yes, they were all Jews who were together in Jerusalem on that momentous day. But they came from the ends of the earth—"every nation under heaven" (Acts 2:5). And the vision was much larger. God had declared that they were to "be my witnesses in Jerusalem, in all Judea and Samaria, and to the ends of the earth" (Acts 1:8).

When some didn't seem to "get it" completely on the Day of Pentecost and insisted on drawing lines, suggesting that only Jews could be part of this new movement, God came again through Peter and Paul and convinced them, saying, "We believe that we will be saved through the grace of the Lord Jesus, just as they will" (Acts 15:11).

Gentile and Jew, Palestinian and Greek, and Roman and Persian—all were to be welcomed, all had a place.

How strange and foolish it would have been had I said to one of those hospital staff persons, "Sorry, but I don't want a Russian administering anesthesia. I don't want a Norwegian in this room when I'm sedated. I don't trust a Pakistani doctor." Indeed, how foolish.

And are we not equally foolish when we in the church draw lines that exclude anyone?

~ hwc

❖ ACTS 1:6-9 ❖

❖ Our Mystery Guest ❖

I was a young professor of religion in the early 1960s. When a pastor asked me to give a series of lectures on the Holy Spirit I agreed to do so. The moment I hung up I wished I hadn't made that promise. I realized that I had given little thought to the subject.

Surely there was something in my seminary notes to aid me. I found almost nothing. I searched for books. Again, very little. It meant that I needed to dig on my own.

The weeks that followed proved to be some of the most enriching and enlightening of my ministry. It began a quest for understanding the person and work of the Holy Spirit that continued for years.

As I might have expected, the greatest help came from the Bible itself and the words of Jesus. When he knew the time was drawing near for him to leave his disciples Jesus made some promises about the Holy Spirit that were not only for them, but for us as well.

Jesus gave a name to the Holy Spirit. In the Greek language in which the New Testament was written it is "paraclatos." In every edition of the Bible translators try to find a word that we might more easily understand. But that proved to be easier said than done. Thus, the older King James version uses the term "Comforter." Newer versions use "Advocate" and "Counselor" and "Helper" and "Friend." One even uses the paraphrase, "Someone to stand by you."

Anyone who is bilingual knows of this problem. It is impossible at times to find a single word that adequately expresses the meaning of a word in another language.

Here is the good news: *Everything* you need for your life as a Christian is provided through the help of the Holy Spirit. So we embrace all those terms and pray confidently: "Come Holy Spirit. Come!"

~ hwc

❖ JOHN 14:15-21 ❖

❖ Visits and Redeems Us in Our Unbelief ❖

This is the story of Luke—how God visits and redeems us in our unbelief. It begins in the first chapter, with Zechariah's unbelief. For him, it began while, as priest, he was officiating at worship and all the people were praying. Suddenly an angel interrupted worship! "Fear overwhelmed him" (Luke 1:12). But the angel said, "Do not be afraid," because your prayer for a son is heard and it's going to happen.

Fear in God's presence came from his unbelief. All through Luke's chapters we see it: Mary (Chapter 1) and the shepherds (2), Peter (5), and the people of Nain (7), the woman with the hemorrhage (8). Even those who walk close with God are constantly in danger of unbelief. This is the deepest core of original sin, common to all people. But God visits us in the midst of our unbelief. God gave Zechariah the gift to believe. Just as for him and others in the chapters of Luke, God also visits and redeems us in our unbelief.

The good news is that our unbelief does not disqualify us from receiving the gift of faith and from receiving gifts that follow faith—gifts of joy, gladness, and rejoicing. Luther taught us that when God gives gifts, they are of God's own self—God's very heart, mind, and will. To be filled with the spirit is the activity of God. And that indeed, is grace.

For Zechariah, this powerful action of God happened right in the midst of his workday. He was "on duty," serving "by lot" his assigned eight-hour shift as it were. So take heart, dear friend. Know that when your faith seems dull, God doesn't disqualify you from grace. Or when your life is all too full, God still can, and will, visit and redeem you in your unbelief.

~ ecc

❖ LUKE 1:8-25 ❖

❖ Mary Visits Elizabeth ❖

Today we commemorate and learn from Mary and Elizabeth. We listen in on their amazing visit after something electrifying has happened in both of their lives. If Mary were living today, she'd text Elizabeth or call on her cell. For her, it meant a visit to tell her, "I have such news!" She already knew Elizabeth was pregnant. The angel had told her. Neither were ordinary pregnancies. What a miracle that Elizabeth had conceived in her old age. And Mary had been visited by an angel telling her three things: not to be afraid, she was favored by God, and she would conceive and bear a son, Jesus. The big question was "How can this be?" (Luke 1:34).

How? "The Holy Spirit will come upon you, and the power of the Most High will overshadow you . . . For nothing will be impossible with God" (Luke 1:35, 37). Not only was Mary "favored" by God, but she was also given miraculous passive action. It was God who pursued her. The word in Greek tells us that this favor comes with compassion and generous grace that is full of power. This grace enabled her to comply, saying, "Here I am, the servant of the Lord; let it be with me according to your word" (v. 38).

Then notice three things that happened when Mary and Elizabeth came together (vv. 42-45):

1. With Mary's greeting, Elizabeth felt the babe in her womb leap because she realized Mary was blessed with God's favor.

2. Elizabeth is humbled that "the mother of my Lord comes to me (v. 43). She knows the one Mary carries is "Jesus my Lord."

3. There's a benediction. Why is Mary blessed? Not because of carrying this child but because she "believed that there would be a fulfillment of what was spoken to her by the Lord" (v. 45).

What impossible thing looms in your life today? Can you allow God's miraculous favor and the Holy Spirit's overshadowing to do the impossible? Blessings as you believe.

~ ecc

❖ LUKE 1:26-56 ❖

❖ Planting Good Seed ❖

My maternal great-grandfather Carl Lindgren died on this day in 1928, well into his 80s. He was a master shoemaker in Skåne, the southernmost province of Sweden. He and his assistants constructed shoes from scratch.

Even more important for his family and future generations was that Lindgren was a godly man. Regular attendance at worship plus prayer and Bible reading in the home were part of his daily routine.

Lindgren kept a daily log of income and expenses for his shoe factory. Here and there he added notes of other kinds. Most outstanding are references to the support he and his wife gave to "the black man Onesimus in Stockholm." An Ethiopian convert to Christianity, Onesimus came to Sweden to study theology in the 1880s. He returned to Ethiopia and translated the Bible and *Luther's Small Catechism* into the native tongue of his people. Out of those seeds has emerged one of the largest Lutheran families of faith in the world—the Mekane Yesus Church, today numbering more than 5 million.

Lindgren had not seen his three daughters for more than a quarter century when he died. But letters, usually at birthday time and often taking weeks to cross the Atlantic, brimmed with a deep sense of trust in God.

In his last tear-stained note to my grandmother, Lindgren begins with words of hope. "God will certainly give to each and every one of us his abundant grace, he who is our God and Father who gives us all good for body and soul. Glory be to his good name!"

Lindgren died without ever knowing how his gifts to his family and to Onesimus would flourish. Neither do we know the outcome of words we speak, gifts we give, or deeds we do. Like Lindgren, we sow in faith and in hope, believing that the Lord of the harvest will see that no seed is planted in vain.

~ hwc

❖ MARK 4:27-29 ❖

❖ Sharing the Honor ❖

At this time of the year we honor our graduates. A few rise to the top, and we set them apart with special recognition—cum laude, magna cum laude, and summa cum laude. These have worked hard to achieve their status. We gladly single them out for distinction.

On a number of such occasions I've been awarded an honorary degree—doctor of divinity or doctor of letters. The award is always accompanied with a bouquet of lovely comments, spelling out the reasons someone thinks I'm worthy of this honor.

As I listened to those accolades I must confess that there were times when I found myself tempted to laugh. No, it would not have been kind of me to do that. Those who gave the honors were sincere. But I couldn't help but ask, "Are they talking about me? Am I really deserving of this much acclamation?"

Helmut Thielicke was a well-known German pastor a generation ago. While attendance at churches in his country was falling, Thielicke drew large crowds on Sunday mornings. His preaching was stimulating for both mind and soul. Students were especially drawn to his church.

The story is told that when he retired from the parish Thielicke was feted at a huge dinner. "These words," he said in his response, "mean more to me than a medal." But then he added that he actually felt some embarrassment. And why should he have felt this way. Because, said Thielicke, "I knew how fragile the vessel was in which I had to keep safe and manage the treasure."

When we are singled out for an honor, we should, of course, accept it graciously. But we should also remember that it is only by God's grace that we are able to accomplish anything in life. Every honor is one to be shared with those who love and support us. And, most of all, shared with the Giver of all gifts.

~ hwc

❖ LUKE 17:7-10 ❖

❖ Beloved Pope John XXIII ❖

It's hard to imagine anyone who lived at the time who did not admire Pope John XXIII. Today is his commemoration day.

Though I never met him, I found myself drawn to him for a number of reasons. He came from a family of thirteen children; we were eight. He, as I, was born into a farm family. Both of us were shaped by spiritual experiences in our youth. We each became bishops at the relatively young age of forty-four. Not surprisingly, we found ourselves embroiled in conflict in the church during those years. We both fostered ecumenical understanding between divergent churches. Not least, we both traveled widely, in my case visiting more than fifty countries over the years.

For these and many other reasons, it was a very distinct honor when Viterbo College, a Roman Catholic school at La Crosse, Wisconsin, presented me with the Pope John XXIII Award in 1989. Though he had been dead for some time, I could not help but feel a deep kinship with him on that day.

I used the occasion to call for greater understanding and unity between our Evangelical Lutheran Church in America and the Roman Catholic Church. Just a few weeks prior to that day I had participated with a Roman Catholic priest in the wedding of my niece and her new husband, a devout Roman Catholic. Though the ceremony was lovely and the occasion solemn, I could not help but ponder on how much more complete it would have been had we been able to share the sacrament as part of the service. On that basis, I called for renewed efforts to bring that longed for day to reality.

Unfortunately, the ecumenical spirit of John XXIII did not persist with the same intensity. Today, more than twenty years later, we are no closer to that goal of shared communion. Let it be our prayer.

~ hwc

❖ ACTS 15:1-11 ❖

❖ Highest Values ❖

Graduation addresses follow an expected pattern: Work hard; make connections; take advantage of opportunities; and inevitably, you will succeed in whatever you do.

Nothing wrong with that advice, is there?

Yes, as a matter of fact, there is something incredibly wrong with that approach to life—especially if we listen to what Jesus says: "Those who want to save their life will lose it, and those who lose their life for my sake ... will save it" (Mark 8:35).

A friend attended the installation service when Medardo Gomez became bishop of the Evangelical Lutheran Church in El Salvador. He noticed a woman in the front pew. She was radiant, exuding great joy. "I must meet her," my friend said. "I need to know why she seems so happy."

Then he learned her sad story. Her husband and all of her children had been killed in the civil war in El Salvador. "How then can you be so radiant?" he asked. "Because," she said, "I am a midwife. Each time I help a baby to be born I say to myself, 'Maybe through this child God will bring a special blessing to the world.'"

Should not that be our goal, no matter what our work may be? Yes, to serve others so that God will use them, in turn, to bless our world.

I've attended a number of high school reunions over the decades. In the early years there was boasting about how rapidly one was rising in one's profession. By the twenty-fifth year I heard much more about the values of family and community. By the fiftieth there were mostly words of gratitude for the good things that had happened, with little reference to accomplishments.

It would be well to reverse that order, to begin with a focus on the values that endure. And among the highest, Jesus would tell us, would be service for others.

~ hwc

❖ MARK 8:34-38 ❖

❖ Keep Balance ❖

We truly did claim New Jersey as our residency during the eight years we lived there. However, my neighbor reminded me one day that whenever I spoke of Minnesota I said, "back home." She was from Holland and that was her "back home." We shared in common an emotional dual citizenship.

As Christians, we too have a dual citizenship, loving God but also this world and all the people and things we're so attached to here. Because we're citizens of both this world and heaven, St. Augustine calls us, "resident aliens." Also, 1 Peter 2:11 says we're "aliens and exiles." By redeeming and claiming us for his own, Christ has won for us full rights as "citizens with the saints and also members of the household of God" (Eph. 2:19), where God has prepared a city for us (Heb. 11:16).

When an expert of the law comes testing Jesus, pressing him to prioritize and name the one greatest commandment, Jesus' answer silenced him: "You shall love the Lord your God with all your heart, and with all your soul, and with all your mind . . . [and] your neighbor as yourself" (Matt. 22:36-39).

We do live in tension with two homes, or two loves as St. Augustine explains. On one hand, if we love this world and self too much, we forget God and seek self glory. Religion sometimes pulls folks too far the other way—to think so much, and only, of the beyond that we forget to love and care for this earth and work for justice.

God says, we must learn to love ourselves. "Intelligent self-love," Augustine says, opens us to know our true identity so that we can love others. "The one who knows that he loves himself loves God. That one who does not love God, even if he loves himself, it can be truly said of him that he hates himself." May God help us keep a balance.

~ ecc

❖ MATTHEW 22:34-40 ❖

❖ A Memorable Day ❖

I was a teenager at the time World War II was drawing to a close. I scanned the newspaper every day to see where the Allied troops had advanced in various parts of the world. Major attention, however, was on England and France. Everyone knew that General Dwight Eisenhower and his colleagues were planning an invasion. Speculation ran wild. Then on this day—June 6, 1944—the news broke. A massive invasion was underway.

Sixty years later I was in England. A friend asked if I would like to visit Eisenhower's command center near Southampton. Of course, I leapt at the chance to see that place. It was awesome. On a huge wall in front of us—probably twenty-five feet by thirty feet—was the map showing the location of ships, troop encampments, and the French shoreline. I was spellbound. To think that it was in this very room that all that action was centered.

The price we paid in dead and wounded soldiers was enormous. We laud them even now as "the greatest generation."

Then recently I listened to an interview of a soldier in the German army. He survived the Allied invasion. But the words of this Christian man were haunting: "We were praying and killing each other at the same time." No wonder even "the good war" in the end was "a bad war."

I know, as you do, that Jesus said, "You will hear of wars and rumors of wars" (Matt. 24:6) as long as the world stands. Since World War II our country has been almost continuously involved in a war somewhere in the world.

No matter how patriotic we may feel we must examine our own motives. So I remember this day in 1944 and all the horrendous days of war since then and I pray, "Lord, have mercy. Help us to find a better way to resolve our differences."

~ hwc

❖ JAMES 4:1-3 ❖

❖ Must There Always Be Change? ❖

In 1958 we arrived at Pelican Rapids, Minnesota, and my first parish. It was a sleepy village of 1,500. Most citizens were of Scandinavian descent. One could hear older folks speaking in Norwegian on Main Street. Even down to the third and fourth generation many spoke English with an unmistakable Norwegian lilt.

At that same time a small turkey processing plant was set up to provide labor for local citizens. As turkey consumption took off the plant expanded time after time. Soon Spanish-speaking Texans arrived to fill the labor gap. A decade later refugees from Vietnam came to town. Then it was Bosnians and Ethiopians and Somalis. Change was swift and breathtaking for that little town.

If we ever think for a moment that "this land is our land" and will remain so forever, we have only to look back a decade or two to realize that change is everywhere and it is unrelenting. We can wish for some kind of stability, but even in the smallest of villages change is constant.

Today we honor Chief Seattle, that venerable Native American who gave his name to one of America's great cities. He was not only a peaceful man; he was also a realist. He saw the inevitability of change. He spoke of "the untimely fate of my people." But then he added a word that is sobering for every generation: "Your time of decay may be distant, but it will surely come, for even the White Man . . . cannot be exempt from the common destiny."

Some of us may recall those days when the pastor began his announcement of a death with the words, "For here we have no abiding city." Those words come from Hebrews 13:14 where the main purpose of the author is to underscore the passing nature of this life and the enduring nature of the life to come.

~ hwc

❖ HEBREWS 13:14 ❖

❖ Resurrection Is Real ❖

In a Harvard research of people ages sixty to eighty, participants were asked to name their greatest fears. In this order they had fear of: 1. meaninglessness, 2. being alone and unloved, 3. feeling lost and not belonging, 4. dying. Are you surprised that meaninglessness is number one?

Meaninglessness is also associated with mid-life crisis that people experience in their forties. That's about the time one begins asking, "Wasn't I suppose to be something by now?" Dante, at age 55, in *Inferno,* is said to be first to describe mid-life crisis: "Midway through life's journey I was made aware that I had strayed into a dark forest and the right path appeared not anywhere."

Loss of meaning is like partially dying while still alive. It's a bleak outlook with nothing of importance to live for and death the final end. Then, what about resurrection? Is there no possibility of resurrection now in the midst of crisis? At that point are you doubting Christ's resurrection as well as your own? Resurrection is so radical an idea for then, as well as for now.

That is what happened to the Corinthians after Paul had preached the good news. They had once believed, but did no longer. They were like Thomas, who needed to see before he could believe, could not believe until he had touched the hands and side of the risen Jesus (John 20:24-27). It is almost too much to believe that Christ was raised from the dead. Or that our bodies will be. Or that Jesus offers resurrection out of meaninglessness for us each and every day. He does promise, "I came that they may have life, and have it abundantly" (John 10:10).

> Christ is risen! Alleluia! Risen our victorious head!
> Sing his praises! Alleluia! Christ is risen from the dead!
> All the doubting and dejection of our trembling hearts have ceased;
> Hail the day of resurrection! Let us rise and keep the feast
> (*ELW* #382).

~ ecc

❖ 1 CORINTHIANS 15:1-26 ❖

❖ City Whose Builder Is God ❖

The legend is told about a Baghdad servant who went to the marketplace for his master. A woman with a scary look on her face came toward him. Somehow he knew that her name was Death. He was so frightened he ran to his master, begging for a horse so he could flee to Samaria. Receiving the horse, he rode away. Later that day at the same marketplace, the master saw this woman named Death. He asked why she had frightened his servant. She replied, "The look on my face was only my surprise at seeing him here in Baghdad, for I have an appointment with him tonight in Samaria."

Death will catch up with each of us. No fleeing when our time comes. In this life there is "no abiding city." But we, like Abraham and all who have died in faith, are assured of "things hoped for, the conviction of things not seen" (Heb. 11:1). We look forward beyond death to entering an abiding city, "the city that has foundations, whose architect and founder is God" (v. 10). Our real citizenship, already as Christians, is in heaven. That is why we are merely "strangers and foreigners on the earth" (v. 13).

Herb's mentally challenged brother, David, lived with a certain hope of going through what he envisioned as "the golden door" where God and loved ones waited for him. The day we explained to him, as cancer symptoms were quickly worsening, that there was nothing more doctors could do, he looked up saying, "I just want to go home." When he saw tears in our eyes, he said confidently, "Don't feel bad!" A sure and certain hope followed him as he said his last gasping words, "I'll be . . . ALL RIGHT."

Let us like Abraham ask God for "faith to go out with good courage, not knowing where we go, but only that your hand is leading us and your love supporting us" (*LBW*, p. 137).

~ ecc

❖ HEBREWS 11:1-16 ❖

❖ PRAY WITHOUT CEASING ❖

On Saturday mornings my mother tuned in to the "Back to the Bible" broadcast from Lincoln, Nebraska. She liked Theodore Epp's homily, and I liked the perfectly blended male quartet, peppy and mellow. I was twelve the summer they offered kids a Bible verse memorization program that would earn a Bible. Faithfully I memorized my forty verses, recited them to my mother, and was thrilled the day my black, zippered Bible arrived in the mail.

One verse stood out from all the others because it was the shortest and also the most perplexing, "pray without ceasing" (1 Thess. 5:17). We prayed in church, at bedtime, before meals, and at breakfast time family devotions. But without ceasing? All the time? Not possible, at least for a child to understand.

But as we experience life we learn that St. Augustine was wise when calling us "resident aliens" in the *City of God*. He writes, "Give me one who longs, who hungers, who is a thirsty pilgrim in this wilderness, sighing for the springs of the eternal City; give me such a person; that one will know what I mean."

In pain or sorrow, we feel helpless by ourselves to pray and are left only to entrust the Holy Spirit's interceding for us "with sighs too deep for words" (Rom. 8:26). It is then that we begin experiencing a closeness to and longing for God that we have never known before. Augustine explains how this inner yearning, continual longing, is also praying. So, "It was not for nothing that the apostle Paul said, 'Pray without ceasing.' [We don't continually bend our knees but it] is another way of praying, interior and unbroken. . . . the way of longing, of desire. . . . if you long for that City, that eternal homeland you are not ceasing to pray. . . . your unceasing desire is your unceasing prayer."

~ ecc

❖ PSALM 42:1-6 ❖

❖ Hold on to Eternal Life ❖

One Sunday afternoon, two young men put their kayak in the backwaters of the swollen Minnesota River. Fun, until their kayak capsized, thrusting them into cold water. One swam strongly to safety. The other, tugged at by river current, grabbed on to a tree, fighting desperately to hold fast with all of his might until rescued. The fight that kept him holding fast to the tree was worth achieving the goal of life itself.

Can we see ourselves in this story—in our fight of faith clinging to eternal life? We struggle against the cold waters of disbelief. Against the strong river current of temptation, turning inward caring only for self. Insisting on our own way.

For those two young men, saving their lives was their only goal. Life had never been so precious as they both fought those cold waters. And they attained their goal. Our goal is eternal life, to which we've been called in baptism. Eternal life, already now. Abundant life now, living each day "in the presence of God, who gives life to all things" (1 Tim. 6:13).

But we live constantly in danger of being capsized by the devil, the world, and our own flesh. That's why we're given the imperative to "take hold of the eternal life" (v. 12). Seize it. Hang on to it for dear life—in regular worship and in time alone with God, daily grasping the promises. Rescued again today by Jesus Christ—cleansed, renewed, refreshed, and filled with God's love. God's love within us and through us for others. Eternal life now and in heaven forever. So, "fight the good fight of the faith; take hold of the eternal life to which you were called" (v.12).

> I need thee ev'ry hour, stay thou near by;
> Temptations lose their pow'r when thou art nigh.
> I need thee, oh! I need thee; ev'ry hour I need thee;
> O bless me now, my Savior! I come to thee (*The Hymnal*, #462).

~ ecc

❖ 1 TIMOTHY 6:12-16 ❖

❖ Faith That Bears Fruit ❖

Sitting bowl-shaped in the Sonoran desert, the agave cactus reaches her majestic bluish green arms heavenward. Although appearing robust, this cactus is short-lived. Building up energy makes it beautiful. But the energy build-up is not for a secure long life. It is for bearing fruit. After a few short years, a spectacular flower will appear on a fast growing tall slender stalk. Bearing the blossom causes the parent plant to die.

We raised one at our Arizona home. The extraordinary burst of bloom is an amazing sight. But being gone for the season, we missed seeing it happen. Our neighbors watched and gave us a running account. Every morning looking through their window blind, they reported, "it had grown three slots higher!" Then it died, having given all of its energy into the producing of the flower.

Like this cactus, we as children of God are given the gift of faith, not just for our own security, but for fruit-bearing. God told Abraham he was blessed to be a blessing to others (Gen. 12:2). It's for fruit bearing. Jesus said, "Those who abide in me and I in them bear much fruit, because apart from me you can do nothing" (John 15:5).

One may think of faith as a possession stored up for personal security, perhaps making oneself more pleasing to God for accumulating so much faith. We even feel puffed up because others notice how much faith we have and the good works it produces. But true faith is for bearing fruit, and it comes from abiding in Jesus Christ. Knowing our helplessness, we receive God's grace that forgives, makes us whole, and causes fruit bearing—a daily death and resurrection.

> I have been crucified with Christ; and it is no longer I who live, but it is Christ who lives in me. And the life I now live in the flesh I live by faith in the Son of God, who loved me and gave himself up for me (Gal. 5:19-20).

~ ecc

❖ GALATIANS 2:15-21 ❖

❖ Gifts We Will Always Have ❖

Of our nine sisters, three have birthdays in May. A friend who was with me when I was carefully choosing three sister cards said, "And I have no sisters." Even thinking of being without a sister hit me like a stab in the heart. Her comment caused reflection of so many wonderful sister memories. Happy memories of their precious presence in our lives. Thankfulness for the unique gift of whom each of them are for us. Gifts we'll always have for they have become a part of us. Gifts to celebrate and cherish.

In praying for his disciples before going away, Jesus is praying also for his followers of all time. Even for you and me in this heartfelt prayer to God. He's pleading that we have eternal life, which is to know the love of God and Jesus Christ. We hear Jesus thanking God for giving us—you and me—to him as his beloved children. Jesus is even saying that he is glorified in us. He's honored to have us! We're each a unique gift to him. So he is asking God to guard us from the evil one snatching us away from him. That we will be filled with God's love in us and through us to others. And that God's love will unite us into one fellowship together.

To make himself real and because we need something we can taste and touch, Jesus comes to us in the Supper, giving us his body and blood. He assures us that his suffering, death, and resurrection have given us eternal life with a full and open relationship with God. What we could never earn. And when we receive his body and blood, he unites us with all others who also receive him. Together then, we are sent to proclaim God's love in Jesus to all the world. Gifts we'll always have. Gifts to celebrate and cherish.

~ ecc

❖ JOHN 17:1-26 ❖

❖ IN PRAISE OF ADMINISTRATORS ❖

I always wince when I hear a pastor declare, "I love to preach. What I don't like is administration."

That is unfortunate. Every member will tell you if the congregation has a great preacher. A pastor is often complimented if she or he delivers a stem-winding sermon. But administration? Even when it's done well it is scarcely noticed.

In my opinion effective administration is as important as effective preaching. In fact, it could be argued that it may be even more crucial. At its best, administration is the means by which a leader enables others not only to join in the work of an organization, but to actually enjoy doing it.

It's no surprise that when he writes about the "gifts of the Spirit" Paul lists leadership, or administration, close to the ministries of preaching, teaching, and healing, all of them very public by comparison.

Today we honor a man who even became known as the "Administrator" because of his unusual gifts for enabling others to do works of mercy. He is Basil the Great, a resident of Caesarea in Palestine in the fourth century. Born into wealth, he sacrificed it at a time of famine and carefully administered its benefits for the poor. He was good at raising money for good causes, including relief efforts. He forbade anyone working with him to withhold benefits from non-Christians. Later he organized missionary efforts and used his skills to settle disputes in the church.

Over the course of my ministry I have known dozens and dozens of women and men who have enriched the life of church and society because they used their administrative skills to help others reach their full potential. Most of them were not well known beyond their immediate organization. They simply did—and now do—what is most natural for them.

Thank God today for the good administrators you have known.

~ hwc

❖ 1 CORINTHIANS 12:27-30 ❖

❖ Is There a Place for Pride? ❖

This time of year a growing number of congregations celebrate "Pride Sunday." It's a day to remind ourselves that everyone is welcome in that congregation. It includes those whose sexual orientation is different from the majority.

It took me a long time, many years in fact, to recognize and admit that I carried prejudice against these brothers and sisters. Just as my negative attitude had been shaped over many years, so my positive attitude needed to be reshaped over several years.

What made the difference? There were two factors. First, it was not what changed my view, but who changed it: David and Anita and Peter and Joy and Randy and Ginny and Mark and Charlotte. These are not phantom names plucked out of thin air. These are real honest-to-goodness human beings whom I know as friends. All are homosexual. They represent hundreds of others I have come to know over the years who are homosexual and who share my belief that Jesus is our Savior. They helped challenge and reshape my view.

A second factor, even more important, has been my study of the Bible. There are two questions: What is at the core? What is at the periphery? A key passage is Galatians 3:27-28: "As many of you as were baptized into Christ have clothed yourself with Christ. There is no longer Jew or Greek . . . slave or free . . . male or female, for you are all one in Christ Jesus." This is the great leveler, a passage that wipes out distinctions we might try to make about what it means to be a Christian. There is only one thing that matters, writes Paul. We are all children of God by baptism.

Does this mean that any of us—gay or straight—can live as we please? Not at all. We are called to live by the highest ethical standards. Our pride is rooted in grace.

~ hwc

❖ GALATIANS 3:23-29 ❖

❖ Whose Land Is This Land? ❖

My friend Cecil lives on the edge of a small town in northern Minnesota. Because he has more property than he needs for himself, he invites others in the community to have garden plots in his back yard and grow vegetables for their families.

One day a younger friend, who didn't know this story, asked Cecil if this was his land. He pondered the question for a moment and then replied, "Well, I pay taxes on it—which I don't mind doing. But I can't say that I really own it."

That young lady learned a simple but also profound lesson in stewardship that day. No, as Cecil put it so well, we never own anything. That includes not only land, but also homes, bank accounts, retirement funds, and anything else of which we are tempted to say, "This is mine."

Good stewardship has to be learned. A young child does not need to be taught to say, "It's mine." And unless we learn to be Christian stewards "my doll, by toy, my bicycle, my clothing" turns into "my house, my farm, my business, my car, my inheritance."

The words that open Psalm 24—"The earth is the Lord's and all that is in it"—stand like a banner over every book of the Bible. God's call to the people of Israel was to be a blessing to the whole world (Gen. 12:1-3). Jesus put it this way: "From everyone to whom much has been given, much will be required; and from the one to whom much has been entrusted even more will be demanded" (Luke 12:48).

You may think you have little, or are, at most, a "middle class" person. But by comparison with the rest of the world, we are incredibly wealthy. Look around. Think of what God has given you. Then, like Cecil, let's keep reminding ourselves that everything is on loan. Nothing is ours.

~ hwc

❖ DEUTERONOMY 8:11-20 ❖

❖ Always on the Way ❖

The first thing I did after I retired as presiding bishop of the ELCA was to take a course to become a Master Gardener. Fifty hours in length and taught by professors from the University of Minnesota, it was both demanding and very satisfying. Having grown up in a gardening family, I thought I knew something about the field.

I soon discovered that I had taken only a few baby steps into a world that stretched to the far horizons. Our professors kept reminding us that when others came to us with questions, assuming a Master Gardener knew just about everything, we would probably be able to answer only one or two queries out of ten. We would have to go to good resources to find solutions. Yes, it was humbling to realize how little I knew.

Isn't it that way in our venture as Christians? We all embrace certain basic teachings of the Christian faith. But many of us feel very uneasy with those who seem to have simple and pat answers to complex questions. We learn that there are sometimes several answers to a question. And we even discover that there are things we will never fully comprehend.

Our walk with Christ is for a lifetime, not for those looking for an easy short course. At times it is mind-boggling. We have moments when we wonder and feel confused. And just when we think we have made some progress we realize that we have a long way to go. We also learn on this venture that it is well to listen to those who have gone before us—the writers of Scripture, the great saints from Christian history, and our pastors and informed lay teachers, and mature friends.

The good news is that if we persist in our quest for greater understanding, we, like a faithful gardener, will be rewarded with a harvest of blessings.

~ hwc

❖ 1 CORINTHIANS 2:1-10 ❖

❖ Open and Laid Bare ❖

Sitting in a highchair, the toddler likes to play hide-and-seek. To hide, she knows she need only cover her face with little, fat chubby hands. Once hidden, she knows no one around can see her; if she can't see them, they can't see her. It's magic. When she again wants them to see her, all she needs to do is remove her hands. And presto, she's out of hiding. They now can see her.

It seems real for the toddler.

Are we like the toddler, thinking we can cover our hearts and hide what's in it from God? Not only do we try to hide it from God but also from ourselves. Scripture is stark in bringing us this truth: "Before him no creature is hidden, but all are open and laid bare to the eyes of him with whom we have to do" (Heb. 4:13, *RSV*).

Ditlev G. Monrad (*For All the Saints,* Vol. I, p. 959) says there's no pretending with God and that we are not given false names to justify ourselves:

> Deceit is called cleverness; greed is called concern for spouse and children; hatred and anger are called zeal for truth and justice. No sinful desire is found in the human heart that does not sail under a false flag and steal a name that does not belong to it. It is a great step forward when we are able to give the right name to all that lives within us. . . . Self examination . . . brings us into the light of God's countenance that which steals around in our souls. . . . Everything that lives within should be laid bare in prayer.

Someone said the only prayer is an honest prayer. "Let us then with confidence draw near to the throne of grace, that we may receive mercy and find grace to help in time of need" (Heb. 4:16 *RSV*).

~ ecc

❖ HEBREWS 4:12-16 ❖

❖ Give Thanks to God ❖

The Velveteen Rabbit is a story of toys all dreaming of one day becoming real. But they are afraid. Afraid of how that might feel. They wonder if becoming real, hurts. So they question older toys who have more experience in knowing if it hurts to become real. They go to the old velveteen rabbit that by this time has become real. He's real because he's been loved and cuddled nearly to death. They've handled him until his coat is now rubbed bare and he isn't really pretty at all anymore. But still so loved. The rabbit admits it hurts to be rubbed bare, but wisely answers their question by saying, "When you are real, you don't mind that it hurts."

Afraid to be real is a human thing. The process of getting real does hurt. But on that journey of what feels like being rubbed bare, we are opened to great joy in receiving God's love and mercy—opened to what Jesus Christ won for us on the cross. That experience of becoming real in Jesus' presence was so real for Augustine that it evoked in him a growing voice of thanks and praise. In both of his books, he begins the same, "The blessedness of the inhabitants of Holy City is to be always praising God." It is our highest calling, and it becomes our schooling for the City of God.

Oh, but wouldn't one grow weary and bored of praising and thanking God through all eternity? We earthlings certainly may wonder. Augustine answers: "Let us rest assured, we shall not be wearied by the praise of God nor by His love. If your love fail, so would your praise; but if love will be everlasting, fear not that you will lack power ever to praise God whom you will have power ever to love."

Being real evokes thanksgiving. "Let the redeemed of the Lord, say so" (Ps. 107:2).

~ ecc

❖ PSALM 136 ❖

❖ Beware of Envy ❖

Free-range chickens we call them now. Ours were free to roam the farm place until one was needed for Sunday dinner. Every evening at dark, they filed into the chicken house for safe shelter and sleep. But it was not always safe. Occasionally at night, a weasel would sneak through the darkness and into their shelter, looking for a meal of their warm blood. A weasel would literally suck the life out of several chickens, and in the morning we would find them lying dead.

Envy is like that, often moving insidiously under the cover of darkness. Maliciously, it leads to harm. Harm to others, but also to the one holding it within. Scripture warns us that envy flows out of the heart, defiling us. Joseph's brothers were envious of him. And jealous. This sin doesn't lay quiet but tends to grow. That happened in the hearts of Joseph's brothers. They began conspiring how they might kill him. But they came upon an easier less conspicuous way to get rid of him. A way in which they could weasel out of being caught. They stripped him and threw him into a pit to die. But then a better solution presented itself when traveling traders came by. They sold him and he was taken away.

Envy ripens easily into deceit. And it did for them. Wanting him to believe Joseph was dead, they devised a scheme to deceive their old father who loved Joseph very much. They presented to their father his coat they had torn and stained with blood so he would think he'd been killed by a wild animal. When envy and jealousy is full grown it brings forth death (James 1:15). And it's in every human heart.

So what can we do with envy and jealousy in our hearts? If we name it and ask, the Holy Spirit will root it out. Another chance for resurrection!

~ ecc

❖ GENESIS 37:5-35 ❖

❖ ABBA, FATHER ❖

Mack grew up under the cruel hand of an alcoholic father. He attended worship but was left with dark, untrusting feelings about God. This only increased after the violent death of his precious little daughter. After that, his accident. And then he had a life-changing dream. It's written into a book, *The Shack.* It's about the dream that took Mack, invited by God, to a mountain shack where he was hosted by God, Jesus, and the Holy Spirit, each humanly personified. Mack, who always wanted a father whom he could trust, now found God as Papa, a black woman who lavished him with listening love, good food, and understanding. Here in this beautiful place, Papa patiently helped Mack empty out all his grief and his old stereotypes about God. Until the tears began to flow. At last, Mack's heart was opened to receive God's transforming love.

"Abba," in Arabic, means Papa, a most enduring term for father. This is what Jesus called God in his most desperate Gethsemane hour. He cried, "Abba, Father, for you all things are possible; remove this cup from me; yet not what I want, but what you want" (Mark 14:36).

In teaching his disciples the Lord's Prayer, Jesus teaches us to know God as our dear, loving Papa, our Abba, our Father. Martin Luther says in *Luther's Small Catechism,* "Our Father in heaven," means that "God wants to attract us, so that we believe he is truly our Father and we are truly his children, in order that we may ask him boldly and with complete confidence, just as loving children ask their loving father."

If you, like Mack could not trust your earthly father, be assured that "the Spirit helps us in our weakness; for we do not know how to pray as we ought, but this very Spirit intercedes with sighs too deep for words" (Rom. 8:26). May you be bold enough to enter the loving presence of Almighty God as your dear "Abba Father."

~ ecc

❖ MARK 14:32-42 ❖

❖ God Uses Ordinary Folks ❖

Now and then we meet someone who has an over-inflated notion of their importance. They not only boast of feats we suspect they've never done, but also try to do things that are beyond their capabilities.

For most of us, the problem is quite the opposite. We tend to underestimate our gifts and shrink from challenging quests. We are not alone. The record of shy and reluctant persons runs from one end of the Bible to the other:

> Moses had to be persuaded against his will to lead the people of Israel out of Egypt. He also thought his gifts to persuade others to follow him were insufficient.
>
> Saul was so shaken by his selection as king that he tried to hide among the baggage.
>
> David, the youngest of several brothers, was almost overlooked as a prospect to lead Israel.
>
> Esther was certain God could not use a common woman like her to persuade the Babylonians to let her people return to their land.
>
> Isaiah was certain he was too sinful to be a prophet of God.
>
> Mary thought it unlikely that God could use a peasant girl from Nazareth to be mother of the Messiah.

None of us is worthy of the high calling to bring good news to our world in word and in deed. We feel inadequate. But God has promised that we will be given the wisdom and strength to do the task to which we have been called.

Ask yourself a few questions: Is there someone I should call or visit today who needs a word of encouragement? Is there a task at my church I should volunteer to do? Is there a letter I need to write today to someone who is facing a difficult challenge?

Surely each of us can find an opportunity to be useful today.

~ hwc

❖ ISAIAH 6:1-8 ❖

❖ SPEAKING DIFFICULT WORDS ❖

Kermit is the retired publisher/editor of a weekly newspaper in a small town. I asked him one day if he wrote an editorial every week over his long career as a newspaperman. "I seldom wrote editorials," he replied. "If I offended even one major advertiser, I was out of business."

I understood his dilemma. Every pastor knows the same tension as she or he prepares a sermon. Step on certain toes and you may be "out of business." Church members, like newspaper advertisers and subscribers, can simply walk away if they hear something they do not agree with on a Sunday morning.

What is a pastor to do? After studying the biblical texts for a given Sunday one may be overwhelmed with the conviction that a word must be spoken about an injustice in the community or a war in some far off land or a moral issue on which the pastor may stand with only a small minority in the congregation.

I recall wrestling with the issue of the war in Vietnam in the early 1970s. The son of faithful members of the congregation had been killed in that war just before I came to the parish. In memory of him the parents gave a beautiful liturgical piece that hung on the front of the pulpit. How could I mount those steps and preach my conviction that the war was wrong and, at the same time, honor the memory of that brave young man?

It seemed at the time that the most I could do was to raise questions about that war, at the very least helping listeners to give second thoughts to blind patriotism. Given the disastrous way that war ended I wonder if I should not have been more forthright.

We live with these impossible choices, not only in the pulpit, but in the everyday life of each believer. We never stop praying for wisdom.

~ hwc

❖ EZEKIEL 33:7-9 ❖

❖ When the Sermon Bombs ❖

Introduce to me a pastor who says he or she has never preached a sermon that "bombed" and you will have introduced me to a liar. Any honest preacher will tell you that no matter how much preparation has been devoted to a sermon, there are occasions when it simply is a flop. Preaching the gospel is such an awesome responsibility, that it's little wonder pastors often ask as they descend from the pulpit, "Do I ever dare step up there again?"

It's for this reason that we give thanks for a church that accents the importance of the liturgy. On those occasions when a congregation may get little or nothing from the sermon, the liturgy alone carries the message that they need to hear. Think about it:

We begin with a hymn of praise.
We ask God to forgive our sins, "known and unknown, things we have done and things we have failed to do."
We hear the good word that "In the name of Jesus Christ, your sins are forgiven."
We listen to words from the Holy Scriptures.
We confess our faith in the triune God.
We pray for the needs of others.
We offer our gifts to support our church and others.
We receive the sacraments.
We are sent out into the world with the blessing of God on the week to come.

All of that without a sermon!

Should we then dispense with preaching? Of course not. Weak and even pathetic as our preaching may be at times, every pastor knows that God uses us in ways we never dreamed possible. That sermon we thought was a bomb? More often than not someone will say to us, "Pastor, your sermon was exactly what I needed to hear. Thank you."

So even though all we need is in the liturgy, the sermon can only enhance that message. Yes, even the sermon that bombs.

~ hwc

❖ 1 CORINTHIANS 1:20-25 ❖

❖ JUST FOR TODAY ❖

I love day lilies. Because of their infinite hues and because different varieties bloom for so many weeks, one could have a beautiful flower garden for most of the summer with nothing but day lilies. They are called "day" lilies, of course, because each lovely blossom lasts just one day. What a shame. You look into a single flower and find yourself wishing that it could last longer. By morning it must wither to make room for the next blossom on the stem to open.

I wonder if this is why Jesus chose the lowly lily to teach us what it means to trust in God. The tender flower, he said, "is alive today and tomorrow is thrown into the oven" (Matt. 6:30). I think he might have added, "to be replaced by another." Jesus knew how tempted we are to grasp hold of what is at hand and embrace it like something we would like to retain forever. But he also knew that life moves swiftly along, and that the only certainty we have in the end is the promise that God will never abandon us. Tomorrow, uncertain as it may be, will bring some new word from God, some lovely blossom we could never have imagined today.

At a time when hope was running very thin for the people of Israel, the prophet Isaiah was called by God to speak a word of encouragement. "The grass withers, the flower fades" he said "but the word of our God will stand forever" (Isa. 40:8).

Whatever kind of day we had yesterday, the sun brings new hope this morning. Today God's promise, like the next lily, is fresh and new.

Michael Perry writes in his hymn about "the flower that must surely die." But that is not the end because "hidden from all nature the eternal seed is sown. . . ." (*ELW* #880).

~ hwc

❖ MATTHEW 6:25-34 ❖

❖ Those Unintended Hurts ❖

We have a hummingbird feeder attached by suction cup to our kitchen window. Fearless as they are, I can view these tiniest of God's birds from only a foot or two away as they suck up sweet nectar after their long migratory flight. What delicate beauty! What wonder that they can dart so swiftly, first in one direction and then in another, wings flapping hundreds of times per second!

One day the delivery service brought to our door a lovely hibiscus plant from daughter Mary. The small table in front of the sunlit kitchen window seemed the ideal spot for it. When the first velvety pink blossom opened we thought it was a perfect match for the hummers.

Then tragedy. My heart skipped a beat when I stepped out on to the patio the next morning. There lay dead one of those delicate hummers. I knew immediately what had happened. How could I have been so careless, so thoughtless? Attracted to the hibiscus blossom, the little bird had crashed into the window and fell dead instantly. Why hadn't I anticipated what might happen? No, I surely didn't mean for this to happen. But it did. A little bird was dead.

How often do we hurt someone by a careless word, an irresponsible act, an unintended insult? "How could I have said that? How could I have done that? What can I do to make it right?"

We can go back to the one we've offended. We can learn from our mistakes to do better the next day, all by God's forgiving and loving grace.

Dr. Bernhard Christensen, president of Augsburg College, once told a small group of us that one of his favorite songs was this:

> If I have wounded any soul today,
> If I have caused one foot to go astray,
> If I have walked in my own willful way,
> Dear Lord, forgive.

~ hwc

❖ ROMANS 7:21-25 ❖

❖ Our Next Home ❖

On the day our widowed neighbor was moving from her home of eleven years into an assisted living facility, I stopped to visit. She told me that, while visiting a friend in that very place a few years before, something had happened, and she said to herself, "I'd like this to be my next home." She put her name on the waiting list. As years unfolded and her town home became more than she could care for, she knew the time had come. She was then ready for the move. Her dream had become reality. Anticipation had made her not only ready but eager to move on.

From those early small apartments and rentals, and on to a house, thinking of our "next home" is common as we look to upgrade and increase living space. First a small "starter" home and then, as the family grows, on to a bigger more accommodating one. At a certain point, however, when conditions change, we start going the other direction, scaling down—to a smaller place, condominium, or apartment. Envisioning a "next home" through the stages of life prepares one for what is to come. As needs change or when physical diminishments begin to take their toll, one looks forward to what one could never have imagined in younger years—an assisted living facility and eventually even to living in a nursing home. But best of all, someday, our "next home" will be heaven.

Like my neighbor who knew some years ago that she wanted the place she was visiting to be her next home, we too can have a knowing and eager anticipation. For we claim God's promise, "We have a building from God, a house not made with hands, eternal in the heavens" (2 Cor. 5:1). We can be sure it will be ready, because God has prepared it for us. Our reservation is good because God gives us the Spirit as a guarantee.

~ ecc

❖ 2 CORINTHIANS 5:1-10 ❖

❖ CLAY JARS ❖

First thing after we have moved, in order to feel at home, I would go to the lumberyard to buy an eight-inch wide oak board, stain, varnish, and brackets. I'd prepare the board, and then with husband's help we'd mount the shelf, arm-length high on our new kitchen wall. And there my collection of pitchers, like good friends, would find their home. When they were in place, I would feel at home in our new house.

Each pitcher was unique with its own history and purpose. Keepsakes from ancestral places of origin—Denmark, Norway, and Sweden. Gifts from friends and loved ones. Mementos from travels. Some are new and some antique. Others are short, tall, slender, or squatty. Each has its own graceful beauty and particular usefulness. Each is for pouring out that with which it has been filled. Each is a "clay jar." And each is a treasure.

Similarly, you and I are each an "earthen vessel," treasured by God. Unique in the way God has made us. Unique also in the purpose for which God made us. In God's kingdom each of us is beautiful and useful, to pour out that with which we have been filled. Each of us is a treasure to God.

You and I have also been filled with a treasure. "For it is the God who said, 'Let light shine out of darkness,' who has shone in our hearts to give the light of the knowledge of the glory of God in the face of Jesus Christ" (2 Cor. 4:6). It's a gift beyond any other. That we have been enabled to know God is the gift put within us as clay jars. As such we are vulnerable, but have been given great responsibility in God's kingdom.

May God fill us up, we who are clay jars, beautiful and grace-filled. And may God use us to pour out that with which we have been filled.

~ ecc

❖ 2 CORINTHIANS 4:1-7 ❖

❖ Do Not Lose Heart ❖

Our friend was riding in a car that hit black ice and skidded out of control. After surviving a life-threatening head injury, Ron overcame one challenge after the other before stepping back into his work of ministry. During his process of resurrection, as it were, he learned so much. About "this treasure." About being a "clay jar," so vulnerable. And that "this extraordinary power belongs to God and does not come from us" (2 Cor. 4:7). He believed and radiated "that the one who raised the Lord Jesus will raise us also with Jesus, and bring us with you into his presence" (v. 14). Ron was a living clay jar, useful in pouring out that with which he had been filled.

It was he who came to my bedside on the morning I was to have cancer surgery. And he read life-giving words when I felt afraid. Words of comfort from this Scripture. "Afflicted . . . but not crushed; perplexed, but not driven to despair; . . . so that the life of Jesus may also be made visible in our bodies" (v. 8-10). He had experienced God-given courage struggling through long rehabilitation. So this word of God coming from his mouth was powerful for us that morning. He was literally pouring out that with which he had been filled. It brought strength and peace. And an eternal dimension.

Later, Ron gave us a gift, a framed watercolor abstract. Dark colors formed the background for the words, "Pressed down by troubles but not crushed or broken. We don't know why things happen as they do. We get knocked down, but we get back up." Then around a misshapen bright gold cross these words, "God never leaves us, never leaves us or abandons us."

Ron died too young of a short-lived devastating disease. But he became forever a part of us. He taught us that things seen are transient, but things that are unseen are eternal. And that we must never lose heart.

~ ecc

❖ 2 CORINTHIANS 4:7-18 ❖

❖ LET THE PEOPLE SING ❖

Because the title of this devotional book is taken from a phrase in one of his hymns ("his bounteous grace is *every morning new*"), it's appropriate that on his commemoration day we reflect on the ministry of music of John Olaf Wallin. Though he was archbishop of the Church of Sweden and carried a heavy administrative load, his major legacy is that of a hymn writer.

When the Church of Sweden published a new hymn book in 1819 more than a fifth of the hymns—130 out of 500—came from the pen of Wallin. Many others were revised or translated by him. Thirty of Wallin's hymns were included in *The Hymnal* of the Augustana Lutheran Church. After the Lutheran mergers in the early 1960s and with changes in church culture only a handful of his hymns survived in subsequent Lutheran hymnals.

Though we may feel some loss with the disappearance of Wallin's hymns, most of us would affirm the importance of songs and hymns in our Christian experience. My friend Robert Esbjornson, longtime professor of religion at Gustavus Adolphus College, once noted for me that he found hymn tunes rising spontaneously in his mind as he went about his daily activities. He did not consciously call them to mind. He would find himself humming a melody and then recalling the words. Many of us find that we do the same.

Where do these memories of hymns come from? Clearly, it is out of our lifelong pattern of worship, in many cases stretching back to early childhood when we stood with our families at worship. At the time we may not have comprehended what we were singing. But the melodies and words were being stored away, to be recalled years later with deep blessings.

This is one reason why it is important for children to worship with their parents. Who knows what impact it may have for their entire lifetimes?

~ hwc

❖ EPHESIANS 5:19-20 ❖

Catherine Winkworth, Hymnwriter

How often do you sing except at church on a Sunday morning? Or sing anything but a hymn? Or thank God for those who gave us hymns to sing? Today, as we commemorate Catherine Winkworth (1827–1878), we give thanks for this remarkable servant of God, translator of German hymns into the English language. She grew up in London, but after her mother died, went to live with an aunt in Germany for a time.

Her great work, *Lyra Germanica*, a book of hymns translated from German was published in 1853. She holds the distinction as foremost translator of German hymns into English. The success of her translation is due to her ability to retain the original spirit of the German composer. If you have ever done translation, you understand this difficulty because so much can be lost in translation. She is also known for being in the forefront of supporting women's rights for their advancement in higher education.

Liturgy and singing in worship is the very heartbeat of the Christian community, says von Allmen, in *Worship*. "It is by its worship that the Church lives; it is there that its heart beats. . . . pulsates like the heart by systole and diastole." Like a pump circulating life and energy into its members and through them to the entire world.

When our song breaks into praise of God, Psalm 96 says, even the earth rejoices. The sea roars. The field exults. And trees sing for joy. So we thank God for Catherine and all servants of God who bring us hymns and for all who make music that helps us glimpse God's beauty. One of Catherine's translations:

> If you but trust in God to guide you
> and place your confidence in him,
> You'll find him always there beside you,
> to give you hope and strength within.
> For those who trust God's changeless love,
> build on the rock that will not move (*LBW* #453).

~ ecc

❖ Our Treasure ❖

How delightful to find a healthy rhubarb plant growing in the corner of the lot purchased for building the new parsonage. But delight turned to dismay when the basement was dug. For a huge mound of dirt was dumped on top of that healthy rhubarb plant. So that was the end of that. Or so we thought. But when warm days of spring arrived, we were amazed to see the rhubarb plant pushing up through three feet of dirt, reaching for the sun. What creative energy.

But even more powerful is the power of God in creating all of heaven and earth. The God who said "Let light shine out of darkness" (2 Cor. 4:6). It is this same God "who has shone in our hearts to give the light of the knowledge of the glory of God in the face of Jesus Christ" (v. 6).

A father in desperation brought his son suffering with seizures, begging Jesus to heal him (Mark 9:21-24). "If you are able" (v. 23), Jesus said. Jesus' word pierced through his doubt like rhubarb reaching through a mound of dirt, when he said, "All things can be done for the one who believes" (v. 23). That was when the father's eyes of faith were opened and he exclaimed, "I believe; help my unbelief" (v. 24).

Faith to believe is a wonderful treasure. Faith is a knowing created by Almighty God. It's a pure gift. The evil one works always to blind us from seeing or believing the light of the gospel. But it is God who said, "Let there be light," the God who made heaven and earth; this same God is able also to open our eyes of faith.

This treasure is for you today. Whatever may be your struggle now, God is with you to let light shine into your darkness. And help you believe, "All things can be done for the one who believes." God is waiting for you to claim your treasure.

~ ecc

❖ 2 CORINTHIANS 4:1-7 ❖

❖ Preparing a Place ❖

We know a lot about *preparing a place.* We as humans know about it and so do others of God's creatures. It's so comforting when someone prepares a place for us. An office ready when we start a new job. The guest room when we come for an overnight. A hospital bed when we're ill. A place for us at the table when invited for dinner. It's also a joy to prepare the place for one we love. For our new baby. For a loved one or special friend. These preparations are done full of eager anticipation, concern, and love—with love that bonds us to them.

We prepare a place for our pets, too. Every ten days after bathing our little cairn terrier, we wash his blanket, so that we can tuck it fresh into his bed. When he crawls in, he bites that clean blanket with a particular joyfulness. It seems that he is responding with thanks, knowing he is secure and loved there in his own place. Birds have a strong instinct in preparing a place for the anticipated hatchlings as they work hard packing the nest in preparation for laying eggs. A mother wood duck, we're told, even picks downy fine feathers from her own breast to line her nest. Not only will it provide warmth for the eggs but also comfort to her babies.

Jesus promised "to prepare a place for you" (John 14:2). This is with love beyond what any earthly parent can have for a child. It's a love that longs to be close and protective. Babies, bird or human, have no knowledge about the depth of love that is present already in the preparing of their places. Nor do we know, even now, the depth of Jesus' love in preparing our places. It's a love that wants us to be close and secure with him forever.

So take quiet moments throughout the day, simply to enjoy and bask in God's love for you.

~ ecc

❖ JOHN 14:1-6 ❖

❖ CITIZENSHIP ❖

On July 4, 1776, the Declaration of Independence was adopted by the Constitutional Congress. It declared the colonies' independence from British rule and was rooted in action of God who created all people equal with inalienable rights. John Adams, one of the five who drafted it, declared for all succeeding generations this day should be "the great American festival." And that it should be commemorated as the "day of deliverance by solemn acts of devotion to Almighty God" and celebrated with parades and fireworks. The first such celebration was observed four days later on July 8th in Philadelphia.

We claim citizenship in both our nation and in the kingdom of God. Citizenship gives each of us responsibility and also reason for joyful celebration. In baptism, when we were made citizens of God's kingdom, we were delivered from sin, death, and the power of the devil. So each day as we joyfully claim the freedoms we have as citizens of both kingdoms, we ask God to show us our responsibility to serve.

In our Lord's Prayer, we pray, "thy kingdom come" and "Give us this day our daily bread." Martin Luther teaches us that the kingdom of God includes both the right and left hand of God. The right hand of God refers to the spiritual kingdom. The left hand refers to the earthly kingdom, which is our government that provides protection, good order, and peaceful lives. When we pray for "daily bread," Luther says that means "everything our bodies need" including "upright and faithful rulers [and] good government" (*Luther's Small Catechism*). So let us pray daily for our elected leaders in both church and government.

> Defend our liberties and give those whom we have entrusted with the authority of government the spirit of wisdom, that there might be justice and peace in our land (*LBW*, p. 42).

~ ecc

❖ MATTHEW 6:7-18 ❖

❖ Venturing into the Unknown ❖

On April 1, 1853, my great grandparents, Magnus and Katrina Chilstrom, and six of their seven children boarded a sailing ship in Gothenberg, Sweden to venture to America. The boulder-choked countryside in the province of Småland left them no other option. Eva, their eighteen-year-old daughter was already married and pregnant. She and her husband would remain in Sweden.

I cannot even begin to imagine the pathos of that day. They surely knew, though it may have gone unspoken, that they would never meet again. Neither could they have known that day in Gothenberg harbor that it would take them until July to reach New York harbor. The sea voyage took four months, more than a month longer than usual.

For a time I assumed that the endless days on the ocean were caused by strong head winds. But in my research I learned that as often as not, the cause was ocean calm. During those fog-enveloping days the emigrants would grow restive and depressed, wondering if the wind would ever again blow, watching their meager food larders dwindling each endless day. Would they starve, watching helplessly as first one and then another member of the family was buried at sea?

What a welcome day when they finally viewed solid ground and New York City on the western horizon.

I cannot help but remember Abraham and his family as they set out from Haran to go to the land of Canaan. They, too, had no idea what was in store for them. They went out in faith, trusting that God would somehow bring them to a good land.

The only possession I have from my great grandfather Magnus is his Bible. When I look at it I feel a deep sense of gratitude. And I ask myself—as I ask you—what ventures of faith are you and I called on to take in our time?

~ hwc

❖ GENESIS 12:1-9 ❖

❖ Loving Our Country ❖

When I hear someone waxing eloquent about early American history, I think about what this country was like when my great grandparents arrived in July in 1853. New York City was a far cry from what it is today. No skyscrapers, buses, subways, taxicabs, or automobiles. Charles Brace describes the city with these words:

> You have no idea . . . what an immense place of misery and crime and filth this great city is. Think of the 10,000 children growing up almost sure to be prostitutes and rogues (*The Story of Two Families and Their Times*, p.36).

A nation is never fully formed. America today still wrestles with enormous problems that often seem insoluble. Were my great grandparents to walk the streets of New York City today they would see many of the same problems they witnessed more than 150 years ago.

In this month when we celebrate the independence of our country we would all do well to recommit ourselves to "refining her every flaw," knowing that the task in the twenty-first century is no easier than it was in earlier times.

What about the other nations of the world? Does God care for the United States of America more than for other nations? It would be presumptuous to say that. But this *is* our land and every citizen has the God-given responsibility to do one's utmost to bring peace and justice to the corners where we live and work.

At the very least, we need to pray for those we have elected to office, asking God to give them compassion, wisdom, common sense, and good health.

The apostle Paul would not expect blind obedience to leaders who are corrupt. We are free to differ with them. But when they are dedicated to the highest good of every citizen, we need to remember them in our prayers and cooperate with them for the common good of every person.

~ hwc

❖ ROMANS 13:1-7 ❖

❖ Promises for Hard Times ❖

After surviving the harrowing four-month crossing of the Atlantic Ocean in 1853, my great grandparents and their six children must have felt enormous relief when they reached North America. Though their destination was a Swedish settlement west of Milwaukee, they probably surmised that it would be an easy passage from New York City.

Only later would they learn that the worst was yet to come. After what was probably a pleasant journey through the quiet waters of the Erie Canal, they embarked from Buffalo, New York, on the stormy Great Lakes—Erie, Huron, and Michigan.

Historians tell us that this leg was far more treacherous than crossing the Atlantic. More people perished on the Great Lakes than on the ocean voyage. Everett Arden describes it in these riveting words: "Crowded and unsanitary facilities, coupled with a siege of cholera, turned the inland journey into a nightmare. Men, women, and children died, one after another, and were hastily buried in the sands along the route" (*Augustana Heritage*, p. 98).

Somehow my great grandparents and the children survived the ordeal and settled in Wisconsin.

It is a picture of what sometimes happens in our lives. Just when we think we have seen the worst, a new challenge comes our way. We can cave in. Or we can reach for the promises of God, promises that assure us that in the newest challenge to our faith God will not forsake us.

After those long years in the wilderness Joshua anticipated an easy conquest of the promised land. He, too, would be in for a surprise. The worst was yet to come. Fortunately, God had given him a sure word that would sustain him for the next challenge: "Be strong and courageous; do not be frightened or dismayed, for the Lord your God is with you wherever you go" (Josh. 1:9). Let that be your promise for this day.

~ hwc

❖ JOSHUA 1:1-9 ❖

❖ UNITED FOR THE WHOLE WORLD ❖

A little Scandinavia grew up around Pine Lake, Wisconsin, when my great grandparents settled there at the end of their journey to America. On the east side of the lake the Swedes, on the west the Norwegians. The lake was either too small or too great and served only to bring misunderstanding between the two peoples. Beyond Pine Lake lay territory that only the French had explored.

And so it remained even into my own young adulthood a century later in Minnesota in the 1950s. There was the Swedish church and the Norwegian church in our town, from either of which one could throw a stone and strike the other.

Those in the younger generations cannot even imagine how separated we were no more than a half-century ago. We have indeed made some progress since then.

Now when I go to church conventions I'm amazed at the kaleidoscope of nationalities and cultures that mingle together as one people of God.

I see this as the vision of Jesus when he surrounded himself with those first twelve disciples. From that small corner of the world, led by a man who only once seems to have set foot outside his native land, they looked out on the greater world as a place to bring the good news to all.

Now we have the opportunity to keep spreading that gospel to every new generation and in every land. And the best part of that mission is that we can do it in partnership with churches that were only a collection of small mission stations a century and a half ago. Some now outnumber in membership our entire Evangelical Lutheran Church in America. Thanks be to God!

~ hwc

❖ MATTHEW 28:18-20 ❖

❖ Baptized and Not Forgotten ❖

After a few years in Pine Lake, Wisconsin, my great grandparents and their six children moved on to Morristown, Minnesota. The three daughters married three brothers. Their stories might be called "The American Dream" and "The American Tragedy."

The "Dream" was lived out by Inga. She and her husband moved to Pueblo, Colorado, where they prospered. Ten children were born to them. Their graves are marked by some of the finest monuments in the cemetery.

The "Tragedy" was lived out by the other two sisters—Louisa and Annie. Bare minimum conditions characterized their frontier homes. Both died in their early 20s while giving birth to a child. Their husbands remarried and moved away. No records show where these sisters, my great aunts, are buried in a barren cemetery. Did word of their death reach relatives and friends back in Sweden? Probably not. Indeed, they were forgotten.

But I also ask as I stand there, "Does God forget a baptized child? Once welcomed into the kingdom, are we ever lost from the heart of God?"

Israel felt that way when they were carried into exile in a far off land. Has God forgotten us? they asked. Would their children live and find peace and security?

Isaiah had words of hope for them. His strong message from God is this: "I will not forget you" (Isa. 49:15).

All of us may have seasons of life when we wonder if anyone cares, if even our own immediate family and circle of friends will cherish thoughts of us when we leave this world. Will we also be no more than a forgotten, unmarked grave? At such times we need to grasp firmly the promise from our day of baptism: "You have been sealed by the Holy Spirit and marked with the cross of Christ forever." No, God never forgets us.

~ hwc

❖ ISAIAH 49:13-15 ❖

❖ The Role of Our Pastors ❖

Certainly the classic work on the life of the early immigrants from Scandinavia is *Giants in the Earth* by Ole Rolvaag. The "giants" are all those forces that made life all but intolerable—loneliness, crop failure, raging blizzards, fear of the native Indians, disease, mental illness, and lack of spiritual care from pastors. Infant and maternal mortality were a constant threat. Swarms of mosquitoes plagued both beasts and humans, at times making it impossible to enjoy a simple meal. Little wonder that depression and mental illness were common.

In these settings the visit of an itinerant pastor was often like a fresh stream flowing through the thirsty community. Baptizing the children, sharing the Lord's Supper, preaching the good news, giving a word of hope from the Bible—these were gifts from heaven. On a visit to the frontier Pastor Eric Norelius noted in his journal that "They were very thankful for my visit, and I felt well repaid for my effort in plowing through the snow to find them."

Eventually a few pastors settled among the immigrants. Norelius describes what a typical parsonage was like:

> It consisted of one room (where) they cooked, baked, washed clothes, slept, read, and prayed. . . . the pastor partitioned off (with cloth) a small room for a study. In this little den he had his books, and though he could not shut out the sound of what went on in the house, he could, nevertheless, imagine he was alone . . .

What kept hope alive for many of these courageous pioneers was a deep conviction that God would not forsake them. Surely the account of Jesus in his wilderness temptations was one they cherished. The closing words of that text must have brought special comfort: "Angels came and waited on him" (Matt. 4:11).

Life is different for us. But we, too, wait for the visit of angels.

~ hwc

❖ MATTHEW 4:1-11 ❖

❖ BREAKING BARRIERS OF PREJUDICE ❖

Because I grew up as the grandson and great grandson of pioneers on the Minnesota frontier, it took many decades for me to see things from the perspective of the Native Americans. The common opinion was that they were ignorant, immoral, and "heathen." Yes, even many of the immigrants involved in the life of our Christian churches harbored these views.

For this reason I look back with profound gratitude for the influence of teachers like Joel Torstenson, professor of sociology at Augsburg College. He spoke with passion about the need to move out of our narrow enclaves of prejudice to engage directly with those of different cultures. He was convinced that in contact with others our prejudices and warped opinions could not stand. In the light of new understanding we must change.

Paul Schultz, an Ojibway Native American, was that kind of person for me and others. As a member of the Lutheran church he brought with him the best traditions and most helpful insights of his native culture, enriching our understanding of our faith with his views.

Jesus, of course, spent his entire ministry trying to open the hearts and minds of his people to God's broader love for all. Steeped in their traditions and narrow religious views, the scribes and the Pharisees could never seem to understand that God's love, care, and mercy were more comprehensive and universal than they could have dreamed possible.

When the early church faced the question of who could be a member of this new community of faith, they had to change their views. Held together by a common faith in Jesus Christ, they believed that Jew and Gentile could be part of the same family of believers.

It is a lesson to carry to every Christian congregation. Who are the "outcasts" in our neighborhoods? Who needs to hear that they are welcome?

~ hwc

❖ ACTS 15:6-11 ❖

❖ Who Knows What a Day Will Bring Forth? ❖

The year was 1892. The day—July 12—began as a normal July morning on the farm of my grandparents, John and Hattie Chilstrom. Life was good. Their homesteaded farm in south central Minnesota was on fertile land. They had put up several buildings to accommodate cows, hogs, and chickens. Their seven children seemed destined for a bright future. Their four sons, including my father Wally, would surely grow up to become prosperous farmers.

At morning devotions that day they read from Romans 14, including verse 8: "If we live, we live to the Lord; if we die, we die to the Lord; whether we live or whether we die, we are the Lord's."

After noon lunch John and eighteen-year-old Edward decided to work on improving the open well. Edward descended first. When John saw him slump over he knew what was happening. Edward had been overcome by deadly methane gas. What would any father do? John descended, hoping to save his boy. In moments both father and son would be dead. Neighbors were quickly summoned, but it was useless.

All the dreams of this prairie family collapsed that day. After all those years of hard work and struggle, all was ended.

Some folks seem to live a charmed existence. Life offers up only the best they could expect. Tragedy never seems to cross their paths.

For most of us, however, there come times when all seems lost, unexpected moments when all of the hopes and expectations of life evaporate into thin air.

It is what we do at such times that determines not only our own destiny, but that of others as well.

I thank God that Hattie chose life; that she persevered in the faith. Had she not done so, I might well not have been sitting here writing these words of hope for you and for others.

~ hwc

❖ ROMANS 14:7-9 ❖

❖ If It Were Not So ❖

Do you remember the first time you made a legal agreement signing for a loan to purchase something you could not otherwise afford? Using the lender's money to pay for it, you then agreed to pay interest to the lender. You were confident that the loan was solid because you believed the lender was trustworthy. You believed the agreement would hold securely until the time when, by agreement, you would have the loan paid back in full. But what if along the way you started doubting? Thinking, "if it were not so."

Jesus raises this, "what if" question. When you think about the fantastic story of Jesus being raised from the dead and the promise that our bodies, too, will one day be raised and live forever with God, are you not tempted to think, "what if it were not so?" The good news is that long ago God had this plan, "prepared beforehand" (Eph. 2:10).

When the apostles got word from women that the tomb was empty and that Jesus had been raised from the dead, it seemed to them "an idle tale" (Luke 24:11). And still as they walked with Jesus on the road to Emmaus, their "eyes were kept from recognizing him" (v. 16). It wasn't until at the meal as Jesus blessed and broke the bread, that their eyes were opened. It was in the breaking of the bread that they recognized and believed it was Jesus raised from the dead.

You know the happiness when a friend or loved one tells you they are so glad and looking forward to your coming for a visit. And that they're making plans and getting everything ready for your time together. Jesus tells us he is doing that now. He's getting everything ready for you in his eternal home—for whenever you arrive. Would Jesus be telling us this "if it were not so?"

Do not let your hearts be troubled (John 14:1).

~ ecc

❖ JOHN 14:1-6 ❖

❖ Eyes Were Opened ❖

Imagine that you were one of Jesus' followers there, walking sad and so exhausted with grief after you had seen him die on the cross. You had pinned your hopes on him to save your country. And now he was gone. You were talking about your disappointment when a stranger came walking beside you. You couldn't believe that he, or anyone being in Jerusalem these past days, would not know about this terrible thing that had just happened. Not until you told him about it. So you told all the details, including the rumors women were telling that he had been raised from the dead and was alive. That was when the stranger began explaining how the Scriptures foretold this. You wanted to hear more. So you invited him in for supper. A most amazing thing happened when he blessed and broke the bread. Like removing blindness, he opened your eyes. And you saw he was Jesus. You understood the Scriptures. Your blindness was gone. Jesus had *opened* your eyes. What you could not do for yourself, Jesus did for you.

The meaning of "opened" in Greek helps us understand the miracle. It's an opening complete beyond what we can make happen. Complete like what happens in birthing when a first born opens the womb so birth is possible.

In my first career, I worked as a labor/delivery room nurse assisting mothers through the birth process, which is miraculous. The mouth of the uterus that had been thick and closed tightly to protect the growing fetus, now with each contraction, begins thinning and opening. Finally, when the cervix opens to ten centimeters, dilatation is complete so the baby can be born. No scientist or physician has ever been able to explain how and why labor actually begins.

Neither can anyone explain how our eyes are opened to see and believe in Jesus, our resurrected Lord. Yes, give us this miracle again today.

~ ecc

❖ LUKE 24:13-35 ❖

Mess Up Today; Start Over Tommorrow

Though sight-challenged, I still enjoy a couple of rounds of golf every week. Thanks to my patient partner, Terry, who keeps track of my shots, I enjoy envisioning a straight drive or hearing the echo of a twenty-foot putt falling in the cup.

Golf, however, is a very humbling sport. No matter how diligently one works on the driving range, no matter how good the swing feels in that setting, the course itself is another story.

And so it is with the life of a believer. As with golf, confidence is essential. But over-confidence is a nemesis.

Paul knew the danger. He is mystified again and again by his failure to live up to his own better judgment. "I do not understand my own actions," he writes. "For I do not what I want, but I do the very thing I hate" (Rom. 7:15). He goes on to say that "I can will what is right, but I cannot do it" (Rom. 7:18). Like the golfer who has taken lessons and read the instruction manuals and knows exactly how to grip the club, how to judge the distance to the hole, and how to read the sloping green for an easy putt, we find that in our Christian life we look back at the end of the day and say, "I knew better. I've made those mistakes before. How could I have been so careless? Why did I lose my concentration?" We are tempted to give up the game.

But there is hope, for the golfer and the Christian. The answer comes at the beginning of the next chapter: "There is therefore now no condemnation for those who are in Christ Jesus" (Rom. 8:1). We accept our limitations, knowing that by God's grace we can tee off again tomorrow.

~ hwc

ROMANS 7:14--8:1

❖ Keeping Good Worship Habits ❖

Many of us look back with gratitude to parents and grandparents and generations beyond them who were faithful members of a Christian congregation. Because of this we may tend to think that most early Americans eagerly embraced church life when they came to this country.

The record tells another story. Only a minority joined a church. A Minnesota pastor wrote in his annual report in 1856: "The spiritual conditions at the close of the year were not very encouraging. There were but few people who had any genuine spirituality, and the people were slow to attend services. No one wanted to submit to the disciplines of the church."

Whenever I hear folks yearning for "the good old days" I feel I must remind them that human nature does not change over the generations. And if they refer to New Testament times as the ideal for church life, I know they have never studied their Bible thoroughly. Peter, Paul, and others chastise the Christian community for laxity in spiritual dedication.

The Letter to the Hebrews was probably written some time near the end of the first century. By that time some of the early flame of the faith had begun to flicker. Members of the Christian community were neglecting regular worship. The author is unsparing. No, there are no accusations of heresy. Instead, they are reprimanded for simple neglect. Neglect, however, is more subtle and dangerous than heresy.

Times change, but habits do not. Polls tell the story. With each passing year the percentage of Americans who belong to a church slips downward. And the percentage of members who worship also descends. The advice of the author of Hebrews is relevant: "Provoke one another to love and good deeds, not neglecting to meet together, as is the habit of some, but encouraging one another, and all the more as you see the Day approaching" (Heb. 10:24-25).

~ hwc

❖ HEBREWS 10:19-25 ❖

❖ Courage from God ❖

Raoul Wallenberg's courage saving thousands of lives from the holocaust needs telling. His execution at Lubyanka prison in Moscow was reported on July 17, 1947. But because of varying versions of his death and that different witnesses claimed later to have seen him, his supposed death remains a mystery.

In Stockholm, Sweden, Wallenberg worked for an export-import company owned by Kalman Lauer, a Hungarian Jew. In 1944, when Hungary leveled heavy restrictive measures against Jews, traveling in and out of there became difficult for Lauer, so he assigned Wallenberg to be his trusted representative in Budapest.

Persecution of Jews began and soon some 12,000 were being deported daily. Wallenberg rented thirty-two buildings where Swedish flags waved and signage designated them as Swedish, such as "Swedish Library" or "Swedish Research." There, thousands were sheltered against persecution. Wallenberg devised protective passports naming them as Swedish subjects awaiting repatriation; therefore, they must be treated as Swedish citizens and not required to wear the yellow badges.

Wallenberg's courage is best told with the story of his climbing onto the roof of a train loaded with Jews headed for Germany's concentration camps. Before the doors of the train were sealed, Wallenberg stood atop the train handing out protective passports to reaching hands from within the train. Then he ordered all with passports to walk off the train and into waiting Swedish flagged vehicles. All the while, he ignored German soldiers ordering him to stop and Arrow Cross soldiers shooting over his head. It was as though they missed hitting him because they were so dumbfounded at his courage.

> When through fi'ry trials your pathway shall lie,
> My grace, all sufficient. shall be your supply.
> The flames shall not hurt you; . . . . oh, be not dismayed,
> For I am your God and will still give you aid;
> I'll strengthen you, help you, and cause you to stand,
> Upheld by my righteous, omnipotent hand (*ELW* #596).

~ ecc

❖ DEUTERONOMY 31:6-8 ❖

❖ A Man with a Vision ❖

When I visited Geneva, Switzerland, the first time, I noted two important buildings standing next to each other. One is the headquarters for the Lutheran World Federation; only a few steps away is the headquarters for the World Council of Churches. As I entered the World Council of Churches building one of the first things that caught my attention was a white marble bust of a distinguished-looking man. As I got closer I saw that it was a representation of Nathan Soderblom, archbishop of the Church of Sweden a century ago. Is the bust misplaced? I wondered. Given that Soderblom was a Lutheran, should it not be next door at the Lutheran World Federation building?

I quickly realized that the bust is in exactly the right place. Soderblom, whose life and vision we commemorate in July, was more than a Lutheran. He was a leader with a vision for the unity of the whole Christian church in the world. Soderblom believed in the central core of the Christian faith. He affirmed the Bible as the written word of God. But he asked some important questions:

> Did all revelation stop when the Bible was completed? Or is God still at work in the world, giving new insights into how we should live together as believers?

Should we do nothing to bring about greater Christian unity? Are there things various church bodies should be doing together rather than separately?

It was primarily out of Soderblom's efforts that the World Council of Churches was formed just after World War II. Indeed, his bust very definitely belongs in the headquarters for this organization that unites hundreds of church denominations in a common mission.

While some progress has been made in bringing divergent Christians together, we are constantly threatened with disunity. We should never cease our efforts to find common ground with other believers.

~ hwc

❖ 1 PETER 2:9-10 ❖

❖ VANISHED OUT OF SIGHT ❖

God is still revealed to us in dreams, just as in biblical times. Let me share a three-part dream when I was devastated shortly after the sudden death of our son, Andrew. Act I, highlighting the utter loneliness of grief, saw me walking with a good friend who seemed to know nothing of the sorrow. Act II revealed how meaningless life felt without my son. I walked with others searching through debris in an Old Cairo city block. No one found anything to salvage. Act III brought me to the corner of the next block with stores ahead. On the corner sat four heavy wooden trunks with lids standing open. Inside of each were valuable silver pitchers and heavy serving spoons. Upon impulse to find someone to protect them, but before I could even take a step, a slight Mediterranean man stood tight against my left shoulder. I felt his compassion and that he understood my loss, loneliness, and the overwhelming fear of another tragedy in our family. He then took a step, closed the trunks, and sat on them. I knew they were safe. And that we, like the trunks, were safe, valued, and protected by Jesus. He had purchased our salvation, not with silver or gold, but with his innocent suffering and death.

Jesus forewarned his disciples (John 16), in a little while they would see him no more but later see him again. In today's reading, they did not recognize the resurrected Jesus until he opened their eyes. And then Jesus vanished. Or more specifically, he became invisible so they could not see him. He was still there, but they could not see him.

Whether today you see him or not, be very sure Jesus is as close as your left shoulder. It took a dream to make me sure. He knows our every thought and fear. He is beside us to guide us, stepping ahead of us to protect us, and within us to comfort us.

~ ecc

❖ LUKE 24:28-35 ❖

❖ Through One Man's Hands ❖

Rising out of an unhappy childhood, Toyohiko Kagawa's life story (1888–1960) is amazing when we realize what God can do through one man's hands. His father worked in the inner circle with Japan's Emperor. His mother was a concubine, which relegated him to an inferior status. Only four years old when both parents died, he lived with loneliness and rejection until, in adolescence, two missionaries entered his life. Through them he learned to know Christ and found God's purpose for his life—to serve the poor.

After graduating from the Presbyterian College of Tokyo, he entered the seminary of Kobe. During that time he lived and worked in the Shink slum where there was filth beyond description. We're told he actually lived there with some twenty thousand outcasts, prostitutes, criminals, paupers, and beggars. What sustained Kagawa was his mystical communion with God, evidenced in poems, such as "Discovery," collected in *Songs of the Slums*:

> A sweet plan is hid in my hand;
> that hand is big, big, because of this plan.
> That God who dwells in my hand knows the secret plan
> Of the things he will do for the world using my hand!

After studying at Princeton Theological Seminary, Kagawa became both a religious leader and an organizer of labor unions. He carried heavy burdens doing God's will, leaning hard on the Lord, as seen in, "The Burden":

> Take thou the burden, Lord;
> I am exhausted, stumble along the way.
> Oh, lead with thine unfailing arm again today.
> Unless thou lead me, Lord, the road I journey on is all too hard.
> Through trust in thee alone can I go on.
> Yet not for self alone thus do I groan;
> My people's sorrows are the load I bear, Lord hear my prayer.

> I know the plans I have for you, says the Lord, . . .
> to give you a future with hope (Jer. 29:11).

~ ecc

❖ JEREMIAH 29:10-14 ❖

❖ It's in the Stars ❖

When I was a young lad I would sometimes slip out of our house on a moonless night and lie flat on the soft green grass, gazing into the starlit skies. I was both fascinated and frightened. Those endless reaches of space, the movement of planets and stars, the fiery tails of objects entering our atmosphere—yes, fascinating and frightening.

I wondered how it all came to be. Was the universe nothing more than physical matter with no creative force behind it all?

I once served on a task force with the famed astronomer Carl Sagan. He was a man of enormous curiosity. He had a profound respect for all of nature. He cared for the earth, naming it the "pale blue dot" that hung mysteriously as the only known planet hospitable for human life. But Sagan was not a believer. He was an agnostic, not ruling out a divine Creator, but unwilling to make a commitment without clearer evidence.

I could never prove Sagan to be wrong, of course. All of us look at the same evidence. Some believe; some doubt; some disbelieve. At some point in my life I took a leap of faith. I said, "I believe in God, the Father almighty, creator of heaven and earth." And that has made all the difference.

The writers of the psalms were often shepherds, "keeping watch over their flock by night" (Luke 2:8). No doubt some were skeptics. Others, however, looked into those same skies and said, "I believe."

The nighttime sky is not as brilliant as it was when I was a lad. But I encourage you to search for a dark corner and look heavenward. You may find yourself confessing with that long-ago psalmist: "When I look at your heavens, the work of your fingers, the moon and the stars you have established, what are human beings that you are mindful of them?" (Ps. 8: 3).

~ hwc

❖ PSALM 8 ❖

❖ Saint Mary Magdalene ❖

Since the tenth century, the church has celebrated the Festival of Saint Mary Magdalene on July 22. She is honored for being the ointment bearer to the tomb, first witness of the resurrection, and first to announce the resurrection to the disciples. Let's go now with Mary.

It is the first day of the week, very early. Jesus died only yesterday. Some of you know what it's like to bury loved ones. It doesn't seem possible that they're gone, ones so alive to you. You'd do anything to have them back. Bedtime comes. You need rest but you can't sleep. Maybe you did a little. But mostly you were praying, crying, and remembering. Waiting for dawn to go again to the grave. I'm not surprised to find Mary there, already at dawn. What a surprise, the stone is rolled away and Jesus' grave is open. Instead of his body, two angels are there asking, "Why are you weeping?" (John 20:13). And then the gardener (must be the gardener) asks, "Why are you weeping?" (v. 15). Desperate now to find his body, afraid and sorrowful, Mary hears her name—"Mary" (v. 16). He knew her. Said her name! That's what made her recognize Jesus. She wanted to stay and hold him; but no, he told her, go tell my disciples. Mary was transformed from sorrow to joy. She ran with the news, "I have seen the Lord" (v. 18). Mary Magdalene, first witness of the resurrection. And from her this good news echoes through the centuries to this day.

Today, Jesus calls you by name. He's known it since your baptism. Like Mary emptied her tears, we may now empty and leave with him our unbelief, fears, and shame. Making room for his resurrection power.

> Come, celebrate; your banners high unfurling, your songs and prayers against the darkness hurling. To all the world go out and tell the story of Jesus glory! (*ELW* #665).

~ ecc

❖ JOHN 20:1-2; 11-18 ❖

❖ WAS THERE LIFE BEFORE THE REFORMATION? ❖

As I entered the cavernous St. Peter's Basilica in Rome I saw statuary everywhere. It seems there is no end to the number of saints who are honored in that place. One marble piece that stops some Lutherans in their tracks, however, is dedicated to Birgitta. How, they wonder, did a Swede make it into this holy place?

The root of our problem is that many of us grew up at a time when we looked at "those Catholics" as virtual unbelievers. The wall between Lutherans and Roman Catholics was so high that we seemed to forget that Christianity was alive and even vibrant in Scandinavia and northern Europe prior to the time of Luther. Little wonder that he was so reluctant to leave that church.

A good example of that pre-Reformation piety is Birgitta, the woman we honor today. Born in 1303, she experienced the presence of God in dreams and visions from early childhood and throughout her life. But she was no recluse who withdrew into solitude to only pray and meditate. She married and had a family. She threw herself into public life both in Sweden and Rome. After her husband died, she dedicated her life to bringing reform to the church and the secular world. Like Catherine of Sienna, she dared to criticize and give advice to both popes and kings.

Today I'm thinking of women like Ruth Youngdahl Nelson, Grace Ryding, Evelyn Stark, Doris Spong, and Delores Bergstrand. I remember them from my years as a young pastor when only men were permitted to be ordained. Any one of these women—and countless hundreds more—might have been ordained had they been born a few decades later. But, like Birgitta, they refused to be repressed. They broke through barriers to make a deep mark on the church and the world.

Give thanks today for women like these whom you have known.

~ hwc

❖ JUDGES 4:1-7 ❖

❖ FACING LIFE REALISTICALLY ❖

I didn't like my doctor's diagnosis: "age-related degeneration." It all started with some pain in my back as I moved into my late 70s. I assumed there had to be a cure. What I learned was that this was a condition I would have to live with. Yes, certain exercises would aid to some degree. Yes, shots would bring some temporary relief. Yes, lifting properly would be important. Yes, surgery might help. But a permanent cure? No, this was "age-related." It's all part of recognizing that I am mortal.

This can be depressing. Where can one find help for the spirit? Ironically, I turned to one of the most curious books in the Bible—Ecclesiastes. How did this book ever make it into the Bible? It starts off with words like these: "Vanity of vanities! All is vanity" (Ecc. 1:2).

That's enough to tempt one to leapfrog over this seemingly *pessimistic* dirge and land in the next book, the cheerful Song of Solomon. I didn't do that. Instead, I sat down one day and read Ecclesiastes from beginning to end. Then the light dawned. This book of the Bible is not pessimistic. No, it is *realistic*. Yes, life can be difficult, even impossible at times. Yes, we feel the inevitable effects of aging as described in Ecclesiastes 12:3-5:

> Tremors set in: "the guards of the house tremble"
> Weakness overcomes us: "strong men are bent"
> Teeth decay: "women who grind cease working because they are few"
> Vision diminishes: "those who look through windows see dimly"
> Sleep becomes more difficult: "one rises up at the sound of a bird"
> Mobility decreases: "the grasshopper drags itself along"
> Sexual urges lag: "desire fails"

So how do we face these inevitable changes? Ecclesiastes says, in effect: "Live and enjoy every day." The book ends with these wise words for all ages: "Fear God, and keep his commandments; for that is the whole duty of everyone" (Ecc. 12:13).

~ hwc

❖ ECCLESIASTES 3:1-12 ❖

❖ Called to Be Christ-Bearers ❖

Saint Christopher, whose day is celebrated on July 25, was martyred about 250 A.D. Because he is known to be the patron saint of travelers, people carry their St. Christopher medals, believing he will protect them while traveling. Although we know little of his life, there is legend telling us that he was a ferryman who transported people across a river. One day he carried a child who grew ever heavier with each step he took walking deeper into the river. When he arrived safely on the other side, he said his burden had been like carrying the whole world. Realizing what a heavy burden the man carried, the child knowingly informed him that he carried not only the world but also him who created it.

Luther used this story in a sermon shortly before he died, saying St. Christopher bore the little Christ joyfully and easily at first but the burden of the child dragged him down when he got in deep water. Like faith, it's lovely early on, but difficult when tested. It's easy to confess faith in Jesus Christ until hard times come. Unbelief may then challenge our faith. Adversity may threaten it too. When God leads us into the thick of battle standing up for those who are exploited or to speak for those who have no voice, enduring gets difficult and faith may falter. It's often when stepping into the deep waters that faith is tested and the Christ child seems too heavy to bear.

Christians of the early church were tested severely and persecuted for the faith. Many were martyred. It was at this time that the Spirit inspired John to write words of encouragement to all Christ-bearers, then and now. It is recorded in Revelation 2:10. He wrote in cryptic language so persecutors could not understand it. God, who is faithful, calls us to, "Be faithful until death, and I will give you the crown of life."

~ ecc

❖ REVELATION 2:2-11 ❖

❖ Build Up Each Other ❖

In a college dorm one night, five girls got their heads together devising a plan for the next morning. It was told to me by their college nurse. Not good, you say, but this is what they did. The first of them to see Jane the next morning told her, "You look like you're not feeling well." Successively, the other four, upon seeing Jane, would each in turn make some comment to her about her not looking well. By noon, Jane came to the clinic to see the nurse saying she did not feel well. Because she had no symptoms, there was no treatment given. However, she did spend the remainder of that day in bed. When this devious plot came to light, the college nurse had a talk with the five schemers. They were embarrassed and sorry for the distress they had caused. Reconciliation followed. But, this is a good example of what harm can come from negative comments and/or body language. We carry within us power to tear one another down—physically, psychologically, and even spiritually.

But on the other hand, we can be instruments of God to encourage and build up one another. Like the high school teacher who saw and encouraged a student's gift for public speaking that set him on his course toward a successful career. Or the young woman in a new job who from an older worker received encouragement that boosted her toward success. And how many can you name who have encouraged and built you up in your walk with God?

We, like the Christians in Thessalonica, sometimes become discouraged. We need for ourselves, but also for others, to gather in worship. To sing hymns, receive the sacrament, and hear God's word. We never know what grief or discouragement might lie beneath someone's smile. So day by day, wherever, and in whatever way possible, we need to "build up each other" (1 Thess. 5:11).

~ ecc

❖ 1 THESSALONIANS 5:1-11 ❖

❖ Untangling the Snags of Life ❖

I've fished as long as I can remember. It started in an old rowboat with my mom and dad and a drop line over the edge. I recall vividly the day I took my after-school earnings and purchased the longest cane pole I could find at the local bait shop. Next, it was my first rod and reel, the kind you cast with your finger on the spool, hoping it wouldn't snag. Inevitably it did, and you were left with a mess.

One of the lessons every fisherman learns is that you can't keep fishing until that snag is unsnarled. It's especially frustrating when the other occupants of the boat are pulling in one nice fish after another. But, no matter, you simply have to deal with that snag.

C.S. Lewis compared it to trying to solve a mathematical problem if you know you've made a mistake in your early calculation. No matter what you do, the problem cannot be solved until you go back and correct your mistake.

Life is that way. Whether the sin is deliberate or unintentional, we must deal with it. Until we do, life will only get more frustrating. If it's confession to God, we know what we must do. We can't hide from the One who sees all and knows all.

If the offense is against another person, we also have no option. Confession is the only way to get the snag out of the relationship. If the person accepts our confession, well and good. If not, we can rest in the assurance that we have done what we could. God will give peace.

It is believed that Psalm 51 is David's confession after he committed adultery and tried to hide it. When the prophet Nathan confronted him, David knew he had no other choice. He needed to deal with the snarl he had created. He confessed and found peace.

~ hwc

❖ PSALM 51:1-12 ❖

❖ In Praise of Organists ❖

There may have been occasions when a congregation wished someone would chase me out of the pulpit. But on only one occasion has it actually happened. It was at the famous St. Thomas Church in Leipzig, Germany. I was leading a tour group. I wondered how it would feel to stand in that famous pulpit. When a member of the church staff rushed down the aisle hurling incomprehensible German expletives at me, I knew I was trespassing and quickly descended the stairs.

In spite of my transgression, I was grateful to have been in the church that Johan Sebastian Bach made famous. Here he composed some of his greatest music, among them one of my favorites—the *St. Matthew Passion.*

What distinguished Bach was that he was more than a talented composer and technician at the organ. He was a man of prayer. He not only practiced the organ; he practiced his faith. Little wonder that he was given the name "the fifth evangelist."

Today on Bach's commemoration day I'm thinking of some of the great organists I have known, musicians who combined high talent with a commitment to Christ and the church. Among them are Paul Manz, David Cherwein, David Fienen, Christine Johnson, and Chad Winterfeldt. Unlike so many members of our congregations, I linger after a service to listen to the musical offerings these persons give us. It seems a shame that we pay so little attention to women and men who work so hard to lead us in hymn singing and then, as an added gift, play music that aids us in our quest to reflect more deeply on our relationship with God.

You may not have the world's most talented organist where you worship. But try to imagine what worship would be like if on a given Sunday every organist across the church took a day off. We would welcome them with open arms the next Sunday.

~ hwc

❖ PSALM 33:1-5 ❖

❖ A Place for Full Acceptance ❖

John and Idell were exactly the kinds of folks a young pastor and his family needed. With no children of their own, they "adopted" us and our children as their family. On a Sunday evening when the pace of life had slowed a bit, we would often drive to their place in the country, an idyllic farm nestled between small lakes and wooded hills. After John finished milking his half-dozen cows, we would settle in easy chairs in the living room and enjoy Idell's chocolate cake with a cup of coffee.

Here was a place where we didn't need to be on guard. We could open our hearts. We shared stories from the previous week as well as the distant past. We laughed. It was safe to cry. We lingered at the door, wishing the evening had not passed so swiftly.

This is the kind of home I envision when I read the stories of those dear friends of Jesus—Martha, Mary, and Lazarus. We commemorate them today because they are among the great saints. Were they well-educated? Did they have some wealth? Why weren't any of them married? What did they do for a livelihood?

All those questions go unanswered because they aren't really very important. What is important is that Jesus felt completely at ease in their home. Here he could "kick off his sandals" and be totally himself. He didn't need to be careful about every word he spoke. Here he could share his fears, his frustrations, his dreams, his hopes.

This is a good day to remember with thanks the places where we feel at ease and to ask about our own homes. Are they places where others can be at ease, where they can bare their souls, where they can find a word of encouragement to help them move through another week of life's challenges?

~ hwc

❖ JOHN 12:1-3 ❖

❖ As Christ Welcomed You ❖

The Gay Men's Chorus of a West Coast city rehearsed weekly in a church sanctuary, a place chosen for its good acoustics. After having used this space for some months, the director came one day to the pastor announcing that they would no longer be meeting there. Puzzled as to the reason for this change, the pastor first reassured them of their welcome and then asked why they were leaving. The answer was simple and direct. It was because the sanctuary itself and the feelings of rejection that happened to them there, brought back too many recollections from growing up gay. Feelings of being condemned for something they had no more chosen than the color of their eyes. It was too painful for them even to practice now in a church building. The memories were devastating, so they had to leave.

It is devastating to feel others look down on you as an outcast. But there is one who understands and cares. From of old, God has reached to comfort and heal. "The Lord . . . gathers the outcasts of Israel. He heals the broken-hearted, and binds up their wounds" (Ps. 147:2-3).

Outcasts in New Testament times were the lepers. And in Old Testament times they were the foreigners and eunuchs. Isaiah sounds the trumpet that soon salvation will come for them, and God's deliverance will be revealed. To eunuchs who hold fast God's covenant is the promise, "I will give, in my house and within my walls, a monument and a name better than sons and daughters; I will give them an everlasting name that shall not be cut off" (Isa. 56:5). Further, God promises to "make them joyful in my house of prayer; . . . a house of prayer for all peoples. Thus says the Lord God who gathers the outcasts of Israel" (vv. 7-8).

So we are called to "Welcome one another, therefore, just as Christ has welcomed you" (Rom. 15:7).

~ ecc

❖ ISAIAH 56:1-8 ❖

❖ Needing the Faith of Others ❖

Some folks say they can believe in God without going to church, that worshipping God in isolation is all they need. The fact that others need them at worship has never occurred to them. There is something important about our being together in worship.

Think of the old campfire. Remember sitting there mesmerized by flames leaping up the logs. Then watching as the fire dies down until only embers remain. But when the scattered coals are pulled together, the fire blazes again.

Perhaps your faith once glowed from a vibrant relationship with God. You worshipped regularly. There was joy in active service with others until something happened. Some change in your life. Children grew up and left home. Maybe a new responsibility that left you exhausted. Or trials and suffering overtook you. You kept it all inside so others didn't even know what you faced. You grieved the loss of joy you once knew as embers of faith died out with seemingly no way to pull them back together.

Luther agonized over the thought of anyone losing the Christ they had once known, of losing the Christ who suffered and died for them. He said the sorrow would be almost unbearable. If this describes your relationship, Christ waits to fill you again with his presence.

When our relationship with God is dull and lifeless, like dying embers, joining the body of Christ in worship can pull faith back again into glowing flames. Within the body of Christ there are pillars of strength we can lean on. And you will become a pillar for others, with no idea of someone looking to you as a tower of strength. One who really misses you if you are not at worship. We need regular worship to keep the flames of faith leaping high.

~ ecc

❖ HEBREWS 10:19-25 ❖

❖ Safe behind the Door ❖

We miss so much of what Jesus meant in some of his teachings simply because we do not live when and where Jesus lived. Here is one example.

On several occasions Jesus said, "I am . . . I am the good shepherd. . . . I am the vine. . . . I am the bread of life."

In another setting he said, "I am the door; if anyone enters by me, he will be saved" (John 10:9). Immediately there comes to mind the doors most familiar to us—home, school, office, church. Life is full of doors, from the most costly and ornate to the most inexpensive and simple. Everywhere we turn there are doors.

When Jesus said, "I am the door," he meant something entirely different. For a moment try to imagine yourself in Palestine in the time of Jesus. Suppose you are a shepherd with a small flock of sheep. All day you keep a watchful eye on them as they graze on the green, rocky hillside, searching for nourishment. As the sun sets you bring them to a spring of cool water where they can satisfy their thirst for the long night. Next, you bring them through a small opening into an enclosure surrounded by a wall of brambles that keep out predators. As they settle down for a night of peaceful sleep you go to that small opening and lie down on your soft mat. The sheep see this. They know that now they are safe for the night. They are at peace because you have made yourself—your very body—"the door of the sheep."

Our God is not just a God of the daytime, one who is concerned about us only when the sun shines. Our God is also a God of the night, a God who is on duty 24/7. Only when we stay near our Good Shepherd can we be confident—day and night.

~ hwc

❖ PSALM 121 ❖

❖ Who's in Charge? ❖

I hate bumper stickers. When we visited an amusement park we came back to our car and found a sticker attached to our bumper. I made them remove it. On one occasion I agreed to attach a sticker for a candidate I supported. He lost. When I tried to remove it the adhesive stuck so firmly that the remnants got traded in with the rest of the car years later.

One day I saw a sticker that read: "My God is in control." It irked me. I had just visited with folks who were suffering in ways that seemed entirely unfair. I wanted to shake my fist at the driver and shout, "No, God is *not* in control of the world I've seen this week!"

It helps put things into perspective if we remember the lessons of the first chapters of Genesis. There it's clear that after creating the world in all of its splendor, God decided that the human family—you and I—could not reach our full potential unless we were given an enormous measure of control over what happens in our world. "Be fruitful and multiply," says God, "and fill the earth and subdue it; and have dominion over . . . every living thing that moves upon the earth" (Gen. 1:28). That suggests if we want to plaster our bumper with a sticker it might better read: "Beware! Humans are in control!"

Yes, that's the risk God took. The remainder of the story spells out how we messed up. And the daily newspaper heralds the same grim news, namely, that we're still messing up.

Should we despair? By no means. God did not abandon us and creation. We still have major control. But now the sticker reads: "We're in control. But God never gives up. God helps us make the best of it."

Drive slowly. It will take your neighbors a full block to read your new bumper sticker.

~ hwc

❖ PSALM 8 ❖

❖ Comfort ❖

In our Stephen Ministry program we were given a model and an image to help us better understand how best to walk alongside one who grieves in order to bring comfort. The teaching tool used a negative image first and then the positive one.

The image pictures a griever walking alone in a pit with a rim circling above. Comforters come in two kinds. The first walks the rim, looking down upon the griever, offering pity. And pity always has the effect of making grief worse. The second comforter comes right down into the pit, walking with the griever, feeling with the griever. That is the meaning of true empathy—feeling with. That is real comfort.

Suffering of any kind, including grief, often causes one to wonder and ask, "What have I done wrong." One may believe God is causing this suffering as punishment. Luther taught that in times of adversity, our sinful flesh thinks God is angry, therefore comfort can never be spoken enough.

Often in the midst of trials, out of sadness, we ask, "God, why this suffering, WHY, WHY?" Have you ever noticed when you ask that question, you're almost immediately drawn to others who are also experiencing the same? And you find yourself walking with them, feeling with them, understanding them in ways you never could have without your own difficult journey. I believe that is what this word of God helps us understand today.

"Blessed be the God and Father of our Lord Jesus Christ, the Father of mercies and the God of all consolation, who consoles us in all our affliction, SO THAT WE MAY BE ABLE TO CONSOLE THOSE who are in any affliction with the consolation with which we ourselves are consoled by God" (2 Cor. 1:3-4).

May we allow God, in Christ Jesus, to console us. And may we allow true sympathetic consolation of others to heal us so that we can become arms of consolation to others.

~ ecc

❖ 2 CORINTHIANS 1:3-7 ❖

❖ The Bare Word ❖

The story is told of a family group meeting where a woman forcefully boasted of her strong faith. She had faith that like a mountain could not be moved. Repeatedly, she named, "my strong faith," gesturing as though it were contained in a box, her very own possession. Thankfully, the leader saved the day. For this was a group of parents feeling quite overwhelmed and helpless with concerns for a family member destroying their life with drugs. In a sense, this woman represents all of us who need to be in control. It's part of original sin, inherent in us all.

We have a need somehow to rev up our faith, making of it a possession for which we can boast. Not a gift, but something we've earned with diligent work, proud of being able to do it by ourselves. We've prayed enough. Read the Bible enough. Obeyed God's law enough. Or maybe, done good works enough. So that we've come a long way in making ourselves right with God. By ourselves. Then we don't need what Jesus has done for us in his death and resurrection. Nor do we need the gift of Christ's justification (just-as-if-I'd-never sinned) that gives us God's righteousness (makes us right with God). "They are now justified by his grace as a gift, through the redemption that is in Christ Jesus" (Rom. 3:24). Martin Luther says this righteousness comes only through the bare Word:

> Our life is simply contained in the bare Word; for we have Christ, we have eternal life, eternal righteousness, help and comfort, but where is it? We don't see it. We neither possess it in coffers nor hold it in our hands. But only in the bare Word (*Luther's Works,* 1906).

> Lord, keep us steadfast in your word;
> curb those who by deceit or sword
> Would wrest the kingdom from your Son
> and bring to naught all he has done (*ELW* #517).

~ ecc

❖ ROMANS 3:19-28 ❖

❖ God's Little Giants ❖

Have you ever heard about a "trim tab"? Unless you've been in the Navy, probably not. A trim tab is a small device that's attached to the edge of a ship's rudder. It's like a miniature rudder. When the captain moves that tiny trim tab, it builds pressure on other parts of the rudder and pulls it around. It takes very little force for this small object to set off other actions that can turn a gigantic ocean liner.

I've known many "trim tabs" over the years. They attract little attention to themselves. They may even be out of sight to most everyone. They just go on day in and day out doing what they were created to do.

Over the years I've also been in positions where a good deal of attention has come my way. I often meet folks for the first time who say to me, "I feel like I know you. I've seen your picture many times. I've read articles and books you've written." Well, I suppose that's all right. Someone needs to stand in those more visible and public places and assume the more noticeable roles in life, whether it be in the church or other places. But in the long history of life God seems to think those small "trim tabs" may be more important.

When the disciples of Jesus vied for positions of prominence in what they thought would be a new political movement, Jesus put things into perspective by bringing a child to his side and saying, "Truly I tell you, unless you change and become like children, you will never enter the kingdom of heaven. Whoever becomes humble like this child is the greatest in the kingdom of heaven" (Matt. 18:3-4).

Can you imagine the embarrassment the disciples felt? A child, a small "trim tab," so inconsequential in the eyes of the world, yet greater than they.

~ hwc

❖ MATTHEW 18:1-5 ❖

❖ Keep It Simple, Stupid ❖

The conversion of Paul looms so large in the Book of Acts that we easily overlook another character whose life was changed just as dramatically. I have in mind the Ethiopian eunuch in Acts 8.

We are not told his name and we have no idea what he is doing in Palestine at the time. All we know is that he was a high official in the realm of the queen of Ethiopia, and that while in Jerusalem he became acquainted with Judaism. He read at least part of what we now call the Old Testament. As he read he became curious. He heart was warmed. But he wanted to know more.

Then comes the encounter with the evangelist Philip. They meet on a desert road. When Philip shares the good news about Jesus, the man asks to be baptized. What happens next is what fascinates me. Philip might have told him that he would need to be instructed for a month or two, or that he should first be circumcised, or that he must make certain promises. Nothing like that is required. They rush into the water and the unnamed man becomes a child of God.

This simple, direct approach fits with the rest of the New Testament. Andrew says to Peter, "We have found the Messiah." Philip says to Nathanael, "Come and see." Mary announces the resurrection with three words, "He is risen."

As I stepped into a pulpit in New England I found the letters: KISS. I knew what they meant, words that every preacher in that pulpit—and every pulpit—needs to remember: "Keep It Simple, Stupid."

We often try too hard to share the good news. We think that if we don't say it just right we'll confuse someone. How about simply saying, "I love Jesus," or "God loves you," or "Believe in Jesus and you will become a child of God."

~ hwc

❖ ACTS 8:34-40 ❖

❖ We Have the Advantage ❖

Would it not be much easier to believe if we had lived in the time of Jesus? We could have felt the force of his dynamic personality. We could have sat on the Galilean hillside to drink in every word of the Sermon on the Mount. We could have witnessed his miracles and talked to those who had been healed. Above all, we could have seen him after his resurrection from the dead. Yes, "seeing is believing," and how easy it would have been to believe had we been there in old Palestine.

Or would it? Luther cautioned his listeners to beware of the tendency to think that because Christ seems to be gone and far away from us that we cannot know him as well as those eyewitnesses in the first century. The very opposite, he said, is the case. While Christ was on earth he was far away from us; now after his resurrection and ascension he is very near to us.

This was the issue that John wrote about in his first epistle. As a disciple, John had been an eyewitness and his readers probably envied him for it. They were probably thinking that it was easier for him to believe. But John reminds them that all who believe have "the testimony in their hearts" (1 John 5:10). Probably the last of the disciples to survive and the one loved so deeply by our Lord, John is eager for his readers to experience the same intimate relationship with Christ that he had known. Can it be? Yes, says John. By believing in Jesus Christ and loving him they stand in the same relationship to Christ as he did.

John Wren captured this idea in his familiar hymn:

> Christ is alive! No longer bound
> To distant years in Palestine,
> He comes to claim the here and now
> And conquer ev'ry place and time (*LBW* #363).

~ hwc

❖ 1 JOHN 5:9-13 ❖

❖ Luther Is So Lutheran ❖

Up early on a beautiful morning, we were already accomplishing goals for the day before breakfast. Then an insignificant thing happened. An angry word. Impatient response. Irritable. All those things love is not. After so many years walking with the Lord and being faithfully blessed by God's grace and mercy, shouldn't one by this time in life be more like Jesus? That's what sanctification is all about. No doubt there's been some mellowing through struggle. And quite a bit of pruning too! After all of that, it gets discouraging to see sin still raging. So that morning, I tearfully said to my husband, "I'm sorry. I don't want to hurt you ever." Martin Luther, in reminding us we're always both saint and sinner, wrote the following:

> It is not possible . . . to become so righteous in this life that thou shouldst feel no sin at all . . . and yet thou art holy notwithstanding. . . . How can I be holy, when I have and feel sin in me? . . . In that thou dost feel and acknowledge thy sin. . . . Despair not. It is one step of health, when the sick man doth acknowledge and confess his infirmity. But how shall I be delivered from sin? Run to Christ the physician, which healeth them that are broken in heart, and saveth sinners (*Luther's Works*, 1953, 1956).

Despair could make us stop praying and reading the Word. We were tempted that morning. But instead, we knew we must run to Christ. That's what Luther did over and over again because he believed that God knows our human weakness and that we are not able to stand against the many dangers of life. Luther believed that God is able to restore us, giving strength to conquer all things that harass us because of our sins. Luther is so Lutheran!

And we did. "Though your sins are like scarlet, they shall be like snow" (Isa. 1:18).

~ ecc

❖ ISAIAH 1:18 ❖

❖ God's Embrace ❖

Although my father was never given to great displays of emotion, we always knew he loved us. Only twice do I remember him holding me. The first time was when I was seven. On a warm summer evening neighbors came to visit. When they were leaving it was dark and their car wouldn't start. But it did when they were pushed down the hill. In that process, Tipper, my favorite kitten, who had been sleeping under their car, was run over and killed. We had over twenty outside cats that kept the farm free from rats and mice. But they were all my pets and each had a name. So I grieved for Tipper. The next day coming in for morning coffee, father, seeing my sadness, took me up in his lap, embracing me with comfort as he wiped my tears. The second embrace was when he came to us after the sudden death of our son. Elderly by then, and mellowed with his own grief, he pulled me in a close embrace with weeping and with fatherly comfort.

Whether or not you know a warm embrace from your earthly father, be sure always of God's loving, welcoming, and comforting embrace. An earthly father's embrace is only for this lifetime, but God's embrace is forever. God's embrace waits for you now—in every place, at all times. "If I take the wings of the morning and settle at the farthest limits of the sea, even there your hand shall lead me, and your right hand shall hold me fast" (Ps. 139:9-10).

The psalmist knew, "My flesh and my heart may fail, but God is the strength of my heart and my portion forever" (Ps. 73:26).

> Oh, let me nestle near thee, within thy downy breast
> Where I will find sweet comfort and peace within they nest.
> Oh, close thy wings around me and keep me safely there,
> For I am but a newborn and need thy tender care (*ELW* #613).

~ ecc

❖ PSALM 73:21-26 ❖

❖ God's Love Poured In ❖

The story is told of a man walking along a seaside bay in England. How astounded he was to see the tragic mess of ships lying helter-skelter against each other in the mud. Pondering how they could be rescued, he imagined hoists and cranes brought in to lift them upright. But while he stood there thinking of solutions, the tide began rolling in. Soon there was wild splashing of water against boats. Mud was being washed off. And then the miracle. As the tide filled the basin, first one ship straightened up and then another. And another. Until every one of the ships stood clean and tall. All so stately as they glistened in the sun.

Some days our lives are like those twisted ships in disarray. We're not letting God pour love into our hearts. Like when one, with a full pitcher of water, tries pouring water into a container with a tightly-closed lid.

Let us open our hearts and listen carefully to hear God's promise from Romans 5. And savor our baptismal gift. We have been justified by faith. We have been given peace with God. We even have access to the glory of God. Furthermore, God's love has been poured into our hearts, cleansing us like the tide washed clean the ships. These gifts are ours, given through the Holy Spirit who dwells in us.

That's why today, and every day, we can rejoice and have no fear of whatever a day will bring. Even in times of suffering, because there's good news. The tide of God's love is rolling in for you and me. And we like the ships can stand tall.

> Love divine, all loves excelling, joy of heav'n, to earth come down!
> Fix in us thy humble dwelling, all thy faithful mercies crown.
> Jesus, thou art all compassion, pure, unbounded love thou art;
> Visit us with thy salvation, enter ev'ry trembling heart (*ELW* #631).

~ ecc

❖ ROMANS 5:1-5 ❖

❖ In Praise of Black Thumbs ❖

Being an avid gardener I'm often complimented for having a "green thumb." Back of that comment is the assumption that folks like me have some kind of mysterious quality that makes it easier for us to grow vegetables, fruits, and flowers.

The truth of the matter is that there is no secret about being a good gardener. For that reason I prefer to think of effective gardeners as having not a "green" thumb but a "black" one. Enjoyable as it may be, the only "secret" to being a good gardener is to learn as much as one can about flowers, vegetables, and fruits and then to work hard—very hard at times.

When I had a greenhouse of my own in northern Minnesota I started some seeds in the dead of winter. Nursing them along in the tender stage meant constant vigilance. At planting time there was hard work in preparing the beds and spreading compost. For the rest of the season there was daily weeding, fertilizing, and defense against disease and pests. At long last, there was the satisfaction of lovely flowers and a good harvest.

I like to think that Jesus understood all this. Raised in a small town by simple folks, he was no doubt acquainted with the hard work that goes into gardening. He understood the value of good soil; he knew about fertilizing; he recognized the importance of pruning for greater production; he knew what weeds could do to a crop; he fell to his knees to look into the beauty of a lily, declaring that even Solomon in all his glory could never match such splendor.

Whether you garden or not, look around and share the sentiments of the Johannes Knudsen, the Dane who wrote:

> I am a gardener, nothing more,
> But what could e'er be greater?
> For all God's given me in store
> I praise him, my Creator.

~ hwc

❖ JOHN 15:1-8 ❖

❖ Painful Pruning ❖

Let's linger a bit with the text we read yesterday from John 15 about the vine and the branches. What is Jesus trying to teach us?

First and foremost, it's not only about us. "I am the true vine," says Jesus. That is the constant. The God who made all things in the beginning and who gives us new life in Christ is also the God who sustains life. The moment we are severed from the vine we begin to wither away.

Baptism is meant to be just the beginning of our life in Christ. It is a lifelong relationship, one that is sustained by Word and Sacrament. We cannot make it on our own. We are in need of daily renewal just as a branch needs the main stock of the vine.

The branches have but one purpose—to bear fruit. Life is growth. At times that growth is accompanied by suffering and loss. We are pruned in order that through our setbacks and disappointments we might learn to trust even more in the source of our life.

The threat of being cut off is sobering, but not new in the teaching of Jesus. He urged his disciples over and over to love him and keep his commandments. As the sap runs from the stock of the vine out into each branch, so we draw our life from Christ. Pruning can only mean greater productivity.

This is the kind of love God wants to see in each of us. This love is not cheap and mushy. It is tough. This image of the vine also teaches us that love is expansive. Though pruned, it only grows stronger.

Most of us can point to times in life when we felt we would never recover from a disappointment. Now we look back and see that it may have been the best thing that could have happened to us.

~ hwc

❖ JOHN 15:1-8 ❖

❖ Here Come the Angels ❖

Ida was deep into senility. Her husband Ernest was with her at the nursing home every day. As we sat in the hall waiting for a nurse to finish caring for Ida, Ernest looked to the far end and said, "Herb, do you see them coming—those nurses down there. They are God's angels."

Today we remember two who set the standards for nurses. I have in mind Florence Nightingale and Clara Maass. They are rightfully named "Renewers of Society."

Born in 1820, Nightingale was a child of privilege. She could have spent her life lounging in the lap of luxury. Responding to what she heard as the voice of God, she dedicated her life to public health. When she learned of horrible conditions among soldiers in the war in Turkey she enlisted other nurses and went to the front. Doctors rejected her and her colleagues at first. But when conditions became intolerable they welcomed them. Working long into the night, the image of the nurse carrying a lamp became a symbol for her and others.

On her return to England, Nightingale continued to work, often against strong opposition, for the improvement of health care. After her own health declined and she became blind, she persisted with her vision of medical help for the needy.

A generation later Clara Maass emerged on the American scene as another angel in white. Like Nightingale, she went to war zones and poured out her life to bring healing to wounded and dying soldiers. When it was suspected that the deadly yellow fever was caused by mosquito bites, Maass volunteered for an experimental research program. In the process she died of yellow fever. But out of that experiment came a cure.

At one time or another most of us end up in a hospital and in need of these angels. Give thanks today for those who follow this calling.

~ hwc

❖ 1 CORINTHIANS 12:7-11 ❖

❖ Perseverance ❖

The Horatio Alger Association of Distinguished Americans is named after the nineteenth century author whose stories about overcoming adversity gripped our country, writes Harvey Mackay (*StarTribune*, 4-20-2009). The association gives over $10 million every year in scholarships to help young folks experiencing adversity. One of their notable members is Oprah Winfrey, whose life experience taught her that, if you want to stay alive and succeed, you must overcome obstacles. Another member, J.C. Penney said, "I would never have amounted to anything were it not for adversity. I was forced to come up the hard way." Adversity, like a grindstone preparing us for sturdiness, happens also in nature. For example, a tree needs wind to become strong. It needs wind also for movement that drives sap up to its leaves for nourishment. A beautiful pearl is formed in the mouth of a mollusk to seal off the irritation from a grain of sand.

Our Scripture today encourages perseverance. It tells of the cloud of witnesses who are our cheerleaders in heaven encouraging us to the finishing line. Remembering those faithful ones now on the other side helps us in our faith journey. Reading stories of others who have done great things after persevering hardships is helpful as well. Looking to their example gives us hope that we, too, can endure adversity and come out strong to do God's work.

But most of all, we look "to Jesus the pioneer and perfecter of our faith, who for the sake of the joy that was set before him endured the cross, disregarding its shame" (Heb. 12:2). And Jesus is even now at the right hand of God interceding for us. With encouragement from Jesus and the cloud of witnesses cheering for us, there is surely strength enough to bravely persevere.

> And when the strife is fierce, the warfare long,
> steals on the ear the distant triumph song,
> And hearts are brave again and arms are strong. Alleluia! Alleluia!
> (*ELW* #422).

~ ecc

❖ HEBREWS 12:1-2 ❖

❖ THAT WE MIGHT LIVE ❖

Pierre Boulle's *Bridge Over the River Kwai* is the story of war prisoners who under duress had formed solid community. Forced into hard labor, they became as close as brothers. One day as they crossed the bridge coming from labor, the cruel guard counted one shovel missing. Believing it had been sold to a civilian in exchange for a morsel of bread, he lined up the men, demanding the guilty one to step forward to be killed. No one moved. Angered even more, he shouted, "Unless the guilty man steps forward, I will shoot all of you!" When no one moved, he readied his rifle for the first man, when, way down at the end of the line, a young man stepped forward. Furiously, the guard rushed to crush the man with the butt of his gun, killing him instantly. After he had left, the saddened prisoners picked up their shovels to bury their friend. And there was one shovel left. Their comrade had died that they might live. That's what Jesus has done for us.

With disaster impending, Jesus' disciples tried to hold him back. But he insisted that he must go up to Jerusalem. Suffering in prayer, Jesus pleaded, "Remove this cup from me; yet, not my will, but yours be done" (Luke 22:42).

Jesus told his disciples, "No one has greater love than this, to lay down one's life for one's friends. You are my friends" (John 15:13-14). Wanting us to have an open relationship with God, Jesus was willing to give his life that we might live. We were reconciled to God by the death of his Son, and saved by his life.

> How pale thou art with anguish, with sore abuse and scorn;
> How does thy face now languish, which once was bright as morn!
> Thy grief and bitter passion were all for sinner's gain;
> Mine, mine was the transgression, but thine the deadly pain
> (*ELW* #352).

~ ecc

❖ ROMANS 5:6-11 ❖

❖ Anxiety or Serenity ❖

On hillsides beside the Lake of Galilee, bright red lilies of the valley open their faces to the sun, happy for one glorious day to bloom. They do bloom only for a day, not caring that tomorrow, after drying up, they'd be harvested and thrown into an oven to make fire to bake bread. That, in fact, was the custom in Jesus' day when he used the lilies for an example.

Jesus wants us to have such complete trust in God so that we, too, can bloom where we are planted, across the landscape of our lives. But knowing our human weakness, Jesus warns, "Do not worry about your life" (Matt. 6:25). The word in Greek, *merimnatay*, means do not be anxious about your life today, distracted from duties of this day, drawn in different directions, annoyed in spirit so you cannot trust God, and having futile anxiety. This kind of worry not only robs one of good sleep, but also harms body, soul, and spirit. Actually, it can be disabling—an obstacle that prevents us from knowing and doing God's will. And haven't you experienced, as I have, that in looking back most of our worrying was unnecessary? We see now, how in past storms we've weathered, that God did intervene. And will continue to do so.

In the serenity prayer, we ask God to help us change the things we can, accept the things we cannot change, and the wisdom to know the difference. May God give us grace to let go when we need to. And guidance to move ahead with confidence and boldness, always allowing God's Spirit to both intercede and work on our behalf. "Cast all your anxiety on him, because he cares for you" (1 Peter 5:7).

What a gift that the Holy Spirit gives us the miracle of faith and serenity—the surety that God is acting, loving, caring, protecting, guiding, and giving new courage. God's peace be with you.

~ ecc

❖ MATTHEW 6:25-34 ❖

❖ Always a Dependent ❖

Today I visited the offices of the State Services for the Blind. Though I'm far from blind, I've lost enough vision to qualify for some of their benefits. The woman who interviewed me was exceptionally helpful and understanding. She could no doubt sense that this was not an easy day for me. After battling with increasing loss of vision, life has been more challenging with each passing year. My strong sense of independence doesn't yield easily to help from others.

This experience does, however, force one to think about our dependence on others. From the moment I was born I needed my mother for nourishment at her breasts. I needed my father to provide food for the table. I needed my older sisters for daily care. I needed my teachers for education. I needed my community for clean water and electrical power to light and heat our home. I needed college and seminary professors to open my mind to new worlds of knowledge. I needed my wife for companionship and affection. I needed churches to fulfill my need to be a pastor.

Where does it end? It doesn't. From birth to death we are dependent on others for everything we need and desire. There simply is not a self-sufficient and self-made person.

This is why John 15:16 is among my favorite Scripture verses: "You did not choose me, but I chose you. And I appointed you to go and bear fruit, fruit that will last." I am also reminded of one of my favorite hymns, one that never made it beyond the *Service Book and Hymnal* (the "Red Book").

> I sought the Lord, and afterward I knew
> He moved my soul to seek him, seeking me;
> It was not I that found, O Saviour true;
> No, I was found of thee (*SBH* #473).

Yes, we're dependent for a lifetime—dependent on God and dependent on others.

~ hwc

❖ JOHN 15:12-17 ❖

❖ Help for a Lifetime ❖

Let's continue yesterday's conversation about dependence. I'm old enough to recall the days when there were no "training wheels" for bicycles. When my daughter Mary and sons Chris and Andrew were old enough to ride a bike there was only one way to learn. I would set them on the seat and run behind them, my hand firmly fixed on the seat. If they faltered I would grasp the handlebar to keep them from falling. After a run or two to the corner and back, I was winded and had had enough for the day.

The second day I would lift my hand from the seat now and then and allow them to ride on their own, though they did not know it until we stopped. After a few days they rode like they had been doing it for years.

Next, it was teaching my boys to fish, sharing the secrets I had learned from others. Over time they honed their skills and became excellent fishermen.

A few years later it was time to sit beside them while they practiced driving the family automobile. This was at least as terrifying for me as for them. I gave them tips, and bit-by-bit they gained confidence. With the help of drivers' training they soon took off with confidence.

Then it was teaching my boys to use tools, including dangerous power units. The last thing I wanted to see was for them to lose a finger or incur an injury.

Is there ever a time when a son doesn't need a father or a daughter a mother? No, never.

Our life as a child of God is no different. We never "graduate" in this school of life. Even into old age there is something to learn, some valuable lesson to store away in our book of experience. Today let's all be open to the help God is ready, willing and eager to give us.

~ hwc

❖ PSALM 71:3-6; 17-18 ❖

❖ Please Stand for the Gospel ❖

Our friend Peter has known since he was a young boy that he is gay. His family was always active in one of our Lutheran congregations. From time to time Peter heard negative things about homosexual persons. It hurt. He had never chosen to be gay.

We asked Peter what kept him in the church. His reply was very disarming. "It was the gospel," he said. As a young lad he noticed that when the gospel was read during the worship service everyone stood. That told him Sunday after Sunday that this must be the high point of the service, the most important part of worship. He listened carefully to the gospel lesson when it was read.

What Peter noticed was that Jesus never said a negative word about homosexual persons. That kept him in the church. Peter and his partner of more than twenty years are faithful members of one of our ELCA congregations. Peter is the chair of the evangelism committee.

What Peter learned is what every good Lutheran should know, namely, that the Bible has a center where it all comes together. And that center is the good news about Jesus Christ. Everything else in the Bible is seen through the prism of the gospel. Every time we worship and stand for the reading of the gospel we are saying, "Yes, this is it. Above all else that we believe and teach, it is the word about Jesus Christ that is most important."

Churches take positions on a variety of issues from war to the death penalty to care for the environment to abortion to divorce to human sexuality and many, many other matters. That is well and good. But we are free to disagree on those issues and still be part of the same family of faith. At one point, however, there is complete unity: "For God so loved the world. . . ."

~ hwc

❖ JOHN 3:16-21 ❖

❖ Growing Pains ❖

Gail Sheehy, in *Passages*, uses the metaphor of the lobster to describe our growing. A lobster grows by developing a series of hard and protective shells. The old shell breaks, not by pressure from without but from growth within. After each time the confining shell breaks off, the lobster is left exposed and vulnerable again, until in time a new covering grows to replace the old. This is like our passages in life. In each of these passages, Sheehy says, "we become embryonic again, capable of stretching in ways we hadn't known before."

Growing toward maturity is often painful. And like the lobster, we are vulnerable after shedding the protective shell of what had been—comforts of childhood protection or a familiar terrain. Vulnerable in a new situation with no role model or past experience. During those crisis times we can no longer be spoon-fed like children, but instead we must find resources of mentors and ways to cope. Embryonic and vulnerable, we're open to receive God's sufficient grace. And the Holy Spirit helps us in our need to hear God's promises with our ear so that the heart believes. We're stretched with new vision, new vitality, and a new covering of faith. This is how Christians are born and reborn in faith and hope. It is a maturity we hadn't asked for. But a maturity that enables us to reach out with God's love to others who are vulnerable in their growing.

In growth toward maturity we need an "Epaphras, . . . a servant of Christ Jesus . . . always wrestling in his prayers on your behalf, so that you may stand mature and fully assured in everything that God wills" (Col. 4:12).

So let us thank God today for those who have upheld us in prayer. And pray even now as we continue growing into the servants God calls us to be. And may we be that also, for others.

~ ecc

❖ EPHESIANS 4:11-16 ❖

❖ Self-Worth ❖

Some years ago I was invited to speak at a church women's conference under their chosen theme, Self-Worth. Women requested this topic because several in the grass roots sensed low self-esteem. Not an uncommon need. Perhaps that's why we loved the little elf-like character Charlie Brown. He was created by a man who felt that way.

As a boy, Charles Schultz was always put down by an older, high-achieving brother. Growing up insecure, it was difficult for him to express himself, maintain relationships, or reach out for help. So it seemed natural that he should develop good ol' Charlie Brown who always struggled and failed.

In regular visits with a parishioner struggling with terminal cancer, I one day asked what her most difficult feeling was. Without hesitation she replied, "I feel unworthy and worthless." What could be her reason, and ours? One could blame parents. Or siblings who placed you at the bottom of the pecking order. Or a lifetime habit of feeling that you don't deserve anything and never will amount to anything. It's difficult to erase a bad tape playing in the mind. Affirmation from others may never be enough. It must come from within. The change needs to begin with listening to God who created us.

God said, "Let us make humankind in our image" (Gen. 1:26). Both male and female. Could there be any higher honor in any ancestral or family root? Isaiah spoke to people who had forsaken God in failing to be a light to the nations. But God gave them a new name, saying, "You shall be a crown of beauty in the hand of the Lord, and a royal diadem in the hand of your God. . . . for the Lord delights in you" (Isa. 62:3-4). For Israel and for each of us, let us savor Almighty God treasuring us.

Don't let anyone, especially yourself, convince you otherwise. Let's celebrate.

~ ecc

❖ ISAIAH 62:1-5 ❖

❖ Be Perfect ❖

At the end of a two-year preparation for confirmation, Pastor Molstre scheduled a private talk with each of us. Relating to him was easy, so it was not threatening. When asked if anything troubled me, I said it was that Bible verse where Jesus demands that we "Be perfect, therefore, as your heavenly Father is perfect" (Matt. 5:48).

At age thirteen we were idealistic. Everything was still black and white because we had not yet learned about the gray areas of life. You're sure you will someday have a perfect life mate. Perfect children. Perfect job. Not like the Smiths or Jones. But like the Mays and Andersons. On and on. But I was already starting to discover perfection was not possible. That I could not control some of my own thoughts and actions. So that day I told Pastor Molstre that, even though I didn't want to, I had bad thoughts about people and sometimes felt selfish. In fact I realized doing good was sometimes for selfish reasons. And then I worried about judgment day and what would happen to me. He listened with a big heart. With understanding, he explained two things. Jesus was perfect for us and shed his blood, covering our sins with his perfection. Having been covered with Christ's perfection, we have already passed judgment day. How thankful I was for a good confirmation pastor so able to help a thirteen-year-old both speak her heart and understand this gospel.

> When you were buried with him in baptism, you were also raised with him through faith in the power of God, . . . when he forgave us all our trespasses, erasing the record that stood against us with its legal demands. He set this aside, nailing it to the cross (Col. 2:12-14).

> My heart is longing to praise my Savior
> and glorify his name in song and prayer;
> For he has shown me his wondrous favor
> and offered me all heav'n with him to share (*LBW* #326).

~ ecc

❖ COLOSSIANS 2:8-15 ❖

Give Thanks for Your Local Congregation

One of the brightest lights among Lutheran leaders in the twentieth century was Conrad Bergendoff. Born into a family with deep roots in Swedish Lutheranism, he went on to become president of Augustana College in Rock Island, Illinois. Bergendoff's influence stretched not only across the Lutheran churches in this country, but around the world. He was in high demand as a preacher and lecturer.

Bergendoff, however, never forgot his roots in the local congregation. He knew that there in that setting one found the deepest expression of the church. In his book *I Believe in the Church*, he writes:

> The most important work of the church . . . is the enthroning of Christ in the unity of the parish church. If there is to be a regeneration of American communities, be it in the metropolis or in the highway-crossroads village, it must come from the small unit of a Christian congregation whose members have Christ as King in their lives.

While the rest of the world is not to be forgotten, in the New Testament believers are urged to begin their works of love right in their own local communities of faith. That makes sense. If we can't love those closest to us, including our own family, what point is there in trying to love those who are out of sight?

When I was presiding bishop of the Evangelical Lutheran Church in America I was inundated with an avalanche of problems. At times I was tempted to despair. What always kept my hope alive and what always made me feel confident in the midst of stresses and strains was the assurance that in more than 10,000 local congregations believers were gathering around Word and Sacrament. Faithful pastors and members of those churches, bound together by a common faith and joined in prayer—that gave me confidence.

Thank God today for your local congregation.

~ hwc

EPHESIANS 1:15-23

❖ IT TAKES ALL KINDS ❖

I've always been fascinated by the disciple named "Nathanael," also known as "Bartholomew." Today is his commemoration day.

Legend is full of stories about Nathanael. One says he went to India as a missionary; another places him in Egypt. In the Bible there is little about him. What there is marks him as a special person. He did not get a direct invitation to follow Jesus. It came second-hand through Philip, another disciple. When Philip tells Nathanael that Jesus of Nazareth is the promised Messiah, does he leap at this news? No, Nathanael scoffs, "Can anything good come out of Nazareth?" (John 1:46). He reminds me of one of my professors at New York University who regularly denigrated the culture of any place in the United States west of the Hudson River! Likewise, Nathanael thought of Nazareth as a seedy, hick town.

Everything changed when Nathanael met Jesus. Jesus saw in him the qualities of a thoughtful person who had the potential to be a disciple. When Nathanael felt this power in Jesus he was persuaded that "You are the Son of God" (John 1:49).

I have known many wonderful Christian people over the years who have never experienced a dramatic conversion. They have seen no bright visions and have had no startling dreams. Their lives were entirely ordinary. But as they thought about the faith and examined it more carefully, they became persuaded that this was what they had been looking for, though they did not even realize they had been searching.

C.S. Lewis comes to mind as a prime example of this kind of believer. He was an avowed atheist. He was certain there is not sufficient evidence to prove that there is a God. Then he literally thought his way to faith. And when he arrived he pronounced that he had been "surprised by joy"—that God had been there all along, though he never knew it.

~ hwc

❖ JOHN 1:43-51 ❖

❖ MAKING SNAP JUDGMENTS ❖

My garden looks a bit tired by this time of summer. The scenes I drooled over on the cover of the seed catalog last January are nowhere to be found.

Corinne and I were standing near my vegetable garden one day when a young woman came by. Not knowing that the garden was mine, she looked at rows of beans and said, "The gardener has certainly neglected this place." None of the beans, she noted, had been picked.

My wife said gently, "You're looking at the gardener." To save her any embarrassment I quickly pointed out that the beans she was looking at were actually "dry" beans—the kind one allows to grow to full maturity before harvesting. They are destined for clear jardinieres of multi-colored beans, delicious crocks of baked beans, and simmering bowls of soup.

The incident reminded me of some of my own embarrassing moments, including a visit to a Greek Orthodox church in Athens many years ago. There was only one woman in the dark sanctuary. She was standing in silence before an icon, completely enrapt in its scene. As we left the church I made the unkind remark that what she was doing seemed like idolatry. My more understanding friend turned to me and asked, "Did it occur to you that she may have been illiterate?" I was crushed with shame. The woman was simply drinking in the gospel story through her eyes. It was the beginning of a venture in understanding another expression of our Christian family—the Orthodox faith.

It is easy to make quick judgments. We would do better to ask questions in the hope that we will learn something. There may be good reason why someone worships in ways that seem alien to us. By asking questions and searching for answers we may have our eyes opened to a new way to praise God.

~ hwc

❖ MATTHEW 7:1-5 ❖

❖ CONTENTMENT ❖

There's a saying, "more wants more." If we get a new luxury, it soon becomes a need. We're ambitious for our children, giving not one Christmas gift, but many. Too much breeds early selfishness. We're all in this lifelong struggle together.

The apostle Paul wrote, "I have learned to be content with whatever I have. I know what it is to have little, and I know what it is to have plenty. In any and all circumstances I have learned the secret of being well-fed and of going hungry, of having plenty and of being in need. I can do all things through him who strengthens me" (Phil. 4:11-13).

Contentment means satisfied with ease of mind in whatever situation. The opposite of contentment is seen in Tantalus of Greek mythology. After killing his own son, this evil king was sent to the lower world. For punishment, he was made to stand under the threat of falling rocks and chin deep in water, but he could never get a drink because with each attempt at drinking, water disappeared. Hungry, he reached for delicious grapes. But with each attempt to grasp the fruit, their branches bounced out of reach. From his name comes our word *tantalize*. When tempted to what is just beyond our reach, we are never satisfied or content.

Advertisers tantalize us to buy, trying to convince us we need more things. Industry thrives on our discontent. God calls us to another way—being satisfied when basic needs are met, with thankfulness to generously share with those in need. We're warned about the danger of riches and the "Love of money [that] is a root of all kinds of evil" (1 Tim. 6:10). It breeds temptations that draw us away from God. May God give us contentment with help to give instead of grasp.

> Jesus calls us from the worship of this vain world's golden store,
> From each idol that would keep us, saying, "Christian, love me more" (*LBW* #494).

~ ecc

❖ Rekindle the Gift of God ❖

Saint Augustine (354–430) in his early years lived out on the edge, defying God and the faith of his pious mother, Monica. Brilliant, yet doing poorly in his studies during early years, he was often punished for not applying himself and for bad behavior. But gradually as he grew older, he became a serious student in university years, devouring philosophy. And entertaining Manichaeism, a popular cult. He certainly accumulated wisdom, but was left feeling empty.

He had learned the name of Christ at his mother's knee. It was deeply imprinted in his soul. At her breast and in her loving care, as he describes. God's mercies overwhelmed him with those memories. At last he realized that reason alone could not quench his thirst for God. This truth came alive under Bishop Ambrose's preaching and from Scripture that truly the "letter kills but the Spirit makes alive." And his eyes of faith were opened.

Many of us know, like Augustine and Timothy, that we have received and so became forever thankful for faith handed down to us from a mother, a grandmother, or someone who has been like a mother to us. When we needed it most, God's mercy brought those memories to our hearts, moving us to yearn for God's will and fresh faith. Like Augustine, we may have had periods of rebellion against both God and believing parents. May we lift our hearts today in thanks for the faith of those who have gone before. And hear God's word challenging us to, "Rekindle the gift of God that is within you" (2 Tim. 1:6).

~ ecc

❖ 2 TIMOTHY 1:3-12 ❖

❖ Augustine, Bishop of Hippo ❖

St. Augustine (354-430) was born in North Africa, some forty years after Constantine legitimized Christianity in the Roman Empire. While a professor in Milan, he was converted under the preaching of Bishop Ambrose. After this experience, Augustine became one of the church's greatest teachers and theologians. He is noted especially for his teaching on the Trinity.

His mother, Monica, had prayed earnestly for him during his early years of rebellion. He resisted God's call for many years. But finally after hearing and studying the Scriptures, his past life of sin caused deep sorrow. For him the message was coming clear, "It is now the moment for you to wake from sleep" (Rom. 13:11). One day in crying out his pain before God, when no child was there, he heard a child's voice cry, "Take up and read." Believing it to be God's command, he opened to read Romans 13:13-14: "Let us live honorably as in the day, not in reveling and drunkenness. . . . Instead put on the Lord Jesus Christ, and make no provision for the flesh, to gratify its desires." What happened then he tells in *Confessions* of his immediate conversion. "I did not desire to read further, nor did I need to. Instantly, at the end of this sentence, a light of serenity flooded my heart and all the darkness of doubt vanished away."

For the witness and insights of Augustine that influence and bless the church even to this day, we give thanks to God.

If you are rebelling like Augustine against or simply don't understand God's will in a certain area of your life right now, you can claim God's promise from Matt. 7:7: "Ask, and it will be given you; search, and you will find; knock, and the door will be opened to you." May the Holy Spirit lead you today into God's loving purpose. Then fresh joy and peace will be yours.

~ ecc

❖ ROMANS 13:11-14 ❖

❖ PRAISING GOD ❖

Today, as we commemorate St. Augustine, our thoughts turn to praise of God. In Augustine's *Vestigia Trinitatus* (Vestiges of the Trinity), he writes about seeing vestiges of God in all of creation, especially in the human soul. For we have been created "in the image of God" (Gen. 1:27). There is an imprint of the Triune God, Augustine says, in the human soul. Consequently, the highest and best way we can relate to God is by worshipping and praising God.

In our early years living in New Jersey, I joined the evangelism committee at church and was paired with Charlotte, an older woman. Together we made calls on inactive members. I was timid then. She was not. So, I mostly listened as she took the lead. I admired Charlotte for her love of God and her love of people. It was all so plain to see. She could be so out front in speaking her mind, yet never offensive. I watched the softening effect on inactive members as Charlotte would say, passionately and so directly, "You need to worship. You need to praise God." From experience, Charlotte knew her own need to praise God, and she did it. That was the reason, I was sure, that she was an effective channel of God's love for others. This is what we see in the psalmist; he knows his need to praise God and he's doing it. Psalm 104 can be our vehicle of praise today.

Our first thought about prayer is often that of asking. What would happen if most of our praying would be praising God? When we are praising God, I believe that you and I are closest to our own identity as persons, closest to being real, the persons God made us to be.

Augustine wrote, "Since we are part of your creation, we wish to praise you . . . our hearts are restless until they rest in you."

~ ecc

❖ PSALM 104 ❖

❖ The Educated Person ❖

Chances are someone in your immediate or extended family is packing bags these days and preparing to head off to a college or university. If it's the first time, there's a strong mixture of feelings in the household. "I'm so grateful for our colleges. But how can it be," parents ask, "that our 'baby' is already going away?"

The other day I found a homily I gave at Augsburg College more than forty years after I graduated. Here are a few excerpts that accent the value of my college experience:

"The decision to follow Christ had been made long before I came to Augsburg. But I have learned from life's journey that no matter what God does, it is still important that I make a decision about God—that I affirm what God wants for me. And I have learned that all of our important decisions in life need to be made over and over again.

"That's what happened here on this campus. Yes, I came with faith in my heart. But it was a faith that needed to be challenged. And it was. I learned to explore uncharted waters, to ask disturbing questions about things I had taken for granted.

"I also learned that it is costly to be a Christian. I was forced to look at the world where there is injustice, prejudice against minority persons, devastation of the environment, and corruption in the political world."

It was during that time that someone gave me a copy of J.B. Phillips's book *Your God Is Too Small.* It was another jump start for a young, somewhat naïve student. I knew that I was on a journey of learning that would continue for a lifetime.

Pray today for those who teach and administer at the colleges, universities, and seminaries of our church. Pray that students will come to see life as a gift given by God and to be shared with others.

~ hwc

❖ PROVERBS 8:10-14 ❖

❖ It's a One-Way Street ❖

Today we honor John Bunyan, who died on this date in 1688. For generations his major work *The Pilgrim's Progress* was second only to the Bible in popularity. In fact, in most homes these were the only two books. Even today it remains a classic book for Christian reflection.

Bunyan's major theme is that the Christian life is not for sissies or those who start off with enthusiasm and then fall by the wayside. His writing came out of personal experience. He was imprisoned for preaching without a license. In jail he ministered to fellow prisoners for more than a decade. When he was released he resumed preaching and caring for needy people. In spite of his strong stands on many issues, he was a warm-hearted and generous person. He was on his way to settle a dispute between a father and son when he was caught in a cold rainstorm and probably contracted pneumonia and died.

We can't help but draw comparisons between Bunyan and Dietrich Bonhoeffer, the German pastor who spoke out against moral evil in Nazi Germany and called for greater discipline among Christian believers. He, too, paid a heavy price for his persistence.

In *The Pilgrim's Progress* Bunyan depicts the Christian as on an upward journey. There is nothing easy about this trek. Temptations to turn back are everywhere. But for the main character "Christian" there is only one path to freedom. That is to keep moving onward and upward. Bunyan writes, "To go back is nothing but death, to go forward is fear of death, and life everlasting beyond it. I will yet go forward."

Jesus warned against starting but not continuing in the faith quest. When potential followers made excuses for not following or asked for time to care for personal matters, Jesus tells them they must make a decision. This is no place for divided loyalties.

~ hwc

❖ LUKE 9:57-62 ❖

❖ INSTRUMENTS OF GOD ❖

It was a magnificent evening of music. Gustavus Adolphus College Orchestra was playing its final concert of the year. Hearing a recording of it would have been great, but how much better being there to watch live musicians in action, director and players in concert. Arms and bows of violinists and cellists moving in beautiful coordination. Brasses and woodwinds making entrances with precision and clarity. Statements of music made with the slightest motion of the conductor's hand. All parts worked together in harmony and unison, the meaning of the word *concert*. Like we as the body of Christ are called to do.

Later, I began ruminating, what if instruments had weaknesses like people. What if there were bad feelings among them? Other instruments refusing support while the flute soloed. Basses looking down on the lesser piccolo and refusing to play together. Or percussions miffed because they were not able to make notes, just rhythm. The bassoon regretful because of sounding somber and never cheerful like a flute. Trumpets upset having to always sit in the back row. Timpani soft and seldom heard. Some instruments feeling not as good as others and afraid of criticism if by chance playing a wrong note. It would be a symphony pathetically in discord!

Scripture gives warning to the body of Christ. There's discord if the foot feels left out because it's not showy like the hand. Or the ear wishing it could be an eye. But hear the word of the Lord. The Holy Spirit has apportioned gifts to each person, and, like a good conductor, positions us and inspires us, seeking always to direct our gifts in harmony for the good of the world.

Dag Hammarskjold, former U.N. Secretary-General, said, "No man can do properly what he is called to do in this life unless he learns to forget his ego and act as an instrument of God."

> Lord, make me an instrument of your peace (from Prayer of St. Francis of Assisi).

~ ecc

❖ 1 CORINTHIANS 12:4-26 ❖

❖ Nickolai F. S. Grundtvig ❖

Nickolai F. S. Grundtvig is commemorated in the Evangelical Lutheran Church of America on September 2 (Feast Day in Episcopal Church USA on Sept. 8) for his gift of over 1,000 hymns. Two of his most famous are "O Day Full of Grace" and "God's Word Is Our Great Heritage."

Grundtvig and Soren Kiekegaard are noted as the most outstanding Danish theologians of the nineteenth century. Thomas Aquinas said, "A hymn is the praise of God with song . . . exaltation of the mind dwelling on eternal things, bursting forth in voice." From the earliest times, singing has been part of worship. We thank God for hymnists like Grundtvig who gave us hymns to praise God.

Grundtvig followed teachings of his pious father who was a pastor grounded in Lutheran Orthodoxy, untouched by the then current wave of European rationalism that relied on reason rather than faith. While studying theology at the University of Copenhagen, he absorbed the joy and optimism of the Enlightenment, was broadened by literature, and found a new world of thought in mythologies of the Northlands. Writing poetry became his profound way of expressing the human spirit.

Grundtvig was a prophetic preacher calling for an awakening, criticizing the Danish church tending toward a philosophical rationalism. But his preaching ostracized him from peers and friends. Firmly, he believed Christianity was an historical revelation of Christ in Scripture, handed down through sacramental Holy Baptism and Holy Communion. More effective than sermons, it was his hymns that brought great change to Danish church services.

Grundtvig is honored as scholar, translator, poet, and as the father of Danish hymnody. He championed freedom in both church and state, promoted education that awakened love of life, and was originator of the famous Danish folk high schools. The Grundtvig Church in Copenhagen was built in 1940 to honor him.

While we thank God for those who have composed music and hymns for our worship, let us also thank those in our congregation who make music.

~ ecc

❖ COLOSSIANS 3:16 ❖

❖ How to Enjoy Your Work ❖

Someone once made an estimate of how we spend a lifetime:

36 % sleeping
10 % eating, dressing, and bathing
34 % leisure, pleasure, and thinking
10 % working

At first glance, ten percent seems too little for working. But when we factor in childhood and youth at one end and retirement years at the other, it makes sense. We spend only a fraction of our lives at our employment.

As we observe another Labor Day about this time of year it's sobering to hear what some say about job satisfaction for the average American. One observer suggested that many persons have good salaries and adequate pension plans but low motivation. By the time they reach forty many are afraid to get out of the rut they're in. They drift for the last twenty-five years.

I'm reminded of a banner I saw in a congregation one Sunday with words from a Langston Hughes poem: "Hold fast to dreams, for if dreams die, life is a broken-winged bird that cannot fly."

How can we hold to our dreams and avoid broken wings? First of all, it's important to recognize that even those who are fortunate enough to have the ideal job they yearned for, even they will admit that not every day is fully satisfying. But what about those like my brother who stood at an assembly line in a turkey processing plant for twenty-five years doing the same task hour after hour?

The biblical view of work and vocation helps everyone to see that simply working, no matter what it is, cannot satisfy. The key is to see all of life as our calling and to be a blessing to those around us no matter where we work or what we do.

Paul's word to the church at Corinth is good advice: "So, whether you eat or drink, or whatever you do, do everything for the glory of God" (1 Cor. 10:31).

~ hwc

❖ 1 CORINTHIANS 10:31-33 ❖

❖ We Need a Map ❖

There was no Global Positioning System (GPS) when I was elected bishop of the Minnesota Synod in 1976. With more than 325 churches scattered across most of the state I needed a good map. I circled in red every church location outside the Twin Cities. Over the next eleven years I unfolded that map thousands of times, often several times on the same trip as I maneuvered my way through a maze of unfamiliar roads. Now and then I got lost. I stopped frequently to ask where I was and where I needed to go. By the time I left office that map was in tatters.

In one of his writings C.S. Lewis comments about believers who only study maps but never go anywhere in their journey of faith. One must actually set out, ask questions along the way, risk a few wrong turns, and even get lost now and then if one is to get anywhere in the journey of faith.

How does God guide us on this venture?

A starting place is the Bible. I don't recommend flipping it open, placing your finger on a page, and expecting to find an easy answer to life's perplexing questions. The key is persistence. Daily reading of the Bible is the surest way to know the mind of God and gain certainty about the way to go.

Being faithful in prayer is another way to understand God's will for our lives.

Stopping to ask others is still another aid. This includes regular worship, Bible classes, and conversations with other pilgrims. We may get lost on occasion, but there are those who are eager to lend an ear and point us back to the way we should go.

Using God-given common sense also helps in finding our way.

Don't forget to use your map. Bibles are printed to be worn out. And don't be too proud to ask for directions.

~ hwc

❖ PSALM 32:8-11 ❖

❖ MOTHER TERESA ❖

It was a thrill to visit Mother Teresa's (1910–1997) Calcutta Mission and learn what one, small woman could do for God. Born in Albania, she heard God's call at age twelve. Trained in a Dublin convent, she went to serve their order in India as a high school teacher. But her concern for the suffering poor outside of convent walls drew her to leave the convent and serve them. Volunteers joined her, and God provided funds to start an open-air school for slum children. In 1950, with permission from Rome, she founded her own order, Missionaries of Charity. Today the order has spread worldwide. She was awarded the Pope John XXIII peace prize in 1971 and won the Nobel Prize in 1979.

After doing a BBC documentary on Mother Teresa, Malcolm Muggeridge, wrote *Something Beautiful for God* in 1971. Leaving her, he felt he was "leaving behind all the beauty and joy in the universe." God's love gave her "luminosity, a shining quality. She has lived so closely with her Lord that the same enchantment clings about her that sent the crowds chasing after him in Jerusalem and Galilee . . . a harbinger of healing." In losing life, she found it. "A nun, rather slightly built, with a few rupees in her pocket, not particularly clever, or particularly gifted in the arts of persuasion. Just this Christian love shining about her; in her heart and on her lips. . . regarding every derelict left to die in the streets as him . . . in every leper's stump the hands which once touched sightless eyes and made them see."

Serenity, simplicity, and cleanliness were the hallmarks we observed at the Calcutta Mission. Sisters began long days with prayer and meditation at 4:30 a.m., followed by Mass. After breakfast, each went to their duties serving schools, lepers, dispensaries, the dying. However overworked or over-crowded their accommodations, none were refused. Christ's presence in morning Eucharist provided energy and love that endures.

~ ecc

❖ 1 CORINTHIANS 13:1-13 ❖

❖ Doubt Is Part of Life ❖

Yesterday, remembering the life of Mother Teresa, we were thankful for what God could do through one, small dedicated person. Today, we learn that she, too, lived with heavy doubts, like the doubting people in Corinth. In that new church, Jews and Greeks alike came from backgrounds where there was no belief in the resurrection of the body. But through Paul's preaching, God's Spirit had given them a convincing faith to believe both in Christ's resurrection and in that of their own bodies. But later Paul hears they are doubting all, and he writes, "If there is no resurrection of the dead, . . . then our proclamation has been in vain and your faith has been in vain" (1 Cor. 15:13-14). He underscores the good news that Christ died, was buried, and was raised.

Mother Teresa, behind her amazing work in the slums of Calcutta, also had grave doubts. Written ten years after her death, *Mother Teresa: Come Be My Light* reveals her secret writings of many years without sensing the presence of God. Pouring out her heart she wrote, "Lord, my God, I call, I cling, I want. . . . No one to answer. . . . Where is my Father? . . . Deep down . . . only empty, dark." It is thought that work was her release as she daily followed the passion of Christ. And that her doubts fueled the amazing efforts of her life and mission. It was a tremendous faith even with such an overwhelming silence of God.

It illustrates for us that doubt and experiencing the silence of God is part of life. Although Mother Teresa had requested this never be made public, theologians have revealed this part of her life because they believe her ministry after her death will help ordinary Christians in their times of doubt. And that her ministry after death will become even greater than all of her heroic work for the poor.

~ ecc

❖ 1 CORINTHIANS 15:1-17 ❖

❖ COME WITH CONFIDENCE ❖

Two young children went happily to spend their summer vacation with grandparents who raised ducks on their acreage. Adventures were aplenty there in the wide-open spaces. Like all boys, Peter loved throwing stones at targets. One day it was a duckling! He never intended to kill it, but when he hit it dead center, the duckling lay dead. He felt terrible. Unfortunately, his sister had seen it happen. Grandmother must not know, so he begged his sister, Peg, not to tell. She didn't tell but did something worse. Each time Grandmother would assign them chores to do, Peg would quietly demand Peter to do hers, saying, "Remember the duck!" Dutifully, he obeyed. Until finally when his guilt got too great, Peter went to his grandmother confessing. How surprised and relieved he was when she put her arm around him saying, "Oh, I saw you do it, and I forgave you long ago." Like God, Grandmother was approachable, understanding, loving, and forgiving.

Today, we're invited to God's throne of grace. Even to come with boldness and confidence. And why? First, because Jesus was human like we are, therefore he knows our weaknesses and feels with us when we suffer. Don't you think that's why Grandmother understood Peter? Certainly she had found mercy after doing wrong. So she was touched watching him suffer and forgave him even before he asked. The second reason God wants us to come is so that "we may receive mercy and find grace to help in time of need" (Heb. 4:16). Don't you know the grandmother was eager for Peter to confess so he could have peace? Likewise, God is eager for you and me to come today.

> Approach my soul, the mercy seat, where Jesus answers prayer;
> There humbly bow before His feet, for none can perish there.
> Thy promise is my only plea, with this I venture nigh;
> Thou callest burdened souls to Thee, and such, O Lord am I
> (*The Hymnal* #408).

~ ecc

❖ HEBREWS 4:14-16 ❖

❖ An Opportune Time ❖

Since moving in, we had seen newspaper articles warning residents to make sure they had secure deadbolt locks on all doors as there were nighttime burglaries in our area. Deadbolts were on our priority list, but so far, not at the top.

At 4:00 a.m. we were awakened by our little dog barking angrily downstairs by the laundry room, between the outside door and the table where the portable sewing machine had been. The door was locked, but someone had been there. When police arrived, they showed us how easily the lock on that door could be opened with one slip of a credit card. A burglar had come at an opportune time, when each of us was sleeping the hardest.

An opportune time it was, when Jesus was hungriest, that the devil tempted him to turn a stone into bread. And the young Jesus, human as we, tempted to receive instant authority without climbing the corporate ladder, heard he could have it if only he would worship the devil. Then from the pinnacle of the temple, the devil challenged him to jump, for certainly the angels would catch him. Notice in each case, the "ifs." The devil planted doubts. He tried it with Jesus and does with us, too.

Jesus understands, "in every respect has been tested as we are, yet without sin" (Heb. 4:15). So let us put on the whole armor of God, take the sword of the Spirit which is the Word of God and "the shield of faith with which you will be able to quench all the flaming arrows of the evil one" (Eph. 6:16).

Martin Luther says, "Keep God's little lantern alight. Take heed to the warning; be prepared, for you must expect at any moment that the devil may knock out a window pane, or tear open roof and door, so that he may blow out the light. . . . He does not sleep" (*Day by Day We Magnify Thee*, p. 39). He waits for an opportune time.

~ ecc

❖ LUKE 4:1-13 ❖

❖ The Challenges of Change ❖

What should we hold on to? What should we change? Those are the questions we often struggle with in church life at this time of year. With children returning to Sunday church school, youth programs gearing up, and new ideas floating everywhere, it's time for change in the life of a congregation. Change, however, is never easy.

I've often pointed to the Broadway play "Fiddler on the Roof" as a good example of the tension between tradition and change. Tevye, the main character, resists change. In scene after scene he raises his finger and shouts, "Tradition!" He sees himself as the preserver of things as they have always been.

But as the play unfolds it becomes clear that he cannot resist change. It is inevitable. In the end the message is that there is a golden mean between tradition and change.

That is what Jesus faced when he began his ministry. Jesus respected his religious roots. But he also saw the need for some things to be set aside in order that a new day might dawn.

Standing in his way was a group known as the Pharisees. They were so beholden to every detail of the law that there were rules for everything from morning until evening. When Jesus and his disciples, for example, were hungry and ate some grain from the field on the Sabbath, the Pharisees attacked him, citing certain passages of the law. Jesus countered with the well-known word: "The Sabbath was made for humankind, and not humankind for the Sabbath" (Mark 2:27). In other words, he was telling them that a deeper law, the law of love, should prevail.

So as new ideas and new programs come along we, too, need to ask if a greater good can be served by a new idea or a new program. We never stop wrestling with the questions: What must we hold on to? What needs change?"

~ hwc

❖ MARK 2:23-28 ❖

❖ Can You See God's Face? ❖

One of the first things I noticed when my vision deteriorated was that the facial features of others became blurred. From across the room familiar faces, even those of old friends, turned more and more into blank slates. This is frustrating for one who has been in the public arena all of my life. Those small nuances we pick up by just looking into the face of another person are gone. The happy or sad smile, the furled brow, the excitement, the roll of the eyes, the wink, the grin, the rosy cheeks, or the pallid complexion—all are gone.

Though I cannot see the faces of others, I can, of course, still hear their words. Now I listen more intently, sensing what I cannot see with my eyes. This puts me to thinking about some familiar words I've heard as long as I have lived. You have heard them too: "The Lord bless you and keep you. The Lord *make his face shine on you . . .*"

Like you, I cannot see the face of God. But I can hear God's words. I can listen for nuances—words of disapproval, words of guidance, words of hope, and, above all, words of grace that assure me over and over again that though I may disappoint God, in the end I can be certain that there is forgiveness for my sin and reassurance for my faith. In those words I *see* the face of God.

I am reminded of the words from the song we sang so often in my days of youth:

> Open my eyes, O Lord, Open my eyes;
> Into my darkened heart let your light arise.
> Show me myself, O Lord, show me yourself, O Lord,
> Show me your truth, O Lord; open my eyes.

In the daily renewal of our Baptism we can say, "One thing I do know. I was blind but now I see!"

~ hwc

❖ JOHN 9:24-38 ❖

❖ Built on a Sure Foundation ❖

Looking to buy their first house, a couple became interested in a cute little bungalow. It had everything they wanted—right size, right location, add-ons, right price, and updates. They were almost ready to sign a contract. But, before they did, they had a good inspector who invited them to walk with him through the house. How shocking it was to discover that the seller had dressed up only the surface. The house was everything but solid. Underneath new siding and a patched exterior were rotting walls and a crumbling foundation.

Jesus longs for us to receive life and salvation and be founded on him, our sure foundation. A foundation that bears good fruit—day-by-day doing God's will, doing justice and peace. Jesus warns about temptations along the way. Temptations to simply put a good-looking façade on our actions. Temptations that entice us to take the easy self-serving way. This, Jesus says, is laying a shaky foundation. "Strive first for the kingdom of God and his righteousness, and all these things will be given to you as well" (Matt. 6:33).

Isaiah also warns us that the easy way leads to death where waters will overwhelm your shelter. But "I am laying in Zion a foundation, a stone, a tested stone, a precious cornerstone, a sure foundation. . . . I will make justice the line, and righteousness the plummet" (Isa. 28:16-17).

We're invited today to Jesus for help in reassessing our lives. To "a living stone, though rejected by mortals yet chosen and precious in God's sight, and like living stones, let yourselves be built into a spiritual house, to be a holy priesthood, to offer spiritual sacrifices acceptable to God through Jesus Christ" (1 Peter 2:4-5). Sacrifice that is serving others as God leads.

> Christ is made the sure foundation,
> Christ, our head and cornerstone,
> Chosen of the Lord and precious,
> building all the church in one;
> Holy Zion's help forever
> and our confidence alone (*ELW* #645).

~ ecc

❖ MATTHEW 7:13-29 ❖

❖ Greetings and Grace ❖

A note came in the mail blessing us in a particular way. Our daughter had carefully chosen this lovely card, and with neat penmanship, every letter spelled grace and love. Kept in a prominent place, the card reminded us of the sender. Kindness in her words, just like the person who sent it. God's word in his letter to us also conveys the goodness of the one who sent it.

Listen to all that God's goodness gives us today. Martin Luther says, "In the Gospel, God has revealed to us His kindness not only that He will help men [women too] and suffer them to be near Him, but yet more holds to them and offers them unceasingly his grace and friendship" (*Day by Day*, p. 62). So our greeting from God today brings his kind presence.

At the very end of our reading today we find "greetings," which is rare before the time of the apostle Paul who regularly sent greetings in letters to Christians of congregations he had established. The word *greetings* at that time meant that one actually wishes to receive you with joy. But since you can't come to me and I can't come to you, I'll send my greetings across the miles. It carries an affectionate embrace, a kiss, my fondness, and my wishing you well. With it come God's grace, love, mercy, and peace.

Because God's nature is too high for us to even comprehend, God submitted himself, sending Jesus to become human like us and show us God's loving kindness. What a gift, that Jesus Christ gave himself for us to redeem us from all iniquity and to purify for himself a people of his own who are zealous for good works (Titus 2:14). Again today, Christ waits to receive us, his redeemed people. As this truth fills your heart and mine with praise and thanksgiving for this good news, we pray for one another, "[God's] grace be with all of you" (3:15).

~ ecc

❖ TITUS 2:11-15; 3:1-15 ❖

❖ WHO'S THE GREATEST PREACHER? ❖

Ask most folks in the United States to name the greatest preacher of all time and Billy Graham would probably garner the most votes. A decade ago Robert Schuller would have picked up a tidy number of nominations. And that Texan, Joel Osteen, would certainly get his share of attention.

The problem with these kinds of contests is that history suggests that we really don't know at a given moment which preachers will have the most enduring impact on the world.

That's why we can confidently cast our ballot today for John Chrysostom. "John who?" you ask. Well, little wonder you may not know him. Born in 349, he lived most of his life in the eastern Mediterranean cities of Antioch and Constantinople. Unlike the preachers mentioned above, Chrysostom made no attempt to cozy up to political leaders. He would never have been an overnight guest at the "White House" of an emperor or governor. He criticized them when he believed they were wrong. He advocated for the equality of women at a time when many saw them a little more than handy tools for a man's use. He opposed slavery when a high percentage of males were slaves. He encouraged the participation of lay persons in the life of the church, much to the dismay of some religious leaders. Chrysostom was, in other words, a nuisance. So much so, in fact, that he spent considerable time in exile, banished from public life.

Yet, in spite of this opposition, those who heard him preach all agreed that he was the greatest. He remains so in church history today and that is why we commemorate him every September thirteenth.

If someone tried to nominate the apostle Paul as greatest preacher, he would be quick to say, "Neither the one who plants nor the one who waters is anything, but only God who gives the growth" (1 Cor. 3:7).

~ hwc

❖ 1 CORINTHIANS 3:5-9 ❖

❖ It's a Big, Big Family ❖

I was hardly prepared for my first visit to Nazareth. Yes, I knew this was the boyhood home of Jesus. But when I saw a gaggle of young boys dashing among the shops on a crowded street I stopped in my tracks and thought, "Could it be that Jesus ran down these same streets with his friends? Was he really *that* human?"

Yes, Jesus was *that* human. Though we have but a single glimpse into his boyhood, we have every reason to believe that he was a normal child in a good family.

As Jesus came to understand himself and his mission in life, his relationship to his family began to change. He saw himself increasingly as part of a much larger family. When told that his mother and brothers were asking for him, Jesus speaks about a larger family: "Whoever does the will of my Father in heaven," he declares, "is my brother and sister and mother" (Matt. 12:50).

I don't begin to understand the mystery of the incarnation, the incredible idea that the Son of God became one with us, ran down the streets of Nazareth, enjoyed life with his family, taught us about God, and then gave his life for us on the cross. It defies reason. It is an insult to my intellect. It is, as some like to put it, a "scandalous" message. I can only say to this One who became completely identified with us as a fully human person, "Lord, I believe. Help my unbelief."

In the end it is a leap of faith for all of us. I always get a catch in my throat when I read these words in the letter to the Hebrews: "Jesus is not ashamed to call them brothers and sisters" (2:11).

Next time you see some boys running down the street stop and think to yourself, "Yes, he became *that* human."

~ hwc

❖ MATTHEW 12:46-50 ❖

❖ Starting with the Tithe ❖

I wonder how many forests have been leveled over the past fifty years for just one purpose—printing stewardship materials for our Lutheran churches.

Helping folks to hear the good news about Jesus was the first priority for me in all of my ministries. But a close second was aiding them to see the importance of generous giving. Over the years I've led seminars that focused on stewardship. I've preached sermons and written letters—all aimed at increasing our giving for the mission of the church.

It's discouraging then to discover that in spite of all of those efforts by me and thousands of other pastors and lay leaders, the percentage of giving among Lutherans remains at somewhere around two to three percent.

I wonder why. If giving is our response to God's love, our answer to God's call, is it possible that we Lutherans are an ungrateful people? Is it fair to say that we are stingy?

I first learned the secret to giving when I was a teenager. I heard that some believers, out of their love for God, gave a tithe—a tenth—of their income to their church and other worthy causes. I decided to try it. In the more than sixty years since then I've never looked back. I've learned, through both good and lean years, that I always have enough left for my own needs and those of my family.

When I was a young pastor I became acquainted with Walter Sundberg, a beekeeper. Walter and I visited congregations in our area. He never apologized for urging others to be generous. To one stubborn church council one night he said, "I want to experience the joy of giving while I'm living."

If you haven't tried to practice tithing, there's no better time to start than right now—today.

~ hwc

❖ LUKE 6:38 ❖

❖ Saying Thank You ❖

Can you imagine the isolation lepers must have felt? Windward, they must remain fifty yards away, and before approaching another, they must cry out in warning, "unclean, unclean." Isolation, but also desperation. For they were required at regular intervals to see the priests who judged the stage of their disease and, when possible, declared one cleansed. They stuck together, whatever race or class, with their common misfortune, like others of any time. In desperation, together, they came begging Jesus to have mercy on them. Right then, as he was sending them to the priests they were healed. Now declared CLEAN! But only one out of the ten returned to say thank you.

What is worse than being ungrateful? A child for instance, who grows up to feel his aged parent is a bother. After many early years of dependency, human infants require parental care longer than any other species. Think of baby birds flying quickly and calves on their feet immediately. Shakespeare's King Lear exclaimed, "How sharper than a serpent's tooth it is to have a thankless child."

What happens when gratitude becomes a habit? What will happen if today you deliberately put gratitude into words? To a parent. Spouse. Child. Coworker. Doctor who has studied long and hard and had years of experience so he or she was able to do a delicate operation that saved your sight. What if today you make a phone call or write a note saying thank you? Well, certainly it will gladden someone's heart. But more especially, it will do something wonderful to your own heart. And what if today you begin saying thanks to God before each meal? And what if you begin now to go regularly to worship where you join and help others say words of thanks to God? It will draw you to God's heart and gladden your days.

> Bless the Lord, O my soul, and do not forget all his benefits (Ps. 103:2).

~ ecc

❖ LUKE 17:11-19 ❖

❖ Remember When? ❖

Why study those ancient, "dead" languages like Latin, Greek, and Hebrew?

In the case of Hebrew, the language of the people of the Old Testament, it turned into one of my most fascinating classes in seminary. One of the best things I learned was that the Hebrew people had a very different way of looking at memory than we do. When we speak of remembering something we think of something that happened in the past, often in the very distant past. We seldom see the connection between that old memory and what is happening in our world today.

For the Hebrew people it was very different. They believed that when you recalled something, especially if it had high significance in your life, that recalled event was present in your current world. The deliverance from the bondage in Egypt is just one example. Over and over again the people of God were told to "remember" that experience. And each time they did so they relived it.

Jesus, of course, was deeply rooted in the tradition of the Hebrew people, their sacred writings, and their understanding of God. Thus, when he gathered his disciples for the last time and shared bread and wine with them, he said at the end of the meal, "Do this . . . in *remembrance* of me" (1 Cor. 11:25).

We ask the question Luther repeated so often, "What does this mean?" For us it means that each time we receive the bread and wine, the true body and blood of Christ, we do more than recall that he died for us some 2,000 years ago. It is much more than that. The death of Christ and the benefit we receive is brought forward in history. It is no longer the past. It is the present: "This *is* my body. This *is* my blood." That old gift is a new gift each time we receive it.

~ hwc

❖ 1 CORINTHIANS 11:23-26 ❖

❖ HAMMARSKJOLD—MAN OF PEACE ❖

My maternal grandfather several generations ago was a watchman in the city of Ystad on the south coast of Sweden. He took his shift in the highest place, the tower of the city church. From that vantage point he had a magnificent view of the Baltic Sea. On a clear day he could catch a glimpse of a German island. His major task, however, was to watch for any sign of fire in a city where nearly every structure was built of wood. The instructions were clear: If he were caught sleeping he would be subject to the death penalty.

When we visited Sweden's south coast in 2007 I thought of another Swedish watchman—Dag Hammarskjold. Not far from Ystad is the place where Hammarskjold found peace and renewal during his life as a diplomat and secretary general of the United Nations. He lived through one crisis after another—the Korean War, conflicts in the Middle East, the Suez Canal crisis, and the civil war in the Congo. It was there he perished in a plane crash on this day in 1961.

We walked to the rise where he sat and contemplated the landscape, including a majestic view of the Baltic. There is a circle of stones where one can sit quietly and seek to recapture the spirit of Hammarskjold. Here in this spot he contemplated how to bring peace to a war-torn world.

It was only after his death and the posthumous publication of his book *Markings* that the world learned that he was a man of deep Christian spirituality. Here was one fully engaged in the secular world, yet in his private life one who wrestled profoundly with the issue of how to live out his Christian convictions in service to humankind. His most familiar lines are a philosophy every believer can adopt:

> For all that has been—Thanks!
>
> To all that shall be—Yes!

~ hwc

❖ ISAIAH 52:7-10 ❖

❖ When Hate Prevails ❖

I've never experienced more intense hatred than on my visits to the Holy Land. These memories linger:

A Palestinian woman who bared her chest to show us where an Israeli soldier had pierced her with a bayonet when she protested the death of her son at the hands of the soldier's comrades.

An Israeli father who feared for the life of his daughter as she drove off for military duty on the Egyptian border each morning.

A Palestinian father who said he felt his newborn son had arrived with a stone in his hand.

An Israeli businessman who wondered every morning as he boarded the bus if he would return home to his family that evening.

A small Palestinian boy clutching a spent bullet that had shattered the windows in his family's home when it was suspected that terrorists were being sheltered there.

An Israeli woman who told us she would gladly give her home back to the Palestinian owners if the United States would force the Austrians to return to her family the home the Nazis took from them in World War II.

Everywhere in the land we call "holy" one can feel this animosity. How can it be that these two peoples, both of whom trace their origin to Abraham, can find no way to be reconciled? After years of trying to see the conflict from all angles and even being engaged myself at times with leaders on both sides, I am at a loss to know how the divide can be bridged. It is tempting to fall into despair.

Despair, however, is not an option. Whether it be in the Middle East or some far corner of the world or in our own country or in our own neighborhood or in our own family, we are bound by our Christian hope to keep trying for reconciliation. The formula never changes: "Love . . . your neighbor as yourself" (Luke 10:27).

~ hwc

❖ LUKE 10:25-37 ❖

❖ Who's Welcome Here? ❖

I served a congregation long ago in a changing neighborhood. When the senior pastor suggested it was time to welcome its new Spanish-speaking neighbors, a church council member spoke up and said: "The doors are open. Let them come." They didn't come. In time the congregation shriveled and died.

Now years later I'm proud and grateful to belong to a congregation that prints this announcement in its service bulletin every Sunday:

> Held in Christ, our Center, and living in grateful response to God's love and grace, we welcome everyone, without exception. We make known our gratitude and appreciation of all, including people of every race, sex, age, color, creed, religion, national origin, sexual orientation, gender identity, marital and familial status, physical and mental ability, health status, socioeconomic situation, education level, and political affiliation.

If our model for the church today is the New Testament church, then it's clear that we must be proactive. Yes, and we must go beyond an announcement in the Sunday bulletin. As Jesus urged, we need to go to "the streets and lanes" to invite all to come to the feast (Luke 14:21).

When the Holy Spirit was poured out on the day of Pentecost it is said that there were pilgrims from the whole known world who were in Jerusalem. If Peter's sermon on that day is a pattern for all preaching that follows, then the vision is clear. This good news is for everyone: all genders—men and women; all ages—young and old; all classes—slave and free; all realms—heaven and earth.

As your congregation moves into the busy fall season when so many programs are launched, is it clear that all are welcome?

This should not be seen as a burden for the church, as something we have to do. Rather, we should see that it is a gift that God gives to us. No, not duty but privilege.

~ hwc

❖ GALATIANS 3:26-28 ❖

❖ How to Measure Success ❖

We tend to measure success by productivity. In business it's the profit margin. In politics it's the number of votes. In baseball it's the batting average. In the church it's . . . Well, that's a good question. How *do* we measure success in the church?

Unfortunately, it's not much different from the world of business, politics, and sports. We measure by the number of members, the size of the budget, and the impressiveness of the building. I admit, as will most pastors, that we get caught up in that same game of numbers.

That's why the disciples of Jesus had such a hard time understanding him. As we trace his ministry through the early chapters of the Gospel of Luke, the direction is upward. He performs miracles that attract large crowds; his teaching is awesome for the growing number of listeners; he is heralded as a dominant figure in Palestinian society.

Suddenly it all changes. In Luke 9:51 Luke writes that Jesus "resolutely set out for Jerusalem" (*NIV*). Jesus knows instinctively that his message will bring increasing opposition. He also knows that it will lead to his death.

We sometimes call this the difference between the "theology of glory" and the "theology of the cross." The theology of glory tallies up numbers. The theology of the cross rivets its message on judgment and hope. Listeners don't like to hear words of judgment, words that call us to accountability, messages that make us feel guilty.

I never resolved this dilemma during my parish ministry. Like others, I wanted greater income for the congregation and got it. I encouraged growth in membership and saw it. I wanted my ministry and the congregation to be highly respected in the community and they usually were.

But as I measure my ministry against the call of Jesus to faithful discipleship I have to pray, "Lord, have mercy. You are the judge."

~ hwc

❖ LUKE 9:51-62 ❖

❖ BLESSED WEARINESS ❖

Three friends in my kitchen, all in their seventy-seventh years shared mutual experiences of feeling more tired after doing less, different than the previous year. Two years older, I assured them, this will increase. I'm glad Jesus, being human, understands with feelings like our own. In passages like John 4:6 we find "Jesus tired out by his journey, was sitting by the well." He needed rest.

George Herbert (1593–1632) was poet and minister in the Church of England. Grounded in Scripture and in theology from both Martin Luther and John Calvin, his work was influential. Hear his poetry, well crafted like Shakespeare, "O Lord! Thy blessings hang in clusters, they come trooping upon us! They break forth like many waters on every side." I like Herbert's poem "The Pulley":

> When God at first made man, having a glass of blessings standing by;
> "Let us," said he, "pour on him all we can. Let the world's riches,
> which dispersed lie, contract into a span."
> So strength first made a way;
> Then beauty flow'd, then wisdom, honor, pleasure.
> When almost all was out, God made a stay,
> Perceiving that alone of all his treasure, rest in the bottom lay.
> "For if I should," said he, "bestow this jewel also on my creature,
> He would adore my gifts instead of me,
> and rest in Nature, not the God of Nature:
> So both should losers be."
> "Yet let him keep the rest, but keep them with repining restlessness:
> Let him be rich and weary, that at least, if goodness lead him not,
> yet weariness may toss him to my breast."

In *Daily Readings from Spiritual Classics*, the Preuses write, "We often think of this (weariness) as an inconvenience, a kind of curse with which we are doomed to live." (Herbert lived with disabilities and through experience knew otherwise.) "The gift of rest is withheld so that in our weariness we would turn to God."

~ ecc

❖ MATTHEW 11:28-30 ❖

❖ The Lost Is Found ❖

Those who have a pet know the trauma that overwhelms us when that good friend gets lost.

Our special little friend is Jonah, a 15-year-old cairn terrier (think Toto in the Wizard of Oz). When he slipped through an open gate on our patio one day our world changed in a moment. We dropped everything we were doing and set out on an intense search. Corinne went in one direction and I in another. I didn't even take time to change from my slippers to a pair of shoes. All that mattered was to find Jonah.

Soon neighbors joined in the search, fanning out in every direction. Even some telephone workers promised to watch for Jonah. As I walked I prayed, "Lord, help us to find Jonah. Please keep him from danger."

Needless to say, we were all relieved when he turned up under a neighbor's pine tree two blocks away, chomping on popcorn that had been scattered for the birds. Such focused intensity for our dear little friend!

How could I help but think of all those places in the Bible where we read about our Lord's impassioned, searching love for us—like the good shepherd who leaves the ninety-nine because just one is lost. No, it's not that there is lack of concern for those ninety-nine. It's just that each of us is regarded as so completely and singularly loved that God will stop at nothing to search and find.

It was, of course, our carelessness that brought on the crisis at our home. That will never be the case with God. If we are lost, it will be of our own doing. The hymn writer says it well:

> Prone to wander, Lord, I feel it; prone to leave the God I love.
> Here's my heart, oh, take and seal it; seal it for thy courts above
> (*LBW* 499).

~ hwc

❖ LUKE 15:1-7 ❖

❖ Ordinary Things; High Value ❖

Long after his father died a son discovered a cigar box tucked away in his parents' attic. In it he found an odd assortment of coins totaling about $12.00. "Not much," he thought. "These coins surely would never have carried my dad through very many rainy days." He was about to spend them when he decided to check their value with a coin collector. To his amazement he learned that their value came to more than $100,000!

We all undervalue the things in our lives that seem so common and ordinary. Then one day we stop and consider carefully their value.

> Baptism: In most cases we never even asked for it, yet we were given eternal life in that moment.
>
> Sunday church school: Week after week we stored up treasures of Bible stories.
>
> Confirmation: A time when we affirmed for ourselves the gift we received in baptism.
>
> Worship: The privilege of living in a land where no one stops us on our way to church and tells us to go home.
>
> The Lord's Supper: An oasis in the desert, a place to linger to be renewed in the faith.
>
> Bible study: Whether alone or in a group, a time to enrich our lives from the richest treasure chest in the world.

One of the dangers of living in a land where there is little or no persecution for being a Christian is that we get lethargic, seldom stopping to count the treasures we easily overlook in the attics of our lives.

The author of Hebrews is heart-broken over the way the believers have fallen away from the faith, taking for granted all the good things God has done for them. Stop today for a moment and ask yourself: "Do I realize the value of all God has given to me?"

~ hwc

❖ HEBREWS 10:19-25 ❖

❖ Those Quarreling Christians ❖

When I was first elected synod bishop in 1976 I soon became aware of about a dozen congregations that were having serious conflict. It was often between the pastor and the church council. But in some cases it was between factions in the congregation, or between the musicians and the pastor, or between the younger and older members.

In my fresh enthusiasm I thought I would plunge into those knotty situations, get them resolved quickly, and then get on with what I thought were more important issues in the synod. My naivety didn't last long. For each troubled situation that got resolved, another arose. For the next eleven years I found that there were always at least a dozen congregations in various stages of conflict. It seemed that eighty percent of my time was eaten up in twenty percent of the congregations of the synod.

That is the human condition, yes, even in the church. The 80/20 rule has been in force in all of church history. Henry Muhlenberg is often called the "Father of Lutheranism in North America." He rode on horseback up and down the American colonies, establishing congregations and caring for scattered flocks. I have a well-worn copy of his book *Notebook of a Colonial Clergyman* in which Muhlenberg writes about his struggles as a leader in those times. There is a gap in his journal between 1775 and 1779. The translator explains why: "Frequently," he writes, "Muhlenberg had to try to mend the relations between pastors and congregations following quarrels." We read those words and sigh, "So what else is new?" Bishops will tell you that a huge amount of their time is consumed today in the same kinds of conflict.

It was no different in New Testament times. Most every letter of Paul addresses conflict of one kind or another. Yet, in spite of these times of stress, the work of Christ moves forward.

~ hwc

❖ 1 CORINTHIANS 13:1-13 ❖

❖ Come to the Table ❖

During my years as presiding bishop of the ELCA I was at times an official guest at dinners in the Middle East. On every occasion I was astounded by their hospitality. I recall a dinner in my honor hosted by the Syrian Orthodox archbishop. Though we were only five in our entourage, the meal could have fed fifty. Nothing compares with the look and taste of a dinner in the Middle East. It's a mark of their culture to be hospitable. They bend over backwards to put on the finest banquet you can imagine. If I had my camera along I often asked permission to take a photograph of the table before we ate.

These experiences help me to understand one of the most seemingly unnecessary miracles that Jesus performed. I have in mind the first one he did, the miracle at the wedding at Cana.

Think about it. There seems to be no great need for what Jesus did. No one is ill or lame. None have leprosy. No one is possessed with demons. No one has died. They are reported to have been feasting for seven days. Can anyone be hungry? And do they really need an estimated 150 gallons of the best wine one can further indulge in? Little wonder some dismiss this miracle as a fairytale.

That would be a huge mistake. The bride and groom and their families were no doubt friends of Jesus' family. Jesus was a man of his time and place. This was a setting for open and honest human happiness. Christ wanted to be there. Providing an overabundance of the best wine for a needy host is exactly what any good man of the time would do. Here we meet Jesus Christ in his full humanity.

Haven't all of us longed for a generous friend like Jesus? I have good news—we have one! So come to the table.

~ hwc

❖ JOHN 2:1-12 ❖

❖ Let's Talk about Money ❖

"Does the church always have to talk about money?"
"Why does the pastor preach so much about money?"

Do you ever hear those questions around your church? Or do you ever ask them yourself? Yes, I'm guessing you do, especially at this time of year. Sometimes I think we've been too apologetic about the money issue. We try to soften our appeal for money by calling it "stewardship." We accent the importance of giving our time as well as our money. We suggest that members increase their pledge by one or two percent for the next year. It goes in one ear and out the other.

The problem with all of these approaches is that they may mask the real issue: We need money to operate our churches. It takes money to pay staff salaries and utility bills and purchase Sunday school supplies. We need money to support the things we do in other places, such as though regional and national church organizations. We need money to send missionaries to the far corners of the world.

But isn't there a better way to do it than to keep haranguing people to give more money? Well, I have news for you. No, there is no other way. In fact, it's always been that way. If we read the New Testament carefully we soon learn that Jesus talked about money more than anything else. The same is true with Paul. He pleads unapologetically with the churches to be generous. To the believers in Corinth, for example, he writes that they should never give grudgingly, but out of a generous heart.

But now comes the good part. Giving money can be the gateway to the most satisfying life one can imagine. The happiest people I've known in my ministry are those who say, "Pastor, keep talking about money. Keep urging us to be more generous. Giving is not a curse; it's a blessing."

~ hwc

❖ 2 CORINTHIANS 9:1-5 ❖

❖ In Praise of Birds ❖

There's always a bit of sadness here in the north country as we watch many of our birds fly south. In the mid-1960s we bought an old lake cabin in northern Minnesota. At first I spent most of my time playing with the kids in the water, fishing, and remodeling our vacation nest.

As the children grew older I began to notice the birds. With a field guide and a pair of binoculars I soon counted more than forty species simply by sitting on the deck of our cabin. I noted everything from thc tiny humming bird to the great horned owl. When the eagles returned to our area it added a whole new dimension to bird watching.

My favorite bird was the purple martin. As house after house went up I was soon fledging more than thirty babies a year, bidding them farewell as they lifted their wings and flew off with mama and papa to spend the winter along the Amazon River.

I think God has a special love for birds. I like the line in the creation story: "Let the birds fly above the earth across the dome of the sky" (Gen. 1:20). A raven and a dove helped Noah know the waters of the flood had receded. In the sacrifices in Old Testament times birds gave their lives for the sins of poor folks. The psalmist must have thought God was a bird-watcher. "I know all the birds of the air" he writes (50:11). Isaiah promises that in time of trouble, "Like birds hovering overhead, so the Lord of hosts will protect Jerusalem" (31:5).

And then there is Jesus. To those preoccupied with the troubles of life he suggests that they "Look at the birds of the air; they neither sow nor reap nor gather into barns, and yet your heavenly Father feeds them" (Matt. 6 26).

Pause today to look at the birds. Thank God for them. Learn lessons from them.

~ hwc

❖ MATTHEW 6:25-27 ❖

❖ Seen Any Angels Lately? ❖

"I've never met an angel. Therefore, there must be no such creatures." I may have agreed with that comment earlier in life. But I've changed my mind.

Certainly the sudden death of our son was one factor. I simply cannot accept the idea that such a bright, talented, and tender person just vanishes forever. I believe he lives. And if I believe that, I can also believe that there are other beings of which we have little understanding.

The other major factor has been my involvement with persons who have experienced sudden loss. In a setting where they can speak freely without fear that what they say will be shared outside that room, I have heard the remarkable stories of reasonable persons who testify to having encountered beings they can only describe as "otherworldly"—angels, deceased family and friends, yes, and even a vision of one they believe was Christ.

I'm told that Billy Graham's best-selling book is the one on angels. Polls also indicate that a high percentage of people, including those who do not embrace a formal Christian faith, believe in angels.

The Bible affirms the existence of angelic beings. If one were to remove all references to angels from the four Gospels it would completely alter those books. Among other things, an angel or angels:

Instruct Joseph to take Mary as his wife
Tell Joseph and Mary to escape Herod's vengeance
Appear to Zechariah assuring him of a son
Announce to Mary that she will be the mother of the promised one
Appear to the terrified shepherds in the field
Comfort Jesus after his temptations in the wilderness
Open the tomb and tell the women not to be afraid

Does all this prove there are angelic beings? No, but I do believe it. If you agree, celebrate "St. Michael and All Angels" today, as the church has done for centuries.

~ hwc

❖ PSALM 103:20-22 ❖

❖ Had Any Dreams Lately? ❖

Yesterday we asked about angels. Today we continue with another mysterious subject: dreams. As with angels, there was a time when I discounted dreams as having any importance in my life. But no more. I have had enough significant dreams and have heard from others of similar experiences to convince me that sometimes—sometimes—the Holy Spirit uses dreams as a way of helping us get through tough times or understand what is happening in our lives.

For that reason, honoring Jerome on his commemoration day is important. Born around the year 350, Jerome is recognized as one of the great intellectuals in Christian history. In a dream Jerome heard God telling him he needed to pay less attention to secular reading and greater attention to his devotional life. In response, he withdrew to the desert for four years for reflection.

Later Jerome dedicated himself to the translation of the Bible from Greek to Latin. It was so well done that it remains the standard Latin text of the Bible. We can only wonder what direction his life might have taken had he not had that dream.

Morton Kelsey, an Episcopal priest who taught at Notre Dame University, has written a thoughtful volume entitled *God, Dreams, and Revelation.* He not only traces the pattern of dreams in the Bible, but also documents their significance in church history from early times until now.

Contrary to the popular belief that dreams primarily predict the future, Kelsey underscores the importance of dreams in helping us understand what is happening in our lives at the moment. By reflecting on a vivid dream and writing it out we often come to see experiences in life from a perspective that aids us in seeing how God is at work and how we need to approach an otherwise impossible challenge.

As I wrote yesterday, I can't prove this. Jerome believed it. And so do I.

~ hwc

❖ ACTS 2:14-21 ❖

❖ WORK OF THE HOLY SPIRIT ❖

In teaching about the work of Holy Spirit, the late Dr. Warren Quanbeck, professor of systematic theology at Luther Seminary, used this example. A man who was excited about building a new house for his family one day welcomed an old friend who came for a visit. He told his friend about the house he was building and wanted him to see it. As they drove to the site, the man described his house in detail. But when they got out of the car, all the friend saw was a big gaping excavated hole, and he exclaimed, "I thought you said it was a house." The man said, "It's going to be, but first you have to excavate so you can build a firm foundation." "That," Quanbeck said, "is like the work of the Holy Spirit."

One day in Old Testament class, Professor Mark Hillmer asked if we'd ever noticed how before God called people to difficult service they went through difficult testings. Think of Abraham, called to offer his son. Moses. And Jesus in the Garden of Gethsemane is our example.

One day we were privileged to worship with folks in a new mission congregation. We met the lay leader working with high passion as this church was being launched. In visiting with him, I asked, "What was the emptying that happened to you making space for the Holy Spirit to fill you with such passion and ability?" He was dumbfounded at first by my question. It clicked. And he told about the trying period of emptiness in his life that preceded the beginning of this mission. And now such unflinching energy and joy in serving. Emptied before the filling.

> Fear not, I am with you, oh, be not dismayed,
> For I am your God and will still give you aid;
> I'll strengthen you, help you, and cause you to stand,
> Upheld by my righteous, omnipotent hand (*ELW* #796).

~ ecc

❖ 1 CORINTHIANS 6:19 ❖

OCTOBER 2

❖ Let Go and Let God ❖

"Let go and let God" is a good slogan, but it's hard to do—even while praying to God for help to change the things we can, accept the things we cannot change, and have the wisdom to know the difference.

We faced a difficult situation. Herb was able to let go, but I couldn't. Anxiety heightened, and then came an event that caused me near drowning in desperation. That night I had a watershed dream that transformed and helped me at last to let go.

I dreamed that together we'd been climbing a rugged mountain. But then I was left alone. The path, growing ever steeper, changed into an impossible summit. And on top, was a flimsy ladder that I must climb before taking the big step across a bottomless abyss to a safe place. Afraid of heights I knew I couldn't, but an unseen someone was there steadying the ladder, which made me certain I could do it. When a warm large hand reached across the abyss, I grasped it, taking the scary step. I had crossed the "letting go" abyss and was at last in a safe place with Herb. God's grace had helped us do the impossible. I awoke transformed and at peace.

Clear meaning in each symbol—God had helped me climb the mountain. God had steadied the ladder. When Herb, already having let go, reached out to me, God helped me take that impossible, scary step. Through the entire journey God had given grace for each and every step of the way.

You may be facing an impossible situation. The path may seem too steep and too long. You may not know to whom or where to go for help. You may wonder if you can hold out. But be sure, you are not walking alone. There is One who not only walks with you but also promises, "My grace is sufficient for you" (2 Cor. 12:8).

~ ecc

❖ 2 CORINTHIANS 12:7--10 ❖

❖ What Must I Do? ❖

Meet Samuel who grew up a shepherd boy on hillsides near Jerusalem. He was bright in synagogue school and lingered at night with the storytelling elders. On Holy Days in the temple he hung around the rabbis, eager to learn, asking questions. When he grew up, he saddened his parents announcing his plan to leave them for starting a bakery in town. It turned into a coffee shop where caravans of silk traders stopped. He grew wealthy, married well, and had beautiful children. He was a good husband and father, honest in trade, and good to parents. "Ideal," you'd say. But something was missing. Here's his story.

One day instead of going to work, I went looking for Jesus. "Good teacher," I asked, "What must I do to inherit eternal life?" I'm successful. Become rich beyond all expectations. Am a good husband and father. And yet I feel empty. When Jesus mentioned the Commandments, I immediately said I'd kept those. I just wanted Jesus to tell me something I could do to fill up the emptiness in my life. You see, like many of you, I was accustomed to setting goals, making lists, and achieving whatever I was after.

But I was shocked at Jesus' reply, "Sell what you own and give the money to the poor, and you will have treasure in heaven; then come, follow me." I couldn't give him my all. Feeling sad and let down, I was turning away when Jesus said some very important words, like he may be saying to you. "For mortals it is impossible, but not for God; for God all things are possible." These words burned in my soul. And the burning was not only the words but also how Jesus looked into my soul with such understanding and love.

Neither Samuel nor we can do anything to earn eternal life. In baptism Christ makes us his own forever, gives us his Holy Spirit, and daily invites us into joyful service.

~ ecc

❖ MARK 10:17-27 ❖

❖ The Path to Happiness ❖

We have had a small statue of St. Francis in our flower garden for years. This patron of birds and animals looks right at home in that setting. One gets a happy feeling just contemplating the thought that faith and nature are so closely linked.

When we visited the city of Assisi in Italy several years ago I encountered a very different statue of Francis. In the courtyard of the church Francis is depicted riding on the back of a donkey, slumped forward in the form of one who is weary and worn from the burdens of life.

Francis, whom we commemorate on this day, was both persons. When he formed what became the Franciscan Order, it was his aim that he and his colleague monks should be happy men of God. Though they had renounced many of the pleasures others took for granted, Francis believed that true happiness could only be found in focusing on God rather than material goods.

But happiness does not mean that one is delivered from the burdens of life. Thus, the slumped figure is also appropriate. Joy is not found apart from the heaviness of life, but rather in the midst of it.

Most of us, unlike Francis, do not find ourselves called to the life of celibacy and poverty. But there are valuable lessons to be learned from him. If we have a loving family, a comfortable home, a sufficient income, an adequate pension plan, reasonably good health, and many other blessings, we should learn to look at them as gifts that are given to us only for a time, even a short time, as we move through life. Francis and his followers could not have done all the good they accomplished had it not been for those others who supported them.

Look around. Is there a St. Francis you should be supporting with what God has given you?

~ hwc

❖ MATTHEW 10:5-10 ❖

The Whole Gospel for the Whole People

Growing up in the Augustana Lutheran Church, I took for granted that all churches cared for the sick, provided homes for needy children, ministered to the physically challenged, and never forgot the elderly. That's the way it was in that church with its Swedish roots.

What I learned later was that this spirit of care and concern for unfortunate ones was not universal. And I also realized that for its rather small size, the Augustana Lutheran Church did far more than one might expect. Hospitals, nursing homes, Bethphage Mission, adoption services, social service agencies—the list went on and on.

What I also came to understand was that the motivation for much of this ministry came not from a Swede but from a German—Theodor Fliedner. We honor him this month. He, in turn, got much of his inspiration from the Moravians and their deaconess program. Soon Lutherans took up the challenge. Among the Swedish Lutherans the deaconesses became a powerful force for good. Like others my age, I learned about these women when I was in Sunday church school. Clad mostly in long, grey dresses with a white collar, we looked at their pictures, heard stories about their work, and felt proud that our church supported persons like these.

Though times have changed, the mission of the church remains the same. We cannot claim to know the whole gospel of good news unless we see that it is intended for the whole people—for everyone.

It all goes back to the commission of Jesus to his first disciples. They were not sent merely to tell the news about Jesus—though that was primary. They were also commanded to address all the needs of those they met.

Pastors and bishops should never have to beg us to give generously so that the church can do this kind of work. It should be as natural as breathing.

~ hwc

JAMES 1:22-27

❖ From Cover to Cover ❖

When my pastor handed a Bible to me on confirmation day, I thought little of it. I expected to place it on a shelf at home and forget it. That same day, however, I went off to Bible camp. During that week my life turned about. My relationship with Jesus Christ became very personal. As the Bible was opened to me it answered a deep longing in my soul.

When I returned from camp I began reading my Bible every night. Often it was a chapter, but never less than a few paragraphs. As I read, the Spirit of God touched my heart. Though I might read for days with no special sense of inspiration, suddenly a verse would leap from the page. Some deep need in my heart was satisfied by a word from that Bible. By the time I finished high school I had read it from cover to cover.

It is for that reason that we give thanks for William Tyndale. He died a martyr's death on this day in 1536. Like Martin Luther, he shared the conviction that the Bible should be translated into the language of the people. Many clergy opposed him, fearing what might happen if common folk read the Bible. Tyndale told his friends that if God spared his life and if his translation of the Bible survived, then even the most common farm boy would know as much about the Bible as the priest.

I was one of those boys, the son of the most ordinary parents one can imagine. But because of Tyndale and others like him, I have been on a lifelong venture of Bible reading.

How about you? Do you recall the words of one of our great hymns—"God's Word Is Our Great Heritage"?

> Through life it guides our way;
> In death it is our stay.
> Lord, grant while time shall last
> Your church may hold it fast . . . (*ELW* #509).

~ hwc

❖ PSALM 119: 9-16 ❖

❖ REMEMBER YOUR LEADERS ❖

When I was a synod bishop I often heard pastors complain about their heavy load of responsibility. And I did my own share of grousing, too.

At times like that I often reminded pastors and myself about the ministry of Henry Melchior Muhlenberg, often called "The Father of American Lutheranism." In 1742 he came as a missionary to Lutherans in the colonies. Not only were they scattered, but there was considerable dissension among them. The German and Swedish churches immediately welcomed him and recognized in him the qualities of a fine leader. Muhlenberg traveled widely by horseback, speaking in German, Dutch, and English. Not only did he organize the congregations into a church body, he also established a worship pattern that continued for generations. For believers who had been part of state churches in Europe, his leadership was exactly what was needed.

I have often recommended that pastors read the journal Muhlenberg kept for most of his ministry. He wrote about the toll it took on his spiritual and physical life to be on the move so much. He expressed a deep longing to spend more time with his wife and children, as well as greater freedom to pray and meditate.

When I was first elected bishop I felt a tad embarrassed when I visited a congregation and special prayers were said on my behalf. That sentiment, however, lasted only a short time. Soon I realized how much I needed the prayers of the congregations to face the challenges that came my way daily.

I like the pattern that prevails in our sister Episcopal congregations. Every Sunday without fail they include in the intercessions of the church their area bishop and their presiding bishop.

On this day when we commemorate Henry Melchior Muhlenberg, I suggest that we not only pray for our pastors and bishops, but that we urge it be done every Sunday at our worship services.

~ hwc

❖ HEBREWS 13:7-8 ❖

❖ When You Pray ❖

A friend, with her husband far away, called urgently needing to meet at a restaurant to talk. Their daughter, planning her wedding, had just arrived and introduced the groom, a man who obviously was a con artist. She'd wept, afraid of what he would do if she did not go through with the plan, so she insisted she must go with her mother shopping for a wedding dress. At the restaurant, she poured out her heart asking for prayer. But what good would it do?

We're invited to pray because God has established a relationship with us. Praying creates "space in the world for God" (Terrance Fretheim, *Primer on Prayer*). It opens a relationship with God, wider possibilities for God, and our involvement doing God's work in the world.

Relationships are determined by closeness or distance. Absence, avoidance, or no contact breeds distance. Warm and frequent contact brings closeness, opening our ability to listen and respond. Prayer brings delight to God like parents swelling with joy when hearing their child first say, "Daddy, Mommy."

Prayer opens possibilities for God to act. When we're silent, God hurts and is shut out—not able to be God as he wants, making more space for ever present evil. God is "less able," Fretheim says, "to bring his power to a given situation." Prayer makes a difference to God who "is now more welcome, given more room to be present and at work."

When God said, "Have dominion" (Gen. 1:28), although never letting go, God takes a risk letting us share his power, tuning us into doing his will and work.

Intercessory prayer makes a difference to God, who certainly knows the need. But in prayer, it's articulated by one with whom God has a significant relationship. In praying, your insight and energy is now placed in the service of God who has more possibilities for the situation.

Any idea how precious you are to God? Or what can happen when you pray?

~ ecc

❖ MATTHEW 18:19-20 ❖

❖ EMBRACED BY GOD ❖

Jesus is creative. Perhaps an object lesson for his disciples will work. So he takes a little child into their circle. The word *exomai* explains that what Jesus does is more a picture than a word. Can you see Jesus? He's gathering the little child in his arms, enfolding the little one with lavish love. The child feels protected and safe. No harm can come—no mean people, bad thoughts, fires, storms, losses. Nothing will separate the child from God's protective love. These eternal enfolding arms will never let this child go. These arms—God's promises—tell the child it is true.

Jesus uses the word *child* to convey the image of one who is weak. Big and rich people are never weak, unless securities are wiped out or until tragedy comes. But there is a little child in each of us. I learned this truth when our son died suddenly. Utter helplessness. Even though surrounded by family, each suffering the same loss, I felt so alone looking that night into the sunset so red. The vastness of space. All signposts gone. Alone in the universe with my youngest child taken away. God heard my spirit crying, "God, where are you in this vast universe you've made?"

God answered my prayer through "the Body of Christ." They came one-by-one with hot dishes and tears and hugs. So necessary and special, holding me together when my world had fallen apart. I felt disjointed, wracked with pain, and wrenched with weeping, but enfolded in the arms of those God sent, bringing a love that yearns jealously to make us whole.

Maybe it takes a tragedy to experience God's love that so gathers us up. It reveals what it means to be forgiven, accepted, and received into the heart of God. It stays fresh as you let God embrace you with his Word and Sacrament. And if it's fresh and new, you have it to give away.

~ ecc

❖ MARK 9:35-37 ❖

OCTOBER 10

❖ Joy in Giving ❖

I knew a young man from a poor family who was putting himself through college. Working hard and frugal, he often wasn't sure how he would pay for his next semester. Faithfully, he gave to God ten percent off the top of every check. I admired how thankful he always was and how he kept trusting God. That is, until we were married and I was drawn into this "faith walk."

Wouldn't it be better to tithe at the end of the month when seeing was believing it would work? How would we make it through his seminary years? And then serving a new mission with a meager $4,000 annual salary and a car allowance used up on long gravel roads. Not much faith, you say. And you're right. But he taught me to tithe off the top. God did supply our needs, and more. For this was how I learned the joy of tithing. The answer is to start somewhere. Make a commitment and resolve to make it grow. Giving and trusting God grow side-by-side.

Then we're drawn into prayer for where our money goes. It gets exciting to see new mission congregations begin and to pray with those pastors walking door-to-door. And seeing the Holy Spirit drawing people in. It gets exciting to follow our missionaries around the world. It gets exciting to see our colleges and seminaries thrive in training young people for all the walks of life. It gets exciting helping advocate for the oppressed together in ways we could never do alone. It gets exciting in our congregation gathering to praise God and be revived with each other at the table, being the body of Christ for one another.

> We offer with joy and thanksgiving what you have first given us—our selves, our time, and our possessions, signs of your gracious love. Receive them for the sake of him who offered himself for us, Jesus Christ our Lord (*LBW,* p. 108).

~ ecc

❖ LUKE 6:37-38 ❖

❖ Those Down Days ❖

I'm in a funk today. I know the reasons for it, but that doesn't make it easier. I tell myself that it's not a good day to try to write a devotional article. The problem is that a deadline is looming and I can't afford to miss a day of writing.

This reminds me of those occasional times when I was in active ministry and didn't feel like preaching on a Sunday morning. Oh, if every Sunday could have been one when I was well prepared, when no one had bugged me during the week, and when I felt it a high privilege to share the word of God. I could run to the pulpit on Sundays like that.

But I remember those times when the steps to the pulpit seemed too steep, when I didn't feel like lifting my eyes from my sermon notes, when I would rather go fishing than preach.

Fortunately, the Bible is a very realistic book. It doesn't sugarcoat the believer's experience. Nor does it evade facing squarely our human frailties.

This is why the lament psalms were included in Scripture. Those honest words tell us that it's all right to be completely open before God about our feelings. "My soul is full of troubles, and my life draws near to Sheol" writes the psalmist. "I am counted among those who go down to the Pit; I am like those who have no help" (Ps. 88:3-4).

Fortunately, a long life helps one put things into perspective. Unlike a teenager who so easily develops "tunnel vision" and cannot see beyond the immediate crisis, decades of walking with Christ helps one to say, "This, too, will pass. Though I may have my ups and downs, God remains the same. I have a sure anchor in troubled waters. Hope and joy will return again if I simply trust in God rather than in my unpredictable feelings."

~ hwc

❖ PSALM 90:12-17 ❖

❖ Our Lutheran Altar Call ❖

A friend grew up in a church where it was customary to have altar calls. He remembers how the minister harangued the congregation to "repent and get right with God" and to show it by coming forward to the altar. My friend was relieved to be freed from that pressure when he became a Lutheran and heard a message of grace.

I agree with my friend. Responding in that way can become another "good work." It tends to put the accent on what we do rather than on what God has done.

Having said that, I also reminded my friend that we do, in fact, have an altar call in the Lutheran church. We call it the Lord's Supper. When we rise and go to the altar it is a public witness that we are saved by grace alone through faith. Having confessed our sin at the opening of the worship service, our move to the altar is a sign that we believe that God has given us everything we need in the death and resurrection of Jesus Christ. As we sing in an old hymn, "Nothing in my hand I bring; simply to thy cross I cling" (*ELW* #623).

This is why I'm thankful I belong to a congregation where the Lord's Supper is offered every week. I never tire of it. I need it at least that often. It refreshes my soul. It prepares me for another week when I know, no matter what happens, I will need more grace for the journey.

We sing it in this hymn stanza:

> My Savior, you here have led me within your holiest place,
> And here yourself have fed me with treasures of your grace;
> For you have freely given what earth could never buy,
> The bread of life from heaven, that now I shall not die
> (*LBW* #542).

Thank God for the Lord's Supper—our Lutheran "altar call"!

~ hwc

❖ MATTHEW 26:26-30 ❖

❖ Who Am I? ❖

During my ministry as a pastor, professor, and bishop, people have tried to figure out who I really am. "What makes that man tick? What motivates him to say what he says and do what he does?"

I decided one day to try to come up with a self-definition, a short statement that would summarize for others how I saw myself. Here's what came out of that effort. I described myself as "An evangelical conservative with a radical social conscience."

I'm evangelical: I believe that I am made right with God by grace and through faith in Jesus Christ. It is by grace alone that I am saved.

I'm conservative: Every Sunday I stand with a Christian congregation to confess my faith, usually with the words of the Apostles' Creed. I believe God has made me and all things; that Christ died for the sins of the whole world; that the Holy Spirit is the creator of the church. That makes me very conservative.

I have a radical social conscience: I believe that if I really believe what I confess, it will make me out of sync at times with popular opinion and broad assumptions of what is right and wrong in the eyes of others. It means that whenever I see someone treated in an unjust or unfair way, I am obliged to speak up and do something about it. One time it may mean writing to an elected official who can change things. Another time it may mean writing a letter to an editor. Still another time it may mean going the second mile to help someone. And again, it could mean marching in a parade to support an unpopular cause. What I do may seem radical to the majority.

What I must do is ask the question: Does my evangelical and conservative understanding of the gospel impel me to act in this way?

~ hwc

❖ 1 THESSALONIANS 2:1-4 ❖

❖ Seasoned with Salt ❖

There's a favorite cooking utensil in every kitchen. Growing up, we had a well-seasoned black pan that browned chicken just right without burning and turned pancakes to perfection. Well-seasoned, it was fit for use.

Wood is seasoned hard to make strong building material. Soldiers are trained and seasoned for endurance. Successful professionals have struggled through hard learning and internship experiences to become fit. Pans and wood and soldiers and professionals are seasoned. All being seasoned need this prayer for God's protection: "that, surrounded by all the changes and uncertainties of life, we may be defended by your gracious and ready help" (*LBW*, p. 50).

Wearied and seasoned through changes and chances of life. And what part does God play in the seasoning? In 300 B.C. the ancient Greek, Epicurus, wrote, "God either wishes to take away evils and is unable, or, he is able but unwilling, or, he is neither willing nor able, or, he is both willing and able. If he is willing but unable, he is not God. If he is able but unwilling, he is not love. If he is both willing and able (which alone is unsuitable to God) then, what is the source of evil? And why does he not remove evil?"

What of earthquakes and floods and droughts? Has God risked sharing power with us and with systems of the natural world, such as moving crusts of earth, bacteria, and cancer cells that bring shocking changes and chances to disrupt our lives? Then what? Do we grow bitter? Or do we allow such refining with salt to cleanse us of self-centeredness and lead us to trust God?

So let us ask God with confidence to deliver us from all the little fears that accumulate to rob us from trusting him and leading us to victory and joy.

~ ecc

❖ MARK 9:49-50 ❖

❖ One Who Is Great ❖

Robert T. Smith's Minneapolis *StarTribune* articles grabbed you. One I saved from February 2, 1975, yellowed now, tells of a scene at a Red Owl supermarket.

Without father, and mother at work, a small seven-year-old boy was shopping for his mother and little sister. With groceries in his cart blocking the line, he asked for help finding an item. Folks behind him grew impatient as the girl left her register to go find it. Some left the line. Others joined the long line. Many grumbled and the child grew very embarrassed. An elderly woman in a blue stocking cap waited patiently with few meager items in her cart. There were bare leather streaks on the fur collar of her coat and a hole in the finger of her mittens.

With groceries totaled, the boy reached in his jacket pocket for money. But it was empty. A man beside him said sharp words while the child fumbled into his pants pocket. Relieved, he came up with food stamps. Short $1.73 and scared, he said his mother was at work and that's all he had.

The elderly woman with the blue stocking cap stepped up to the clerk saying she would take care of it. Smiling, the boy hurried out of the store. When it was her turn at checkout, she paid also for the boy. With her food stamps.

Jesus, just down from the Mount of Transfiguration, found a father begging him to heal his son. With his disciples there, he cast out the demon. Then he told them of his coming death. And right there, in that context, they began arguing. About which of them was the greatest!

For an object lesson, Jesus took a child beside him saying, "Whoever welcomes this child in my name welcomes me, . . . for the least among all of you is the greatest" (Luke 9:48). Lord, help us to be so.

~ ecc

❖ LUKE 9:46-48 ❖

❖ THOSE JEWISH NEIGHBORS ❖

Until I was in my early 30s I never knew a Jewish person. Then suddenly and unexpectedly I found myself living in a community in the eastern United States where one-third of our neighbors were Jewish. We joined with other members of our Lutheran parish in neighborhood interfaith dialogue groups. I soon learned that Jews are as divided as Christians, ranging from the strict Orthodox to the Conservative to the Reformed.

In those conversations I had to wrestle more directly with the question, "How do I share my faith with my devout Jewish neighbor? As I come to know them as friends, is it right for me to insist that they believe exactly as I do?" Out of those dialogues and my own reflections on what it meant to be a Christian I came to several conclusions.

First, I need not compromise or water down my belief that Christ died and rose for all, including his fellow Jews. If I did otherwise I could not expect my Jewish friends to respect my faith convictions.

Second, I needed to honor their equally strong faith convictions just as I expected them to respect mine. It is not for me to make judgments of others and their faith values. I can leave that to God who sees into every person's heart.

Third, we live in a world where people of different religious backgrounds need to work aggressively to find ways to promote understanding among all people. It is a tragedy of history that millions have died because of senseless disagreements among different religions. In most every case, when we look back on those conflicts we see that some effort at communication and dialogue could have averted the bloodshed.

Though he worked passionately for the conversion of people to faith in Christ, Paul also recognized that there was no place on earth where God's presence was unknown.

~ hwc

❖ ROMANS 2:1-11 ❖

❖ Is There a Doctor in the House? ❖

Yes, if you have a Bible in your home there's always a doctor in the house. His name is Luke, the author of the third Gospel and the man we commemorate tomorrow. Luke plays as huge a role in the early church as anyone other than Peter and Paul. In addition to the third Gospel that bears his name, he also wrote the Acts of the Apostles. Given all of the stories from the life of Jesus that appear only in Luke's Gospel, and then the history of early Christianity in the Acts of the Apostles, it is impossible to underestimate Luke's importance to all of Christian history.

Luke was almost certainly a Gentile. This is reflected in how he writes. His world is much broader than it would have been had he been born and raised in Palestine. Little wonder he and Paul were soul mates. Though Paul was a Jew, he too was born and raised outside Palestine. As a physician, Luke probably attended to some of Paul's medical needs as they traveled together.

Much is made of the fact that Luke was a physician. But I wonder if he should not be honored more highly as a historian. In the opening verses of his Gospel he says that he was not an eyewitness of the events in the life of Jesus. But he has carefully documented them. Then comes what is most significant of all: Luke says he has written this account of the life of Jesus for his friend Theophilus "that you may know" (Luke1:4). That's the key—"that you may know." Luke's passion, plain and simple, is that others might know about Jesus.

Luke sets an example for all of us who claim to be followers of Jesus. "Doctor, lawyer, merchant, chief"—whatever our work, wherever we live, we have but one calling—to let others know about Jesus.

~ hwc

❖ LUKE 1:1-4 ❖

OCTOBER 18

❖ Learning from My Dog on My Birthday ❖

We've had three cairn terriers over the years—Toto, Obi, and Jonah. I can't imagine a better companion. Friendly, obedient (most of the time), lively, and attentive, they have all enriched our family life more than I can tell you. What I've liked best about having a dog for a pet is that they simply love to be with you. Their pack instinct motivates them to follow you around the house or yard, simply because they like your company. As I sit here writing this devotional piece I look over at the couch in my study and see Jonah, content just to be near me. If I leave my study and don't return shortly, he comes to find me.

That's the way I like to think of Jesus, my best friend. That's especially true today because it's my birthday. Turning eighty is a bit sobering. Many of our good friends have died in the past two or three years, some younger and many in their eighties. I know my days are numbered, yes, even if I live beyond this decade. Issues of consequence may happen in the seventies; they almost certainly *will* happen in the eighties. Sobering indeed.

I find that as I think of life beyond the current one it is most important to believe that I will be with Jesus. I want to be in his pack. Just to be near him, whatever that means, is enough for me. If my dear little Jonah thinks it's good enough to be near me, then it's good enough for me to know the same about Jesus. The "Father's house" he promises may be entirely different from what we expect. But Jesus will be there. Yes, good enough.

Thanks, Jonah, for teaching me this important lesson about life—here and forever. Is there a reason why "dog" spelled backward is "God"?

~ hwc

❖ JOHN 14:1-7 ❖

❖ LIFE IN THE SLOWER LANE ❖

It was a sad day. My eye specialist told me my vision had diminished to the point where I must restrict my driving to four-lane highways and familiar places. After six decades of freedom to by and large come and go as I pleased, this seemed too much. Though I saw it coming, somehow it never seemed possible. To go to the bedroom dresser the next morning and not casually pick up my car keys and slip them into my pocket—indeed, it was a blow.

Among the feelings I had to deal with was anger. Having been accustomed to going "eighty miles an hour" for all of my life, now I had to adjust to life in the slow lane. It was incredibly frustrating.

But there are lessons to be learned when we hit these speed bumps on life's road. Among them is that while feeling anger is entirely appropriate, harboring bitterness is not. I need only think of my brother Dave who was developmentally disabled. He had never even driven around the block. Then thoughts of gratitude and grace overwhelm my anger. I give thanks for Corinne who has good eyes and excellent driving skills. And I am touched deeply by offers from good friends to be my chauffeur.

I also think about the apostle Paul. He writes about his "thorn in the flesh." Some scholars think it was poor eyesight that hobbled and frustrated him. He writes to the believers at Corinth, saying that he pleaded with God to set him free from his limitation. Life would be so much easier without this "thorn" that kept him from living as he wanted.

Finally, Paul discovers that there may be a purpose in his limitation. He believes that it makes him more dependent on God and less on himself.

Even when we are in robust health we should feel this way. Why does it take a disappointment to learn such a valuable lesson?

~ hwc

❖ 2 CORINTHIANS 12:7-10 ❖

❖ Remembering Who We Are ❖

Not long after I retired I decided to work on my family history. As it became known among siblings and cousins and other relatives that I was interested in this heritage they sent scraps of history my way.

At first the task seemed too daunting. But as I visited county historical centers and explored church records, my interest grew exponentially. I got so wrapped up in the project that Corinne came to my desk one day and said, "I think it's time you paid as much attention to your *living* relatives as your *dead* ones." She was right, of course. It did get out of hand for a time.

Yet I have to say that the venture was not only enlightening, but also sobering. As I learned more and more about our ancestry I came to appreciate the strong foundations they had laid for future generations. Now I also came to treasure that word in Scripture: "We do not live to ourselves . . ." (Rom. 14: 7).

Memory is such an important part of the biblical story. It begins with the promise from God at the time of the great flood: "I will remember my covenant that is between me and you and every living creature . . ." (Gen. 9:15). That promise keeps reappearing through the Old Testament: "I will remember my covenant."

Running as a parallel stream through the Bible is another word. Over and over the people of God are urged to remember their past, to recall God's mercy through the generations. Deuteronomy 32:7 is but one example: "Remember the days of old, consider the years long past; ask your father, and he will inform you; your elders, and they will tell you."

You would do well to sit for a time with grandparents, parents, and others who can tell you of your roots. It will amaze you to learn how much your ancestors have contributed to your life.

~ hwc

❖ PSALM 77:9-15 ❖

❖ THOSE "ILLEGAL" IMMIGRANTS ❖

At this time of year as cool breezes begin sweeping into Minnesota, our thoughts turn to the Southwest. We've enjoyed several years of respite in the lovely village of Green Valley, just a half-hour from Mexico. Our Arizona neighbors think it's an ideal spot for snowbirds. Fine homes are surrounded by uniformly neat landscaping, many of them fronting on verdant golf courses.

There's just one big problem that looms on the near horizon. It's that wall. What wall? The wall just thirty minutes down the road that separates the wealthiest nation in the world from one of the poorest. Every night along that long border from the Pacific to the Gulf of Mexico hundreds slip across the border.

In spite of warm, sunny days, nighttime temperatures often dip to near or below freezing in the unforgiving desert. When I awaken on those mornings I know with certainty that several have died from exposure to the elements.

Who are these unwelcome intruders? Drug couriers? Yes, there are some of those. Studies show, however, that the vast majority are exactly like my grandparents who came to the United States because they simply wanted to find a way to care for their families.

Resistance to immigrants is not new. The earliest German newcomers were looked down on. The descendants of the English Puritans abhorred the poor Irish who flooded into America in the mid-nineteenth century. The Chinese were completely shut out for decades. When others come, whether legally or illegally, they often accept those jobs most Americans do not want.

Do I have an easy solution to the immigration question? No, I'm afraid not. What I do know is that there is a stream running from one end of the Bible to the other insisting that those who have must share with those who have not. Almost all of us are descended from immigrants, many of them despised. Yes, even Jesus was one of us.

~ hwc

❖ RUTH 2:1-10 ❖

❖ Another Bit of Humor ❖

In an earlier devotion, we found a touch of humor in the story of Jonah and the fish. I find still more humor in an unexpected place in the New Testament. Believe it or not, it's in the resurrection story.

Look at it this way. If you could have predicted who would first discover and announce that Jesus had risen from the dead, who would it be? The disciples, of course. They had been his intimate friends for some three years. They had seen him work miracles. They had heard him assert that after three days he would rise from the dead. Yes, they should have been the first to greet him when he arose, the first to tell the good news.

Instead, it's women who play that role. No, the women were no more expectant than they. They came to anoint the body of Jesus. They were surprised.

But isn't it amusing that the women were the first to experience this great event? In those days women were regarded in most circles as little more than slaves. To add to the irony, John tells us that the very first to meet the risen Christ was Mary Magdalene, thought by some to be a former prostitute. If you stand back from the scene you can't help but smile. Once more, God does the unexpected.

Before we are too hard on the disciples we should stop a moment and ask if we would have been any more prepared for our Lord's resurrection. Would we have believed this incredible story? I don't think so. I worked in a funeral home while in college. I can assure you that the dead stay dead.

So it comes down to what Paul said. Either we cast our lot with Jesus or we die in hopelessness. Since for us every day is Easter day, once more we shout, "Chris is risen!"

And that's not funny.

~ hwc

❖ 1 CORINTHIANS 15:50-56 ❖

❖ THE REAL ELECTION ISSUES ❖

Samuel had a problem. He had no son who was worthy to inherit his mantle of leadership. To fill that vacuum the people demanded a king to lead them. Samuel reacted negatively. He thought that if everyone followed the law of God there would be no need for a strong central authority like a king.

In the end Samuel yielded. After warning the people that a king meant taxation and military conscription and regimentation in many areas of life, he caved in to their demands. He agreed that it was necessary in order to hold the country together.

At this time of year we are bombarded with appeals in newspapers, on television and radio and bumper stickers, all suggesting that certain candidates deserve our support. Running beneath all of that falderal is a more fundamental question: How much governing do we want?

At one end are those who desire little or no civil authority. In the extreme, they would rather be a law unto themselves, paying as little tax as possible and letting the victims of unfortunate circumstances fend for themselves or depend on the uncertain generosity of others.

At the other extreme are those who believe that the only way is to have strong central authority with power to tax and the responsibility to defend us and care for the poor and those caught in the tragedies of life.

The answer today seems to be the same as it was in Samuel's time. It is the golden mean between those extremes—respect for individual freedom combined with the acknowledgement that life in community requires submission to law and authority.

I think Jesus was wrestling with this same issue when the Pharisees confronted him with the question, "Is it lawful to pay taxes to the emperor, or not?" (Matt. 22:17) He gives no pat answer. Rather, he says, "Give therefore to the emperor the things that are the emperor's, and to God, the things that are God's" (v.21).

~ hwc

❖ MATTHEW 22:15-22 ❖

❖ Stones in My Heart ❖

The telephone rang this morning. How welcome the voice of our wise and faithful friend of sixty-one years asking, "How are you both?" Did she somehow know we needed her especially today? My husband, Herb, spoke for both of us when he answered, "I have two stones in my heart." Her gifts once again were an active listening and a well-worn familiar presence. In that phone conversation, she became for us an open channel for God's love to pour into our hearts.

Having heavy stones in the heart happens to all of us at times and certainly did for the psalmist. Suffering was most difficult because he had no idea when there would be an end to it. After a broken bone has been repaired we need to know how long we'll have pain. When a loved one is terminally ill we need to know how long until the dying. We seem to know we can survive distress if only we can see a light at the end to suffering. For the psalmist, not only was suffering long, but evil was triumphing and God seemed absent. And he cries out, "How long must I bear pain in my soul, and have sorrow in my heart all day long?" (Ps. 13:2). With heaviness unbearable, it felt like death overtaking him. But he dares to bare his soul to God because of the well-worn familiar presence of one who listens and cares.

When we've cried out our pain in God's presence, the Holy Spirit opens the channel, assuring us again of God's steadfast love, a transforming love that pours in to lift the heaviness, and we, too, can sing, "I trusted in your steadfast love; my heart shall rejoice in your salvation. I will sing to the Lord, because he has dealt bountifully with me" (v. 5-6).

> What a friend we have in Jesus,
> All our sins and griefs to bear! (*LBW* #742).

~ ecc

❖ PSALM 13 ❖

❖ A Steadfast Heart ❖

One morning in our devotions, we read this beautiful challenging prayer from Thomas Aquinas in *For All the Saints*:

> Give me, Lord, a steadfast heart, which no unworthy affection may drag downwards; give me an unconquered heart, which no tribulation can wear out; give me an upright heart, which no unworthy purpose may tempt aside. Bestow on me also, O Lord, my God, understanding to know you, diligence to seek you, wisdom to find you, and a faithfulness that may finally embrace you, through Jesus Christ our Lord. Amen.

Steadfast in the prayer means loyal, unwavering, firmly fixed, unchangeable, and unswerving. The Old Testament word for steadfast love is *hesed.* It means kindness, faithful compassionate love, mercy, and grace. These words describe the goodness of God who is at the heart of all creation. We can trust God's faithfulness by the rainbow, and certainly, by the promise, "As long as the earth endures, seedtime and harvest, cold and heat, summer and winter, day and night, shall not cease" (Gen. 8:22).

Polycarp (69-155), early bishop of Turkey who opposed heresy, was arrested with other Christians and falsely accused of plotting against the government. The governor agreed to save him if he condemned Christ. With sure and steadfast faith, he boldly declared, "For eighty-six years I have been his servant and he has done me no wrong. How can I blaspheme my King and Savior?" (*For All the Saints*). When the fire failed to kill him, Polycarp was stabbed to death for his steadfast loyalty to Jesus Christ. His was a powerful witness that strengthened young churches during a time of great persecution.

In response to God's steadfast love, and with hope from the example of Christians like Polycarp, we ask God for a steadfast heart.

> Lord, keep us steadfast in your word;
> curb those who by deceit or sword
> Would wrest the kingdom from your Son
> and bring to naught all he has done (*LBW* #517).

~ ecc

❖ LAMENTATIONS 3:22-24 ❖

❖ Philipp Nicolai ❖

As pastor in Westphalia during the devastating plague of 1597–1598 that took 1,300 of his parishioners, Nicolai (1556–1608) had as many as thirty funerals a day. From his home, he looked out on the graveyard with its continual death. This prompted him to write both "Mirror of Joy," a series of meditations to comfort his people, and, the following year in 1599, "Wake, Awake, for Night Is Flying," known as king of chorales. The other hymn for which he is famous, "How Brightly Beams the Morning Star," is known as queen of chorales. These two hymns, based on Psalm 45, a royal wedding psalm, have inspired many composers, including Johan Sebastian Bach. Nicolai is said to be the last in the tradition of one who writes all of both text and music.

"How Brightly Beams the Morning Star," became in Germany a traditional wedding song inspired by this royal psalm. Intertwining its political and religious life, Israel deified their king as God's representative on earth to rule with equity and justice. So the psalm begins praising the bridegroom. Then it salutes the bride, hoping their joy would help her forget her homeland in Tyre as she enters her new home and bears children for the king. The psalm is translated now to be our praise of Jesus Christ who welcomes us, the church, as his bride.

Worshipful hymns like these, both words and music, powerfully transform us, raising us to hope and joy. Whether we sing them alone at our piano or together in worship, every verse is prayer and praise.

> Lord, when you look on us in love,
> at once there falls from God above
> A ray of purest pleasure. Your Word and Spirit, flesh and blood
> Refresh our souls with heavenly food. You are our dearest treasure!
> Let your mercy warm and cheer us! Oh, draw near us!
> For you teach us God's own love through you has reached us
> (*LBW* #308).

~ ecc

❖ PSALM 45:1-17 ❖

❖ PAUL GERHARDT ❖

In his early studies at the University of Wittenberg, Paul Gerhardt (1607–1676) was influenced by Paul Rober, professor and pastor who often took his sermon text from a hymn. From him, he learned hymnody to be a great tool of pastoral ministry. While tutoring in the home of a Berlin family, he became a prolific writer of poetry that so impressed their church cantor that he used Gerhardt's poems in a popular publication. Later as a small town pastor, Gerhardt lost his wife and children, leaving him with only one son. Personal sorrow besides the suffering during and after the Thirty Years War affected Gerhardt's writing, which was sensitive, warm, and tender. Through all of this, he became known as Germany's greatest hymn writer. His life-size portrait hangs in the Lubben church, with this inscription, "A divine sifted in Satan's sieve."

Our Scripture today reminds us that, "The Lord looks down from heaven; he sees all humankind" (Ps. 33:13). We are watched by God. Distressing that God knows every thought and feeling, every motive that we gloss over. But it is comforting to know that God loves us anyway. That we are cleansed by the blood of Jesus and clothed with his righteousness. And that God delivers our soul from death. He is our help and shield. And is our comfort at all times. We pray with Gerhardt's words:

> Evening and morning, sunset and dawning,
> Wealth, peace, and gladness, comfort in sadness:
> These are your works; rich in glory divine!
> Times without number, awake or in slumber,
> Your eye observes us, from danger preserves us,
> Causing your mercy upon us to shine.
> Gracious Lord, hear me, pardon and spare me;
> Calm all my terrors, blot out my errors,
> That justified in your sight I may stand.
> Order my goings, direct all my doings;
> Guard me and guide me and stay close beside me;
> All I commit to your fatherly hand (*ELW* #761).

~ ecc

❖ PSALM 33:13-22 ❖

❖ Lessons in Humility ❖

I've been privileged to occupy some fairly important stations in life, including bishop of the largest synod in the church and presiding bishop of the 5 million-member Evangelical Lutheran Church in America. No matter how hard one struggles to keep life in perspective, there is always a strong temptation to think one is quite important when elected to a high office. Yes, even in the church that temptation lurks. We night even say "especially" in the church because it is so subtle and insidious.

These elevated platforms of life only last for a short time. In my case, it happened just a week after I left my role as presiding bishop in late October 1995. I called the church offices in Chicago to speak with a staff person in the office of the treasurer. When she wasn't in I asked the receptionist if I could leave a message. I said, "Please ask Debra to call Herb Chilstrom." There was a brief pause at the other end of the line. Then she asked, "Would you please spell that?" Forgotten after only one week?

I suppose I might have been offended. But I reminded myself that support staff—who numbered in the hundreds—came and went with some frequency. There was no good reason why this person should have known me, to say nothing of spelling my unusual name.

Having said that, the incident was a good reminder that renown does not last very long. Cemeteries are filled with those who thought the world could not get along without them.

The disciples of Jesus were not immune to this temptation. They vied for position, jostling for special recognition. Jesus used a child to tell them that greatness has little to do with status in the eyes of others. Yes, some are given greater responsibility. But all stand on level ground at the foot of the cross.

~ hwc

❖ MATTHEW 18:1-4 ❖

❖ All Are Needed ❖

In late October I used to hunt my way across South Dakota with a group of five friends. We were three bishops, two pastors, and a psychiatrist. We would begin by hunting pheasants in the eastern part of the state, then geese on the Missouri River, then more pheasants in the foothills of the Black Hills, and finally deer in the higher elevations. After a few years of this comradeship we learned each other's strengths and weaknesses. Some could cook; others could not boil water. Some were sharpshooters; others could scarcely hit "the broad side of a barn." Some could tromp the fields and hills tirelessly; others would have to "post," waiting for friends to drive game in their direction. Some could skin out a deer in a few minutes; others needed help. At the end of the hunt all the game was divided equally among the hunters.

There was one gift we shared in common—we were brothers in Christ. As much as we enjoyed the hunt, far more important was that we simply enjoyed being together as sons of a common Father.

This is what a pastor sees as she or he looks out over the congregation on a Sunday morning. No two out there are alike. Each brings to the church unique gifts. There sits one who is a good cook; here one who can fix anything; there one who is naturally outgoing; here one who is quietly reflective; there one who leads; here one who follows; there one with an earned doctorate, here one with little formal education; there one with the voice of an angel; here one who can't carry a tune. And the list goes on. Different gifts but a common Lord.

Is that what Jesus had in mind when he chose his disciples? Bombastic Peter, pensive John, radical Simon, cautious Andrew, doubtful Thomas, confident James. Different disciples, but all needed.

~ hwc

❖ 1 CORINTHIANS 12:4-6 ❖

❖ A BIBLE ON A GARAGE SALE ❖

The other day a neighbor said he wanted to show me a Bible he picked up for a dollar at a garage sale. He noted that my name was written at the bottom of the flyleaf. When I looked at the Bible I affirmed that it was indeed my name.

On the top of that page was the name of Elizabeth, a young girl I had confirmed more than thirty-five years earlier. The Bible was obviously in good condition, evidence that it had never been used. The fact that it was found at a garage sale was further indication that Elizabeth, now a woman in her late forties, had probably never thought it important to read or study her Bible. It was like a stab in my heart.

Every pastor knows this disappointment. After seeking to spark an interest in the Bible and the Christian faith, and praying that each of these students will grow to adulthood as a vibrant believer and active member of a Christian congregation, it's a huge letdown to realize that so many either never catch the flame or turn aside along the way.

We have company in this kind of discouragement. The letters of Paul have references to those who started strong and then dropped away. Near the end of his second letter to Timothy he writes about Demas who "in love with this present world, has deserted me . . ." (4:10).

Jesus, of course, knew this kind of disappointment. He watched as Judas, one of the chosen twelve, succumbed to the lure of money in exchange for betrayal.

All of this reinforces what Jesus said again and again: "He who has ears, let him hear." The listener is as responsible as the one who teaches and preaches. Elizabeth, wherever you are, I pray you will come back and that somehow the good news will awaken faith and a love for the Scriptures.

~ hwc

❖ MATTHEW 13:1-9 ❖

❖ "DOOR TO DOOR" EVANGELISM ❖

Standing before the weathered door of the church at Wittenberg, Germany, was an awesome experience. Yes, I know some historians question the validity of the story that Luther posted his 95 Theses on that door. Whether he did or didn't, the door still holds significance for Christians.

Doors were the most effective means of communication in Luther's day. If you wanted to spread some news, good or bad, that was the place to post it. With the invention of the printing press about the same time, Luther's ideas spread like a wildfire through much of Europe. This was indeed good news—that we find peace by trusting in Christ alone—alone—for our salvation. No more purchase of indulgences, no more counting up good works. Just simple trust. That was the best news the world could hear.

Fast forward to the early twenty-first century. Now with lightning speed news flies around the whole world. I was stunned on my last visit to Tanzania, East Africa, to see cell phones used in the most remote areas. Lies, misunderstandings, false reports—in moments millions hear the word. But so it can be with good news.

That is where we fit into the picture. I'm not suggesting that we get obnoxious about it. But when we send an email or a text message, when we chat by Skype or cell phone or a landline phone, how often do we think about sharing a simple good word about our faith? Luther would have given his right arm to have means of communication like these. He used the best in his day; we should do the same in ours.

Right now I'm using what is still a good means of communication—writing a book. I want to tell you on this Reformation Day that my only hope is in Jesus who died and rose again for you and for me.

~ hwc

❖ JOHN 1:1-14 ❖

❖ All the Saints ❖

It is well-known that in Roman Catholic tradition, among other things, sainthood calls for evidence that a candidate has performed at least three verifiable miracles. Out of it has come the humorous remark from some that they are "three miracles short of sainthood."

There is nothing humorous, of course, about miracles. What we Lutherans and other Protestants emphasize, however, is that sainthood does not depend on what we have done, but on what God has done. Over this year of readings we have singled out a number of persons who deserve to be commemorated. They are ones whose life and work set them apart as having accomplished something unique in this world. Yet, even for such outstanding individuals we insist that their good works do not make them more deserving of God's grace than anyone else. They have simply allowed that grace to flow through them in an extraordinary way.

What about the rest of us—we who will not be remembered long after we die and whose track record is so ordinary that few will recall anything unusual we have done?

Good news. No one is ordinary in the sight of God. This is why on this All Saints Day we accent passages from the epistle to the Romans. In chapter 5, for example, it says, "Since we are justified by faith, we have peace with God through our Lord Jesus Christ, through whom we have obtained access to this grace in which we stand (v. 1).

And again in chapter 6, Paul points to our baptism as the source for our life as believers: "We have been buried with him by baptism into death, so that, just as Christ was raised from the dead by the glory of the Father, we too might walk in newness of life" (v. 4).

So, my sisters and brothers in Christ, give thanks today that all of us are saints.

~ hwc

❖ ROMANS 8:1-4 ❖

❖ Cloud of Witnesses ❖

Yesterday, on All Saints' Day, we thanked God for the life and witness of saints who have gone before us. Some Protestants may cringe at celebrating saints, but we do share a common pre-Reformation heritage with the Catholics. So together we honor such as St. Francis of Assisi and Julian of Norwich. We also thank God for guiding many saints in the secular world who made it a better place.

To understand the practice of commemorating saints, think how in the first century after Jesus' resurrection, Christians experienced persecution and martyrdom, agonizing as Christ did on the cross. So for three successive days after Christmas we remember those who died for Jesus' sake—Stephen, John, and the Holy Innocents, children killed in the effort to eliminate Jesus. We celebrate Saints' death day of triumphantly entering heaven.

Saints are models for Christians to follow. In monasteries, during the morning Prime hour, each person is given a saint to ponder as his example for the day. At baptism, an infant is named for a saint to be a model for his or her life. By the fourth century, All Saints' Day was set to remember saints, the great cloud of witnesses.

At workshops we have often given participants this exercise, and I suggest that you do it today. Take a sheet of paper, draw a dinner table, and set it for eight. Make place cards for persons you would like to honor at your table and for whom you would thank God. Choose persons who have made a profound impact on your life and journey of faith. Write to thank those who are still alive. Then share with someone what each person meant to you.

> Thou wast their rock, their fortress, and their might;
> Thou, Lord, their captain in the well-fought fight;
> Thou, in the darkness drear, their one true light. Alleluia!
> (*ELW* #422).

~ ecc

❖ HEBREWS 12:1-2 ❖

❖ Need a Banquet Hall ❖

Yesterday I asked you to set a table for eight persons who had made an impact on your life and journey of faith. I set my table, but quickly running out of room decided I needed a banquet hall. Perhaps you did, too.

Hebrews 11 invites us into a banquet hall to meet people who through faith "administered justice . . . won strength out of weakness" (vv. 33-34). They are like the persons who have impacted our lives and journeys of faith. Let me share a few.

In thanks to God, my parents tithed ten percent of their farm income. As a child, I watched with big eyes as they tallied the year's income and figured how much more they needed to meet their tithe. If it had not been a good year, they took out a loan to fulfill their tithe. Their faith was a quiet and powerful example to me.

Aunt Alma always sat with her family in the pew ahead of ours. As a child I was eager after worship to step near her. She was tall and stately just like her faith. With her arm around my shoulder, she seemed to see into my soul, making me feel tall and strong, and like herself, confident and able.

When I first got to know Herb Chilstrom, there was something about his quiet witness that grabbed my attention. I saw in him a beautiful combination of humility and what J. B. Phillips described in his paraphrase of the New Testament, a "sane estimation of your own abilities." Having grown up believing pride was the worst sin, I learned the habit of downplaying my abilities. Herb's witness taught me to savor and develop the use of my gifts.

Our table guests and those in Hebrews, all "won strength out of weakness" (v. 34). Their witness is long-reaching; even after their death, they "still speak" (v. 4). Your witness will be so as well.

~ ecc

❖ HEBREWS 11:1-40 ❖

❖ Judge Not ❖

Walking our dog one windy, April morning in Arizona, I suddenly felt something blow into my eye. Maneuvering my eye to get it out didn't help. Nor did my physician's maneuvering that afternoon. Nor did the ophthalmologist's the next day. But ointment he prescribed settled it down. We thought it resolved itself; however, six weeks later it hurt the same way again. My Minnesota ophthalmologist, hearing my story, smiled knowingly as he reached for a tweezers and plucked out an Arizona thorn from the tear duct. It was dormant for six weeks before rearing its ugly head again. Like our penchant for judging. Jesus warned, don't try picking out the speck in your neighbor's eye when you have a log in your own.

Amanda lived in our town. Amanda gathered news and quickly dispersed it. But not before making judgments, sifting it through her own small world of rules. Furthermore, reducing a person to be smaller than herself would always make her feel superior. Relaying her revised version of the news was often hurtful. I did say Amanda lived in our town, but I hear you saying she lives in your town. You know her. Actually on your very street. And if honest, you may say she lives in your heart. And how do I know so much about Amanda? Because she lives in my heart too. Amanda lives within all of us. And Jesus says, "Do not judge" (Matt. 7:1). Like a thorn, dormant but recurring, caught in this web, what can we do? Repeatedly, we must admit our wrong and flee to praying with the psalmist:

> Purge me . . . and I shall be clean; wash me, and I shall be whiter than snow. Let me hear joy and gladness; let the bones that you have crushed rejoice. Hide your face from my sins, and blot out all my iniquities. Create in me a clean heart, O God, and put a new and right spirit within me (Ps. 51:7-10).

~ ecc

❖ MATTHEW 7:1-5 ❖

❖ Body Has Many Members ❖

"What happened to your foot," we asked as we noticed the strange spring under his shoe. He'd been cleaning leaves out of a gutter and his ladder slipped, throwing him several feet to the frozen ground. His crushed ankle had to be surgically fused. The foot doesn't seem like such an important part of the body until it doesn't work right.

The word *foot* in Scripture often represents the whole person. It is also used to highlight the importance of our God-given gifts. No gift, like the foot, should be considered lesser, especially when we think how complex and how important the foot is to health and functionality.

Made up of over twenty-five important bones, the foot contains delicate metatarsals, strong tendons, muscles crisscrossing for various movements, interlacing nerves to guide movement, and a series of arches enabling to bear body weight and to provide leverage when walking. Muscle tone keeps everything in readiness for action at instant command. Some folks talk about wishing for a miracle when a part of the body is not working right. But can you imagine any greater miracle than the workings of a normal foot?

Likewise, God arranged the body of Christ so that there should be no discord. That is why the Spirit gave a variety of gifts. Like a foot working properly and without drawing attention to itself, in the body of Christ we must fully use our various gifts. As Antonio Stradivari, the great maker of violins said, "If my hand slacked, I should rob God."

We, as well as our gifts, are important, so God promises protection: "For he will command his angels concerning you to guard you in all your ways. On their hands they will bear you up, so that you will not dash your foot against a stone" (Ps. 91:11-12).

> My help comes from the Lord, who made heaven and earth.
> He will not let your foot be moved (Ps. 121:2-3).

~ ecc

❖ 1 CORINTHIANS 12:4-27 ❖

❖ The Pulpit and Politics ❖

As elections near it's a good time to ask about the connection between politics and the pulpit.

Most pastors have learned over the years that it's important to stick to issues in a campaign and avoid advocating for specific candidates. There's a long and solid history of prophecy in every major religion. We look to our religious leaders to dig deeply into our sacred writings and make applications to our contemporary world. In those prophetic writings there runs a strong bias in favor of helping the poor, defending the innocent, resisting war, advocating for peace and justice, denouncing greed and immorality, and much more.

Having said that, we also recognize that it's not only unlawful in our country but also unwise to back a specific candidate from the pulpit. If one favors a leader who promises no new taxes, to take just one example, what does one say when it becomes apparent that failure of that office holder to raise taxes weakens the safety net that provides health care, education, food stamps, and other essentials of life for the poor and needy?

Courage to speak out on moral issues belongs in the pulpit. Yes, daring to take a minority stance is necessary on occasion. Yes, risking being wrong on a particular issue may be important.

In the end, however, we also need to trust that lay people who study their Bible and are sensitive to their own conscience will make good judgments on important questions, including the candidates they vote for in an election.

In our churches we have not only a pulpit, but also an altar where we pray.

In our Lutheran tradition we have a prayer that is appropriate for all: "Defend our liberties, and give those whom we have entrusted with authority of government the spirit of wisdom, that there might be justice and peace in our land" (*LBW*, p. 42).

~ hwc

❖ MATTHEW 22:15-22 ❖

❖ Do You Know Father Heyer? ❖

If you answer, "No, I've never heard of Father Heyer," then let me introduce him. John Christian Frederick Heyer was the first Lutheran missionary to go from the United States to another country.

Heyer was born in Germany 1793. He was sent to a relative in Pennsylvania just after he was confirmed. A deeply spiritual young man, Heyer heard the call to be a pastor. He traveled widely among immigrant congregations and was instrumental in setting up Sunday schools wherever he went. After twenty years of parish ministry Heyer felt a call to go to India. He prepared by not only studying Sanskrit, the language of India, but also medicine. At age forty-eight he sailed for India, leaving behind his six motherless children. The youngest was thirteen.

Like other Christian missionaries, Heyer was forbidden to work with those in the higher castes. But the authorities didn't mind if they worked with the "Dalit" people, the so-called "untouchables" who were so low in the caste system that they were not even thought of as humans. Heyer's work prospered. His tireless efforts resulted in the establishment of many congregations and mission stations in the Andhra Province.

When we visited India we encountered evidence of Heyer's ministry almost everywhere we traveled in the Andhra area and beyond. Because of the work of Heyer and others, these believers now have a sense of dignity they never could have imagined. In a culture where the caste system has been officially outlawed, vestiges of it still persist. The church has become the gateway not only to a new life in Christ, but also to opportunities for work and careers that could never have been imagined without the ministry of hundreds of missionaries like Heyer. The affectionate title "Father" was well deserved. He died on this day in 1873.

Again today I urge you to pray for and support our missionaries around the world.

~ hwc

❖ MATTHEW 28:16-20 ❖

❖ WHAT DID THEY DO WRONG? ❖

I want you to linger with me another day in India. On one of our trips we visited a leper colony near Delhi. It is composed of simple homes, some weaving rooms, and a chicken farm. It is supported by our church.

As is almost always the case, our attention focused initially on the misshapen bodies of the people who had leprosy. Missing fingers, hands, arms, legs and ears, white blotches all over their bodies—I admit that it was, at first sight, quite repulsive. I wanted to look away.

That first reaction, however, was short-lived. Smiles, often distorted from the effects of leprosy, were unmistakable. Women in an open courtyard looked up from spinning wheels to greet us. We moved on to rooms where we met people sitting at looms. Missing arms and legs made it difficult for them to operate even simple mechanisms. But emerging from the far end were intricately patterned tablecloths, napkins, and table runners. Soon we thought nothing of their ravaged bodies. Now we saw only the quality of their work and, beyond it, the beauty of their souls. When presented with gifts of their work we felt overwhelmed. Now as we use these items for table settings for guests in our home the memory of that day floods back. How can we but thank God for a Savior and a church that cares!

From ancient times and even until recent history there has been this often unspoken question: "What did their parents do to deserve such a child? What did they do to deserve this punishment?"

Jesus encountered this issue when his disciples asked the same question about a blind man. "Who sinned?" His reply was revolutionary: "Neither this man nor his parents sinned" (John 9:3). Then Jesus went on to suggest that out of the tragedies of life God is able to bring much good. We saw it at the leper colony in India.

~ hwc

❖ JOHN 9:1-5 ❖

❖ Who Are the Special Ones? ❖

With elections on our minds this time of year, we hear many politicians accenting how special the United States is in the world. We pledge allegiance to "one nation, under God." We often hear political leaders end their speeches with a benediction: "God bless you; and God bless America!"

I'm not very comfortable with all of this. I wonder at times if we don't slip into the very subtle state of mind that leads us to think that God cares more for the United States, or our state, or our community, than other places.

That was the problem in Israel at the time of Isaiah. The people were accustomed to thinking they were God's special people, and that others were second class. Isaiah walks in and shocks them. "Do not let the foreigner joined to the Lord say, 'The Lord will surely separate me from his people'" (Isa. 56:3). Then he talks about eunuchs who had been excluded because they were thought to be immoral in some way. Isaiah says, "I will give [eunuchs] an everlasting name that shall not be cut off" (v. 5). His hearers must have been stunned.

I'm reminded of the time a friend asked us to attend his inner city church when new members were being welcomed. Prior to the service the pastor told me about them. Among them was one who had just been divorced, a woman whose husband was Hindu, some newlyweds, a former prostitute, and a gay couple. As they made their commitment to Christ and to the mission of the congregation in the community, I turned to Corinne and whispered, "I think Jesus would be very happy to be here today."

What about your church? Are people of any race, any minority, any financial status, any sexual orientation, any physical appearance, any developmental disability—are these welcome in your church?

Isaiah says, "My house shall be called a house of prayer for all peoples" (Isa. 56:7).

~ hwc

❖ ISAIAH 56:1-7 ❖

❖ The Necessity of Gadflies ❖

Søren Kierkegaard died more than 150 years ago. I'm glad he wasn't around when I was a bishop. He would have made life quite uncomfortable for me and many others. He was a classic gadfly, calling into question anything he thought was not pleasing to God. He felt disturbed as he observed the stiff formality of much that went on in the church. His passion was that each person should experience God in a very personal way.

We need to be careful not to confuse Kierkegaard's concern with an insidious trend in our times. Some speak of "making a decision for Christ," of being "born again." Kierkegaard would have been repulsed by someone who said they had been "born again" and now felt content. He believed that having a true encounter with God was so wrenching, so soul-searching that it left one completely exhausted. But as frightening as this is, he says that this is the only way to find true freedom.

Kierkegaard would agree with Shakespeare in saying that self-love, though a sin, is not as serious as self-neglect. In other words, each of us is called to search until we find who we are and then to have the courage to live it out in daily service.

Kierkegaard died at a relatively young age—only forty-three. He would have been shocked to know that his writings have been the subject for entire schools of thought and hundreds of books.

We should thank God for gadflies, for people in church and society who make us feel uncomfortable and inspire us to think in new ways. But even more so, we should give thanks for those like Kierkegaard who keep reminding us that life calls for making decisions about what we believe and how we will live. As long as we live we must make leaps of faith, trusting that God will be with us.

~ hwc

❖ ISAIAH 6:1-8 ❖

❖ LIFE'S WORST DAY ❖

It was unbelievable. How could it have happened? On this day in 1984 we found the body of our son Andrew in the basement of our home, dead from a gunshot wound.

Any parent who has adopted a child knows the unbridled joy that surges through your heart the moment that little one is placed in your arms. Not having been able to have children of your own making, you can't imagine a better way to fill that void. With his bright eyes, keen mind, humorous grin, and engaging ways, he grew to be everything we could ask for in a son.

It was when he entered adolescence that ominous clouds began to gather at the edges of Andrew's personality. He wondered who he was, why his birthmother gave him up for adoption. "She must have been a slut," he speculated. No matter how we tried to convince him otherwise, he persisted in that belief.

When he went off to college we followed him with our prayers, hoping that he might blossom into the kind of young man we dreamed he would be. Instead—and unknown to us—he descended deep into his personal hell. Finally, he could stand the pain no longer. He saw no other way of escape.

How does one survive? In subsequent days, Corinne will write about grief and how one moves out of darkness and back into the light.

Let me simply say that the shock of sudden and unexpected death brings waves of contrary feelings: guilt, anger, shame, confusion, helplessness, hopelessness, and more. But let me also say that at no time in my life have I ever come to know the presence of the Holy Spirit and the meaning of the "communion of saints" more fully than in those days. How I thank God for my sisters and brothers in the faith! Without them and the Spirit I could not have survived.

~ hwc

❖ ROMANS 8:22-28 ❖

❖ In Grief, Take a Psalm ❖

When overwhelmed with grief, it's hard to pray, and even if you can, your prayer goes round like being stuck in a rut. So praying is more like brooding. The "lament psalms" can be a wonderful help.

Martin Luther warns us not to sit and brood, but suggests using a lament Psalm to help pour out our troubles to God. Using psalms helps give over our sorrow to God, getting beyond grief where we can then allow God to fill us with his presence. It is at such times when we are lead into a new journey of joy that we could never have known without the grief.

A lament psalm helps us cast our agony on God, and its very five-part structure lifts us out of sadness back to trust in God. (Some other lament psalms are 6, 31, 88, 89, 130, Lamentations 3, and Jeremiah 3.) We find each of these important parts in Psalm 102.

Invoking the name of the Lord opens the door and makes speaking to God possible. "Hear my prayer, O Lord; let my cry come to you" (v. 1).

Pleading to God to "not hide your face from me in the day of my distress" (v. 2).

Crying out one's lament, even complaining that what God has done is causing my suffering (vv. 3-11, 23-24). It's healthy to get it all out, as God told Job, "Pour out the overflowings of your anger" (Job 40:11). God can take it.

Recalling what God did in the past (vv. 12, 18-22, 25) helps us realize that, although I am broken now, God has been in my history all along. Out of this grows new confidence of trust (vv. 13-17) that leads us to joy in God's presence with hope and praise.

Vowing to praise God because trust has been reborn (vv. 16-22, 25-28). Out of grief's ashes rises a new creation. A miracle of grace.

~ ecc

❖ PSALM 102:1-28 ❖

❖ God of All Comfort ❖

New in the parish, I began making regular visits in the well-appointed home of an elderly couple, Mary and Sam, who had recently lost their only daughter. In the course of events, Sam became ill and died. Mary's grief compounded as she became more and more bitter, believing that God had targeted her for these disasters. All the while, her bitterness blocked Jesus waiting at her heart's door with his gifts of comfort.

When broken by grief, we can easily become cynical and bitter. It's one of the worst things that could ever happen to us. But there is hope at the cross of Jesus. For he who is the "man of suffering and acquainted with infirmity" (Isa. 53:3) understands and welcomes us. We must go to him, speaking out our feelings and losses. Asking him to carry each loss too heavy for us to bear. And there at his cross, he will lift them one by one and free us again to wholeness and health. Then we can live again and find joy deeper than any we could ever have known without this sorrow. God comforts us so it will flow through us to others.

Grief, not only over the loss of a loved one, comes in various packages. Losing car keys or credit cards. An accident. Burglary. Loss from fire. Financial insecurity. A failing business. Moving away from friends or family. Losing a pet. A failed relationship or expectation. Loss of health or fertility. Loss of a limb or a body function. Loss of hearing or so much sight you have to stop driving. Each is a loss that must be grieved or we risk growing bitter.

The apostle Paul was crushed with affliction, almost despairing of life itself. But it made him rely on God "who raises the dead" (2 Cor. 1:9). If we go to the cross, Jesus will take away bitterness and raise us also.

Blessed be the God . . . of all consolation (v. 3).

~ ecc

❖ 2 CORINTHIANS 1:3-11 ❖

❖ A Sheep of Your Own Fold ❖

During these many years since the suicide death of our son, parents who have been likewise bereaved, have asked us one daunting question: Will God receive the suicide victims into heaven? Since suicide was declared a mortal sin by the church of the Middle Ages, this fear has filled many hearts. No one can erase these fears from our hearts. It must come from God. For me, memorizing God's promises made them readily available for the journey, secured in the shelves of the mind for easy access day or night. God's word would transport me to where Andrew was there with the host of heaven praising God.

The question is asked, "Who are these, robed in white?" (Rev. 7:13). And answered, "They have washed their robes and made them white in the blood of the Lamb. For this reason they are before the throne of God" (vv. 14-15). Andrew was twenty-three days old when it happened, "Sealed by the Holy Spirit and marked with the cross of Christ forever" (*LBW*, p. 124). When the pall was placed over him on November 14, 1984, these words were said, "When we were baptized in Christ Jesus, we were baptized into his death. . . . if we have been united with him in a death like his, we shall certainly be united with him in a resurrection like his" (*LBW*, p. 206).

At Resurrection Cemetery that noontime hour, our family and friends joined us in praying, "Into your hands, O merciful Savior, we commend your servant, Andrew. Acknowledge, we humbly beseech you, a sheep of your own fold, a lamb of your own flock, a sinner of your own redeeming. Receive him into the arms of your mercy, into the blessed rest of everlasting peace, and into the glorious company of the saints in light" (*LBW*, p. 211). With him, even now, God is wiping my every tear and sheltering us with his presence.

~ ecc

❖ REVELATION 7:9-17 ❖

❖ One Little Word ❖

Baptism was foundational for Martin Luther, born November 10, 1483, and baptized November 11 on the feast day of Martin of Tours (therefore given his name). In baptism we are delivered from sin, death, and the power of the devil. We must know who the devil is and face him with the sword of God's word as our defense.

Steve Wilkinson, former tennis coach, in an email from Wimbledon, wrote, "I had fun working with Eric (former student) on handling the hard balls that got blasted at him. It is important to never turn away. Face the opponent and use the racket in a backhand block position to protect the vulnerable spots." So how do we who all struggle against the devil, handle the hard balls that he blasts at us? What is our defense?

The devil is a present powerful force in this world. But Christ has delivered us from his dominion and bondage to sin. Luther in *Day by Day* writes, "Sin is a powerful and cruel master and tyrant over all . . . no one can resist it. . . . All would be slain and devoured by him. . . . Christ alone is the hero who can thwart that cruel and unconquerable foe. But it cost our dear Lord dearly. For He must lose his life in doing it." The center of our baptism liturgy is to renounce the devil. And we must do it daily.

When the devil comes to us in the night with the Ten Commandments saying, "You have sinned," be ready to say, "I am baptized. My righteousness is in Jesus Christ and is more powerful than my sin."

> Though all the world with devils fill and threaten to devour us,
> We tremble not, we trust God's will: they cannot overpow'r us.
> Though Satan rant and rage, in fiercest war engage,
> this tyrant's doomed to fail;
> God's judgment must prevail! One little word shall triumph
> (*ELW* #505).

~ ecc

❖ COLOSSIANS 1:11-14 ❖

❖ SALT AND LIGHT ❖

Yesterday God's word gave us deliverance from the devil's "dominion of darkness" through Christ's redeeming us from bondage to the devil. What other temptations does the devil bring?

Martin Luther says the devil tempts us to withdraw from the world and refuse to see the needs of the poor. Since the devil is not a self, he uses other voices, those of our conscience and of society. And he mimics God's voice as though he had authority. These convincing voices must be identified.

The devil often uses the voice of society, as through advertisements convincing us that we need more things. Only take care of yourself and your pleasure. Please yourself.

The voice of the devil speaks also through our conscience, tempting us to despair and to unbelief, forgetting our identity as children of God. Jesus was human, as we are, in order to give us an identity through his life, death, and resurrection. Tempted as we, he unmasked the devil and is able now to help us in our times of temptation. Founded in Jesus, we, with Luther, can speak boldly to the devil saying, "This is who I am, and therefore I need not submit to despair or unbelief."

With our identity in Jesus to be lifted out of despair and unbelief, we can hear Jesus' voice calling us to be salt and light in the world, as when he called his disciples saying, "I will make you fish for people" (Matt. 4:19). Will you allow Jesus to make you the servant he needs right where you are? The needs are great. Ask and God will create, making you into salt and light for the world.

> Across the world, across the street, the victims of injustice cry
> For shelter and for bread to eat, and never live before they die.
> We have no mission but to serve in full obedience to our Lord;
> To care for all, without reserve, and spread his liberating word
> (*ELW* #729).

~ ecc

❖ MATTHEW 5:13-16 ❖

Meet Elizabeth and Other Saints

The world is fascinated by royalty. Even Americans follow the fortunes of European kings, queens, princes, and princesses. If you study this unusual world of the royals you soon learn that marriage for love is rare and recent. In earlier times it was almost always marriage for political advantage.

Today we commemorate Elizabeth who died on this day in 1231. Believe it or not, she was promised in marriage when she was only two years old! But, contrary to what you might expect, when she eventually married her chosen prince at age fourteen it actually turned into a very happy partnership. She and her husband lived in the Wartburg Castle, the place where Luther some 300 years later translated the New Testament into the language of the people.

Elizabeth was a very devout young wife and mother. She worked tirelessly for the sick and the poor. She established hospitals, including one at the foot of the hill near the Wartburg Castle. Her model was St. Francis of Assisi. After her husband died she gave away her fortune for the poor and devoted herself to works of charity. She died at the youthful age of twenty-four.

Is there a St. Elizabeth hospital near you? Or do you know of one by that name? Most likely it is named after this remarkable woman.

Yesterday I visited my brother Dave who is in hospice care suffering from prostate cancer. I watched as two staff persons came to his room to care first for his immobile roommate and then for Dave. They were simply doing what they do every day, year in and year out. They were doing tasks many of us would find difficult or repulsive. They did it cheerfully. As I observed them I said to myself, "Here, too, are God's saints."

Give thanks today for all of the "Elizabeths" who serve God by caring for others.

~ hwc

PSALM 103:1-5

❖ Raise My Ebenezer ❖

"Come, thou Fount of every blessing, tune my heart to sing thy grace; streams of mercy, never ceasing, call for songs of loudest praise. . . . Here I raise my Ebenezer, hither by thy help I've come; . . . Jesus sought me when a stranger, wand'ring from the fold of God; he, to rescue me from danger, interposed his precious blood" (*ELW* #807).

After singing the hymn, a man came shaking my hand, asking what it meant to "raise my Ebenezer"? It's our story of Samuel today.

His mother, Hannah, bitter in barrenness, prayed for a child. In thankfulness for God's answer, before giving birth, she dedicated him to the Lord. Young Samuel was taken to Eli the priest to serve him in the house of the Lord.

One night God called his name, and Samuel answered, "Speak, for your servant is listening" (1 Sam. 3:10). That was the beginning of Samuel's faithfulness, like his mother before him, and his crying out his anguish to God, listening to God, and obeying God. He became a great leader and tool in the hand of God. (Reading 1 Samuel 1–7 is powerful.)

The Philistines, strong and with weapons of iron, threatened Israel. And one day they captured the Ark of the Covenant, which was like taking away the very presence of God. But it brought disaster to them, including an epidemic of tumors. So they hitched up two fresh milk cows to a cart taking away the Ark. Unbridled and undirected they brought it miraculously back to Israel. When things were hopeless, God had once again intervened. Like at the blackest hour of Jesus' death, God intervened and raised him to new life.

So there at Mizpah, in great thanksgiving to God, Samuel set up a stone, calling it *Ebenezer.* It means, "Thus far, the Lord has helped us." Raising your Ebenezer of thanks, what stories will you tell today? Raising your Ebenezer will fill you with thanks that will overflow to others.

~ ecc

❖ 1 SAMUEL 7:2-17 ❖

❖ Expressing Gratitude ❖

Foundational in his many years of teaching and coaching tennis and life, Steve Wilkinson believed that "expression of gratitude is an important habit." And he lived it, even when metastatic cancer ravaged his body.

A habit is something we practice—a routine, something we continue to do on a regular basis. Something we can choose to do. We can make gratitude our habit. What helps and what hinders making gratitude a habit? And what are the benefits?

Remembering past events can bring joy or sorrow, a blessing or a curse. A chapter giving insight from research on memory in Lehrer's *Proust Was a Neuroscientist* warns how memory can be destructive. Each successive time we remember an event it can become altered until it is less about what you remember and more about you. So if one broods or associates with one who blames, memory can make the past become a curse. And rob us of gratitude.

That's why we need a reinforcement anchor—worshipping regularly with the body of Christ. Receiving Christ's very presence in communion. Expressing thanks to God in liturgy and singing hymns. Remembering what God has done for us through the death and resurrection of Jesus Christ. Renewing our baptism saying, "I renounce the devil in all his works and ways." We need Psalm 136 with each verse announcing a gift God gives and our thankful refrain, "His steadfast love endures forever."

Establish a routine of not only feeling thankful, but saying it! Not always the Scandinavian way. Make a habit of saying thanks to those we live with, and a habit of sending "thank you" emails and notes to relatives and friends. It can be as simple as when one day my brother-in-law wanted to thank me on the phone for serving red grapes on breakfast cereal when they visited seven years ago, teaching him a healthy boost to his immune system.

Let's warm God's heart, saying thanks for specific things. Joy returns a hundredfold!

~ ecc

❖ PSALM 136:1-26 ❖

❖ HERE COMES THE KING ❖

Several years ago Corinne and I were invited to a reception for the king of Sweden and his wife when they visited the United States. Prior to the event we received detailed instructions on how to conduct ourselves in the presence of their majesties:

Stand when they enter the room.
Do not approach them.
Do not initiate a conversation with them.
In the receiving line, do not extend your hand to them. Any contact must be only in response to their initiative.

In other words, saying, "Hi Carl, how's the weather in Stockholm?" or "Hello Sylvia, who did your hair for this trip?" would be quite out of order!

Now give some thought to the King of Kings and Lord of Lords. Yes, we are to hold Jesus Christ in the highest esteem. We should give to him the greatest respect and loftiest praise. We should feel breathless in the presence of him whom God has crowned as the eternal King of the universe.

But then think of how privileged we are to be actually invited to approach him, to speak to him, to bare our souls to him, and to feel his personal embrace. This is the theme in the second chapter of Paul's letter to the believers at Philippi. Christ, he writes, was "in the very form of God . . ." (Phil. 2:6). In the mystery of the Holy Trinity, Paul says that Jesus Christ is one with God. But now comes the miracle of the ages. Christ, Paul says, "did not regard equality with God as something to be exploited, but emptied himself, taking the form of a slave, being born in human likeness" (vv. 6-7).

What can we say to this other than, "Wow! This is unbelievable! This is the best good news we could ever expect to hear. He is not aloof from us. We are actually invited to approach him and touch him and be embraced by him."

Welcome King Jesus!

~ hwc

❖ PHILIPPIANS 2:5-11 ❖

❖ Trimmed and Burning ❖

Rural electricity came to us when I was in seventh grade. Until then, lamp detail was my Saturday responsibility. Wash and shine chimneys. Fill with kerosene. Trim with sharp scissors the blackened char off wicks. The syncopated choir anthem, "Keep Your Lamps Trimmed and Burning," is a favorite anthem, because I'm familiar with the responsibility.

Jesus used the marriage custom to teach Christian responsibility. Bridesmaids prepared the bride for the bridegroom coming with his companions to take her to his home and the feast. Bridesmaid responsibility was to hold lamps high, lighting the way for the bridegroom. Unwise maids ran out of oil. The wise maids had their lamps trimmed and burning. Jesus warns, "Keep awake therefore, for you know neither the day nor the hour" (Matt. 25:13). Jesus is coming. Will we be ready? Will we recognize him? Only if we have our lamps trimmed and burning.

So when and where will we see Jesus? In everyone who hurts. The sick and imprisoned. Naked and hungry. Those experiencing injustice. Then, Jesus must be all around us. We need to start at home with those we love most. Retired, my husband now having time, said "I really want to help more, but you are so fussy in your kitchen." Way too set in my ways from many years of working alone there. I felt so bad. I'm asking the Holy Spirit to take a sharp scissors and trim my wick so that I can do justice right in my own home.

Each of us was given the light of Jesus Christ in our baptism. We've been made right with God through his death and resurrection, given the Holy Spirit to light our lamps with energy to shine in a troubled world. But evil can and will suck up oil right out of our lamps. We need lamp detail. Daily cleaning to remove despair and blackened char on the wicks. And daily filling with the oil of Jesus' presence.

~ ecc

❖ MATTHEW 25:1-13 ❖

❖ Ole Hallesby ❖

Although never ordained, Ole Hallesby (1859–1961) was professor of theology and ethics at the independent seminary of Oslo, Norway. He became an outspoken opponent of the Nazi regime and for that he was detained in the Grini concentration camp. Prolific as an author, he wrote some sixty-seven books, with *Prayer* being the most widely read. This one, we're told, kept its place during World War II on the bedside table of President Franklin D. Roosevelt.

Hallesby believed that prayer was to glorify the name of God.

"If we make use of prayer, not to wrest from God advantages for ourselves or our dear ones, or to escape from tribulations and difficulties, but to call down upon ourselves and others those things which will glorify the name of God . . . then we shall see such answers to prayer as we had never thought were possible."

"The spirit must always be given opportunity to reveal Christ to us. . . . We only need to see Him, and prayer will rise from our hearts."

"To pray is to let Jesus come into our hearts. It is not our prayer that moves the Lord Jesus. It is Jesus who moves us to pray. He knocks. Thereby he makes known his desire to come in to us. Our prayers are always a result of Jesus' knocking at our hearts' doors."

Jesus knocking on a door with no outside handle was the altar painting of my childhood church. I saw Jesus there every Sunday, on my confirmation day, and our wedding day. The message was clear—the first move of Jesus coming into our hearts is not ours, rather it is his will to enter.

Pray today what we sang on our wedding day:

> Lord Jesus Christ, be present now;
> our hearts in true devotion bow.
> Your Spirit send with light divine,
> and let your truth within us shine (*ELW* #527).

~ ecc

❖ REVELATION 3:20 ❖

❖ Done Enough? ❖

Whether walking amidst Matthew's words or under Michelangelo's painting of the last judgment on the Sistine Chapel ceiling, we're drawn into the scene of Jesus saying to some, "Come, you that are blessed by my Father, inherit the kingdom" (Matt. 25:34), or saying to others, "You that are accursed, depart from me" (v. 41).

So much was happening in the parish during the days while I was giving birth to a sermon on this text. We had just buried a pillar of the congregation who gave so generously. I grieved knowing Don would not be in his usual place with his extended family. His van would not be waiting out front as every year on this Sunday, so youth could load donated turkeys for delivery to Logan Square where hungry people hoped for Thanksgiving dinner.

Wednesday morning, Jo came spreading sunshine, carrying a box overflowing with her handcrafted mittens, scarves, and stocking caps for "Street Ministry," clothing for the homeless.

Saturday morning the altar guild women came cheerful and ambitious, readying the chancel for worship and Eucharist for all who hungered and thirsted for God. Annie was dusting the altar.

To all, I heard Jesus saying, "Blessed, inherit the kingdom." Did their doing merit the kingdom? Had Don given enough? Did Jo know if she'd knit enough? Or young Annie, had she dusted enough?

The answer had come with the words spoken when we covered Don with the funeral pall. "We were buried therefore with him by Baptism into death, so that as Christ was raised from the dead . . . we too might live a new life. . . . we shall certainly be united with him in a resurrection like his" (*LBW*, p. 206). It's because of Jesus that we enter the kingdom. So we don't have to do anything. But out of thankfulness we knit and dust and give, seeing Jesus in all who need us today.

~ ecc

❖ MATTHEW 25:31-46 ❖

❖ The Perfect Break ❖

Professors and pastors are accustomed to getting a sabbatical leave, a time to get away from the pressures of their work to study and rest.

Jesus was no exception. But, as I noted earlier, there is only one reference in the Gospels to a time when he "got away" and took a well-deserved break. He goes to the lovely city of Tyre on the coast of the blue Mediterranean Sea. I've been to that coast. I've taken a swim in those refreshing waters. I can fully understand why Jesus chose to go there.

Unfortunately, Jesus soon learned that "the best laid plans of mice and men" often don't turn out to be as we expect. In this case Jesus' growing fame preceded him. As soon as the people learned he was in their community they flocked to him. It's no surprise that a woman with an afflicted child sought him out and pleaded for help. Her courage was remarkable. She's a woman. She should have known her place. If you've ever had a sick child you know why she acted as she did. All hesitation vanishes. You have but one aim—to get help for your child.

Jesus' response to her is what makes this story so fascinating. "It is not fair," he says, "to take the children's food and throw it to the dogs" (Mark 7:27). Wow! Talk about a slap in the face. Talk about rejection.

What's going on here? In my opinion we are seeing the raw, human side of Jesus. He has yearned for a break. He was human enough to get irritated, just as we do at such times. In any event, it is the woman's response that brings us to the heart of this story. She turns to Jesus and says, "Sir, even the dogs under the table eat the children's crumbs" (v. 28).

Jesus must have been stunned. No wonder he interrupts his sabbatical to heal her child.

~ hwc

❖ MARK 7:24-37 ❖

❖ ISAAC WATTS, HYMN WRITER ❖

"Father of English Hymnody," Isaac Watts, like his father, was a nonconformist, imprisoned twice for his religious views. Born in England in the late seventeenth century during troubled times, he was the eldest of nine children. Rhyming early was both amusing and consternation to his parents. One day, seeing a mouse climbing up a rope, he said, "A little mouse for want of stairs ran up a rope to say his prayers." Sacrilegious! Responding to threatening punishment, he said, "Father, Father, mercy take and I will no more verses make."

Recognized for being a very bright child, he was offered a university education that would lead to ordination. Because nonconformists were not allowed at Oxford or Cambridge, he refused and went to a dissenter's academy. After graduating and while living at home for two years, he wrote most of his 600 hymns that literally poured from his pen.

After the Reformation, divisions came when groups questioned hymns. Calvin's tradition believed Holy Scriptures were sufficient, so plain psalms were sung. Lutherans and Moravians, believing that since free prayers are good, free verse can be sung as well. So they began developing a rich tradition of hymns in the vernacular. But because the English had no talent for and did not write hymns in English verse, they used Calvin's verse translations of the psalms, of which there were seventy-eight editions. Isaac Watts, out of discontent, began writing hymns—hymns for praise and prayer.

They poured from his pen with the impetus of a true genius. Many are our favorites, such as these: "Alas! And Did My Savior Bleed"; "Come, Holy Spirit"; "Love Divine"; "From All That Dwell below the Skies"; "Give to Our God Immortal Praise"; "Joy to the World"; "Oh, that the Lord Would Guide My Ways"; "When I Survey the Wondrous Cross"; "O God, Our Help in Ages Past."

> Saints have dwelt secure; sufficient is your arm alone, and our defense is sure (*LBW* #320).

~ ecc

❖ PSALM 121:1-8 ❖

❖ WHAT WILL HEAVEN BE LIKE? ❖

I like my hometown—Litchfield, Minnesota. It was a fine place to spend my childhood and youth. I carry with me hundreds of pleasant memories from growing up in that city.

I can't imagine, however, that anyone would ever describe Litchfield as "picturesque." Situated on the wide prairies of southern Minnesota, there is nothing about the city that would distinguish it from hundreds of other small towns in America's broad Midwest.

For that reason, it's little wonder that I nearly wore out the shutter on my camera the first time I toured Switzerland. With its lofty alpine peaks and verdant green valleys, I said to myself, "This has to be the most beautiful place on earth."

That is, until I visited Norway several years later. Again, my camera was at my eye almost constantly as we sailed its fjord-dotted coastline. I can still easily conjure up visions of the Hardunger Fjord as we snaked our way through the blossoming orchards at the coastline. "This has to be it," I thought. There can be no more lovely place on earth.

That is, until Corinne and I came to the south island of New Zealand on our first trip after retirement. Within an hour one can drive from awesome glaciers to tropical rain forests, from the world's most manicured public gardens to eye-popping rock formations. "Indeed," I said, "this has to be it."

At this time of year we remember those who have died. We wonder, "What is heaven like for them? And what will it be like for me?"

The longer I live the less I need to have an answer to those questions. Just as I could never have imagined those lovely places on earth before I visited them, so I can't possibly paint a picture in my mind of what heaven will be like. I find myself completely content to wait until I get there.

~ hwc

❖ 1 CORINTHIANS 2:6-15 ❖

❖ Be Prepared ❖

On the stair landing at a Lutheran high school in Budapest, Hungary, I saw a statue of Martin Luther planting a tree. It is the only known statue of its kind. It recalls the story told about the time when it is thought that someone asked Luther what he would do if he learned that the world would end tomorrow. He is said to have replied, "I would plant a tree."

Whether the story is true or not is beside the point. It surely represents Luther's views. Whether the world ends tomorrow or not until a million years from now is immaterial. What is important is that we be prepared. And the best way to be prepared is to go on doing our daily work and carrying out what we believe to be God's call for our lives.

This is what I like most about this time in the church year. Sunday after Sunday the Bible readings call us to be expectant and to be prepared. A good example is the parable of the wise and foolish bridesmaids. The foolish ones thought they could slack off because the master of the house would surely be delayed. They let the oil in their lamps run low. But the wise bridesmaids, though they had no certain knowledge of when the master would return, did what they did every day. They trimmed their lamps and made sure the oil basin was filled.

As believers we are called to work while we wait. It is sometimes said that "Just showing up is half the job." For us, just doing what is needed today is what is important. If in the process we touch just one or two other persons and bring light into their lives, then we have kept the lamp full and burning.

This kingdom is not for the half-hearted and the undecided. This is a call to full readiness. So, be prepared.

~ hwc

❖ MATHEW 25:1-13 ❖

❖ Where Are the Saints? ❖

It was an idyllic day. We stood on the Mount of Beatitudes overlooking the sparkling blue waters of the Sea of Galilee on one side and verdant green hills on the other. It seemed only natural to read the opening words of the Sermon on the Mount:

> Blessed are the poor in spirit
> Blessed are those who mourn
> Blessed are the meek
> Blessed are those who hunger and thirst for righteousness

Our sense of peace was deepened by the singing of the birds, the bright red lilies of the field, and the stillness away from busy streets.

Soon our tour bus arrived and it was time to move on. Now the shock of the real world seemed almost too much to bear. Monuments to war assaulted us wherever we looked: burned out tanks, sand-bagged gun emplacements, silvery rolls of barbed wire snaking up one hill and down another, military vehicles filled with soldiers. Suddenly the stillness of the Mount of Beatitudes and the kind thoughts of Jesus seemed like a dream.

We so easily forget that the words of Jesus were aimed at a world of turmoil. Rebellion, insurrection, revenge, and anger were everywhere. The heavy hand of Rome, with intolerable taxation, denial of human rights, and harassment of all kinds were the order of the day.

This text is a strong reminder that we cannot drive a wedge between the world as it is and the world as we wish it were. At this time of the year when we think of the saints and those who have had an impact on our lives, we do not honor those who ran from engagement with the world. No, we bless the memory of those who saw the world as it is and then did as Jesus commanded. They were merciful; they were pure in heart; they suffered for righteousness sake.

And that, too, is our calling.

~ hwc

❖ MATTHEW 5:1-16 ❖

MARKED WITH THE CROSS OF CHRIST

Today is the anniversary of my baptism in 1931. Because my sponsors could not arrive until the afternoon the baptism took place at the kitchen table, with my four, wide-eyed older sisters in the front row.

If Romans 6:4—my favorite verse—is true, then I both died and was born again that Sunday afternoon. I died with Christ and was born a second time by the power of the Holy Spirit. Yes, I believe it.

I find that as I grow older my baptism means more and more to me. Whatever achievements I may have accomplished along the way, whatever diplomas I may have hung on the wall, whatever honors may have been bestowed on me, whatever books I may have written, whatever sermons or lectures I may have delivered, they matter less and less. What lingers now and what looms ever larger is that I have been baptized and sealed by the Holy Spirit and "marked with the cross of Christ forever."

As a young man I thought that making the sign of the cross was "too Catholic." I even made fun of it. What a terrible mistake! I came to learn that making the sign of the cross when I was blessed or when I blessed others was intended to remind us that we died and were raised with Christ in our baptism. At first I made the gesture very furtively, not wanting others to see me doing it. But soon, as I realized its true meaning, I became bold and thought only of the wonder that Christ had died for me and that in my baptism I was joined to him and the whole Christian church—forever.

Luther said we should make the sign every day. I encourage you to try it. Even if it feels awkward at first, do it. In a short time you will discover that it is a natural way to remember your baptism.

~ hwc

❖ ROMANS 6:1-11 ❖

❖ THE NUMBER ONE DISCIPLE ❖

Peter, James, and John are usually thought of as the "inner circle" disciples. They accompanied Jesus to the transfiguration. More is said about them than any of the other disciples.

Today, however, we commemorate the one who was first—Andrew. According to John 1:40, Andrew was the first to follow Jesus. And no sooner did he make that decision than he did his most significant work. He introduced his brother Peter to Jesus. Peter not only became a disciple, but was the one who, along with Paul, brought the gospel to the Gentile world. There are many more churches and cities named after Peter than Andrew.

Everything else about Andrew is shrouded in legend. He is said to have preached in Palestine and areas as far north as the Black Sea. There is also an ancient legend that he was crucified on an x-shaped cross. The church in Scotland has always had a special affinity for Andrew. For us the important thing is what is certain—that he was the first to leave everything to follow Jesus.

Andrew reminds me of Aaron in the Old Testament. Always in the shadow of his famous brother Moses, Aaron played an important secondary role in the history of God's people.

I've known many folks over the years who never made big waves. Their names never appeared in headlines. They never wrote autobiographies. They never left a huge mark when they departed this world. Yet by their eagerness to be the first to raise their hand, the first to do a task that others may later have done a bit better, the first to stir others by speaking up when they see wrongdoing—in all these ways very ordinary folks have made an enormous contribution to the good of the church and the world.

That's why Andrew is the number one disciple. Thank God today for all the "Andrews" in our world.

~ hwc

❖ EXODUS 4:10-16 ❖

WHAT DOES IT MEAN TO BE "SPIRITUAL"?

We live in an age when it is more and more common to hear former members of our churches declare that they are "spiritual" but not "denominational." In other words, they think that they can practice their faith in isolation from a worshipping community of believers. A walk in the woods on a beautiful Sunday morning is as inspirational for them, and possibly more so, than attending a worship service at their former church.

These folks also tend to point to the faults of the church:

> "The church is too concerned about doctrine and not enough about practice."
>
> "They talk so much about money rather than things that are more important to us."
>
> "There's a lot of conflict in the church. We like to avoid all that division and disagreement."

You can add to the list the excuses you've heard. And we have to agree that many of them are legitimate. Part of the issue is centered in ignorance of the nature of the church. It sometimes shocks people when we point out to them that every single letter of Paul in the New Testament is addressed to a congregation that is having a problem of some kind. That's simply how it is. While we believe the church is the creation of the Holy Spirit, we can't get away from its very human nature.

But now let me challenge those who think they can "go it alone." At this time of the year we think of the great saints who have shaped the world in unusual ways. They recognized the weaknesses and shortcomings of the church. But, almost to a person, they did not abandon it. They recognized that we have a long tradition of worship and service that stretches back to Christ himself. They did not run away. They took the church as it was and worked for reform and renewal. We need a new generation of these kinds of saints.

~ hwc

EPHESIANS 2:1-10

❖ Good Excuses Aren't Good Enough ❖

One of the most misunderstood stories in the New Testament is the one where Jesus is calling new disciples to follow him. They offer their excuses:

> Lord, first let me go and bury my father (Luke 9:59).
>
> I will follow you, Lord; but first let me say farewell to those at my home (v. 61).

We tend to be hard on these fellows. What an opportunity! How could they be so insensitive? We think that had we been there we would have dropped everything for this chance to follow the Lord.

But just a moment. Before we make such a harsh judgment we need to look again at those excuses. Did one say, "I'm going to a party tonight; I'll join you in the morning"? Or did another say, "I have a terrible headache right now; I'm sure I'll feel better tomorrow"? Or did another say, "I'm not certain I agree with all you have in mind. Give me a week to think it over"?

No, not at all. Their excuses were very legitimate. Why shouldn't a man respect his father enough to see that he gets a decent burial? If he's not going to see his family for some time, shouldn't one at least be able to go home and bid them farewell? Is Jesus really that inconsiderate?

I think it is clear. Jesus is telling us that there is one invitation that is more important than anything else in life. It is the invitation to God's banquet, the invitation to be a part of God's family. Everything else in life is of lesser importance.

This is the mark of the saints we honor at this time of the year. They have in common one thing: They are single-minded. Once they catch a vision of what God has called them to do, everything else diminishes in importance. What is more important to you than anything else?

~ hwc

❖ LUKE 9:57-62 ❖

❖ Go into All the World ❖

After his resurrection and before his ascension, Jesus summoned his followers to "Go into all the world and proclaim the good news to the whole creation" (Mark 16:15). His own disciples and countless others, in obedience to that call to preach the gospel, have endured hardships, even given their lives.

Paul Mikki was one of them. Before him, the stage was set by Francis Xavier (1502–1552), an early missionary to Asia, first to India and then to Japan. He is regarded as one of the greatest missionaries in the history of the church. As the result of his preaching, Christianity spread rapidly in Japan, taking a firm hold. But because government leaders became alarmed, Christianity was declared illegal in 1614. This set off a time of terrible persecution. Christians were marched through the streets and killed publicly to reinforce the verdict, often killed with swords like Jesus was on the cross. Paul Makki, together with twenty-five Christians from other countries, was among them. For 250 years, any known Christian in Japan was put to death. Yet in 1859, when Christianity became legalized, new missionaries found secret Christian communities still in existence.

There is a long train of men and women who have answered the call to go into all the world with the gospel—to teach and preach and bring ministries of agriculture, education, and healing. And many have suffered hardships, even giving their lives for the sake of the gospel.

Not all of us as individuals will be able to venture to the far corners of the world. But the mandate still stands. You and I are fortunate to be part of a church that takes this call seriously. And together we serve in ways none of us could do alone. We can each take up our task as pray-ers, as encouragers, as givers, or as helpers. Wherever we are, God has a piece of the proclaiming for each of us to do.

"Go therefore and make disciples of all nations" (Matt. 28:19).

~ ecc

❖ MARK 16:15-20 ❖

❖ WHAT SEASON IS THIS ANYWAY? ❖

The pastor says: "Advent is a sober season. It's a time when we recall that God will judge all things at the end." And some folks complain when they get home: "Doesn't pastor know it's Christmas time! Hasn't pastor heard all the Christmas carols wafting through the air as Santa welcomes the children at the local department store? I wish pastor would lighten up. How about some Christmas carols?"

Ah, yes, it's that time again. We call it Advent. I call it "The season that gets crunched."

Why *do* pastors insist that we not skip it? For this reason: We cannot hear the Christmas good news until we hear the Advent bad news.

Think of some of the texts we hear in Advent:

> Let us live honorably as in the day time, not in reveling and drunkenness, not in debauchery and licentiousness, not in . . . jealousy (Rom.13:13).
>
> You must be ready, for the Son of Man is coming at an unexpected hour (Matt. 24:44).
>
> Do not grumble against one another, so that you may not be judged (James 5:9).
>
> O Lord of hosts, how long will you be angry with your people's prayers? You have fed them with the bread of tears, and given them tears to drink in full measure (Ps. 80: 4-5).

Not very "Christmasy" texts, are they? But this is what prepares us for the good news that God comes to us in times of darkness to set us free. For the people of God this is a season when the words of the Bible tell us over and over again that we are to put our trust in God alone, not in material possessions that we work so hard to bring to the foot of the Christmas tree. No, it is at the foot of the cross—that other tree—that we find our hope.

~ hwc

❖ ISAIAH 2:1-5 ❖

❖ You Light Up My Life ❖

One of our most memorable trips was an Advent excursion to Scandinavia. We were accustomed to shorter winter days in Minnesota. But to have the sun linger until mid-morning and then rush off quickly to set by mid-afternoon was a bit much. What we learned in the far north, however, is that you fight darkness with light.

I recall visiting a church in Denmark. In the near pitch darkness of the early evening we stepped into a nave that was bathed in white. Every wall, the pews, the altar—everything was painted in brilliant white. I could feel my spirits rise just standing there.

The same was true in every city in Denmark, Norway, Sweden, and Finland. Candles glowed in nearly every window. It was as though each residence was sending out a message: "It may be dark outdoors, but in this home there is light and warmth."

This theme of darkness and light runs as a strong current through the Advent season. Isaiah 34 and 35 are good examples. In chapter 34 we hear dark judgment: "The Lord is enraged against all the nations, and furious against all their hordes" (v. 2). But in chapter 35—an Advent text—the light breaks through: "They shall obtain joy and gladness, and sorrow and sighing shall flee away" (v. 10).

Jesus spoke about his followers being "the light of the world" (Matt. 5:14). This raises some good questions: Do others see me as a light in their world? Do those who wander in doubt and confusion see me as a source of comfort, hope, and stability?

If we are to be light we must first realize that the illumination does not originate with us. Rather, the light we have to share with others is reflected from the grace we have received from God. God lights up our lives in order that we might light up the lives of others.

~ hwc

❖ PSALM 18:25-28 ❖

❖ A Famous Mystery Man ❖

There are probably more churches and chapels named after him than any other saint in Christian history. He is the patron saint of sailors. He is said to have performed miracles and befriended the poor. He is called the patron saint of virgins. He is regarded as the guardian of children and merchants. All this and more. Yet we know almost nothing about the man the church commemorates on this day. You probably guessed by now that this mysterious saint is Nicholas. Yes, Jolly Old Saint Nick.

All we know for certain is that Nicholas was bishop at Myra on the southwest coast of Turkey. That's it; nothing more. Everything else has grown out of legend and myth. Maybe he deserved to be named a saint. But one has to wonder if this is not an instance where the church let things go too far.

As we approach the celebration of the birth of Christ and the miracle of his incarnation, of his becoming truly human, we would do well to try to separate myth from reality. In the minds of some children even God becomes little more than a jolly old man in a red suit who rewards those who have been not naughty but nice.

The message of the word of God is radically different. In Scripture the good news is that Jesus Christ lived and died for us so that even though all of us are naughty—sinful and unworthy—he will forgive and he will bless us with the greatest gift of all—eternal life.

Isaac Watts had the right idea.

> No more let sin and sorrow grow nor thorns infest the ground:
> He comes to make his blessings flow far as the curse is found,
> Far as the curse is found (*ELW* #267).

There is no uncertainty about this view of Christmas. This is not legend. This is good news for the whole world.

~ hwc

❖ JOHN 1:1-14 ❖

❖ Light Out of Darkness ❖

Since darkness seems mostly representative of evil, what can be good about it? Can darkness be creative or bring hope? But light, when it comes, could never be as glorious as when it shines out of darkness.

The late Dr. Joseph Sittler, when almost blind, preached a sermon about creation in the midst of darkness. He told Shakespeare's *Henry IV* story of tired, unarmored English soldiers preparing to fight the heavily armored French cavalry. Before this great battle, when everything seemed dark and hopeless, Henry filled their cups with wine toasting the coming battle that would secure their victory. Symbolically, it was the lifting of the cup together that filled them with hope and courage.

We speak of the "dark night of the soul," of dark periods in our nation, or of a gathering storm. In each case we sense energy brewing. An energy that can be either destructive or creative.

Job's brooding darkness had creative energy. His anger spiraled until at God's request he poured it forth. That opened him to see the light. And he exclaimed, "I know that my Redeemer lives" (Job 19:25).

The people of God walked in darkness. Creative energy turned them to hope. Isaiah foresaw the Messiah coming to set them free, using phrases recalling a king's coronation—"Everlasting Father" providing steadfast love and care, "Prince of Peace" offering peace and prosperity, and "Mighty God," with divine might (Isa. 9:6). Hope is a powerful thing, enabling one to walk presently in what is hoped for. "People who walked in darkness have seen a great light. . . . For a child has been born for us" (v. 2, 6).

When we come invited to the Lord's Table, we often come with darkness, weighed down with concerns. But when the cup is lifted, rejoice! Christ shines in our darkness.

> O Morning Star, how fair and bright!
> You shine with God's own truth and light,
> Aglow with grace and mercy! (*ELW* #308).

~ ecc

❖ ISAIAH 9:2-7 ❖

❖ Travail and Birthing ❖

Betty came often from next door to play dolls with our daughter. And when she married, was anxious to have her own live ones. But during the anguish of labor, she wondered why she ever became pregnant and was sure there would never be another.

Before ascending to heaven, Jesus promised to return. Didn't say when, for only the Father knows. But the early church expected the Day of the Lord momentarily. Some were so eager, they quit working. Complacent, as is true in every generation, why struggle for betterment of the world if we're soon going to heaven. But "the faithful are responsible for the newness of this human world" (Schillebeeckx). God keeps calling us to do difficult things. There are surprising opportunities to bend history. It's hard work, bringing us anguish as of a woman in travail, some so great that we will want to escape from it. Anguish can even obliterate hope for new life.

God comes now in Advent to deliver us from giving up in times of travail. To set us in motion for the salvation of the world. Giving us courage to face reality and not cop out. To labor and give birth.

Important during labor is rest between contractions, saving energy for the birthing. We, too, need rest between contractions. Rest in God's promises and at the table. Encouragement and refreshment for bringing to birth of what God calls us to do.

Every moment is a fresh and new coming of Jesus. We must be alert and awake, watching always for surprising opportunities that God leads us into. Things are often hard and difficult. There will be travail and anguish. We may be tempted to give up, like Betty. But there is great reward in seeing the fruit. Joy in new life that comes forth. And even joy waiting for God's next call. Like Betty coming with her little daughter, Maggie, announcing with excitement that she will soon be a big sister.

~ ecc

❖ 1 THESSALONIANS 5:1-11 ❖

❖ You Gave Me Food ❖

Paul Simon, late U.S. Senator from Illinois and champion of Bread for the World, grew up when Lutherans, Jews, and Catholics didn't talk to each other. But early experiences taught him to be ecumenical, cooperating with those of various backgrounds for the sake of the world. To earn money when age ten, he sold weekly magazines for five cents each, earning one and one-half cents per copy. One day caught in a downpour, thirty-four magazines were drenched. Dejected, he ducked into Mr. Rothenberger's furniture store. There he found a man who cared so much about a sad young boy that he bought all thirty-four magazines. That loving action forever changed Paul. His prejudices vanished.

Paul and his brother, Arthur, founder of Bread for the World, grew up believing that life is a gift from God, and that when we are reconciled to God we must work for justice for all people. They grew up in Eugene, Oregon, during World War II when U.S. citizens of Japanese origin were rounded up and put in prison camps. Their father was one of few people speaking out against it, and his courage inspired others. Led into public service, Paul believed as his father who said, "Better to build a fence at the top of a cliff than to have an ambulance at the bottom."

Paul served as U.S. Senator from 1985–1997. On his death day, December 9, 2003, we give thanks to God for a life dedicated in public service to champion the cause of hunger and poverty. Bread for the World rallies citizens to urge the nations' decision makers to end hunger at home and abroad by changing policies, programs, and conditions that allow hunger and poverty to persist.

Jesus said, "I was hungry and you gave me food. . . . Just as you did it to one of the least of these . . . you did it to me" (Matt. 25:35, 40).

~ ecc

❖ MATTHEW 25:34-40 ❖

❖ HUMAN RIGHTS DAY ❖

On Dec. 10, 1948, the Universal Declaration of Human Rights was passed by the United Nations General Assembly. Its thirty articles declare rights to such things as life, liberty, personal security, education, employment, paid holidays, and social security. It declares freedom of thought, conscience, religion, freedom of expression, and freedom from torture and cruel punishment. It is a worldwide standard for freedoms, but it is still violated by some countries that have subscribed to the declaration.

After gas chambers and mass killings of World War II, international concern rose up to act. The declaration has brought greater freedoms to people of the world. Yet Amnesty International reports many of the UN member governments who subscribe continue to violate the rights. Many still execute and torture their citizens, but they are being watched. As a result, torture has gone underground, resulting now in more disappearances and secret killings of both citizens and their defenders.

In 1989 we visited churches in Namibia while they were still under the cruel rule of South Africa's martial law. People were being killed without reason or defense. We were hosted by Bishop and Aina Dumeni, who grieved over recent losses. A brother working in his field with cattle was killed by a South African soldier. Their eighteen-year-old Anna died along with twenty other hospital workers cashing their weekly checks over the noon hour at the bank when it was bombed. All were buried in one grave where we stood with grieving parents. Land mines were planted on roads, and we saw many burned-out vehicles. Bishop Dumeni's staff person drove his car in front of the car we rode in, humbling us to realize that in case of a land mine he would be killed and not us.

As long as human nature exists, there will be a need to work for justice. God calls us "to do justice, and to love kindness, and to walk humbly with your God" (Micah 6:8).

~ ecc

❖ MICAH 6:6-8 ❖

❖ Already and Not Yet ❖

Another theme that courses through the season of Advent might be summarized in this phrase: "Already; not yet."

In the Advent Scripture lessons there is an emphasis on the present. God is here now; God is at work in the world; God's grace is new every morning. But at the same time, we wait in expectation for what is to come. We never feel completely fulfilled. There is always something lacking, something we know lies in the future.

This is the spirit in which Jesus shared his last meal with his disciples. When he said, "This is my body; this is my blood," he meant exactly that. All of the grace the disciples needed was right there at that table. The same is true for us. When the pastor uses those same words to consecrate the elements of bread and wine we believe that, as Luther said, "in, with, and under" the bread and wine we receive the true body and blood of Christ.

And yet—and yet—we long for more even in that moment. So it is not surprising that as soon as Jesus had shared the bread and the cup with his disciples he said, "I will never drink of this fruit of the vine until that day when I drink it new with you in my Father's kingdom" (Matt. 26:29).

Take a look at your children or grandchildren. As the packages accumulate under the tree they usually know what they are getting. They feel of the packages, shake them, maybe even tear off a corner to satisfy their curiosity. They get enormous joy in those moments of expectation. And yet, they will not be content until the hour arrives when they can rip them open to affirm their expectations.

So it is with believers. God is so good this day. Life is exciting. Yet we, too, wait expectantly for what God will do in the future.

~ hwc

❖ MATTHEW 26:26-30 ❖

❖ What Do I Have to Do? ❖

I like the way Gerhard Forde once put the question: "What are you going to do, now that you don't have to do anything?"

Start at the end: You don't have to do anything to be a child of God. We believe grace is sufficient even for a baby in the waters of baptism. And it's true as long as we live. There is nothing we can do—or need to do—to merit God's grace.

But then go back to the first part of that question: What are you going to do? How are you going to show your gratitude for God's free grace?

In Advent we hear from John the Baptist, that fiery man of God who prepared the way for the appearance of Christ. When asked that question—What must we do?—he had a ready answer. I wonder if they were prepared for his unexpected reply?

> If you have two coats, give one to a person who has none.
> If you have food, share it.
> Don't charge more than is fair.
> Be content with your salary.

There's no advice about going to the temple more frequently, or giving more to the temple treasury, or saying more prayers. Instead, John gets down into the nitty-gritty of life, the places where we connect with others in a very direct way. We might say that John is interested in everyday living, that is, in living every day as one whose life has been transformed by Jesus Christ.

In Advent we try to spend time preparing our hearts for the celebration of the coming of Jesus into the world. That is God's gift to us. We can never even begin to repay God for that best gift of all. But now remains that unsettling question: "What are you going to do, now that you don't have to do anything?" Do we need to wait for suggestions?

~ hwc

❖ LUKE 3:7-14 ❖

WHERE'S THE EXCITEMENT? ❖

Advent is a season of excitement. We see it in our children and grandchildren. They can scarcely wait until they can open Christmas gifts.

For believers there is something more exciting. It comes through in the prayers we hear during Advent. The phrase "Stir up . . ." occurs again and again. The Latin root of the word is *excita*—"excitement." That's the watchword for these days as we wait for the greatest gift the world has ever been given. We should have the same spirit about the birth of Jesus as the children have about those gifts under the tree.

Waiting is not passive for a Christian. It is active. Like a couple waiting for their wedding day or a student eagerly longing for graduation, so we are active while we wait. We keep busy even as we prepare for that happy day. We involve ourselves in the task at hand, helping the needy, serving the poor, speaking up for those denied their rights. We may not see the fruit of our labors today or tomorrow or the next day. But we keep at it in the full expectation that God will not disappoint us.

This spirit of anticipation often gets deadened during Advent season by the distractions around us. We are tempted to rush to the manger of Jesus, so eager to celebrate Christmas that we are completely exhausted the moment that day comes. Instead of singing, "Hosanna in the highest! Blessed is he who comes in the name of the Lord," we may find ourselves off on one of the side streets of life missing the joy of the Advent season.

This year try to pace yourself. Why not practice what one might call "energetic waiting"?

We would do well to echo the yearnings of the hymn writer Philip Doddridge:

> Our glad hosannas, Prince of Peace,
> your welcome shall proclaim,
> And heav'n's eternal arches ring
> with your beloved name (*ELW* #239).

~ hwc

❖ MARK 11:1-10 ❖

❖ Waiting at Your Door ❖

Prepare. And she always did! Before a family wedding or graduation, there was some major painting or recarpeting redo of the house. Workmen were barely out the back door when guests were knocking at the front.

Prepare. John the Baptist said to get ready because Jesus was coming. Jesus may be waiting even now at your door. When you go to see someone, you knock on the door. If they don't answer, you'll go back or try other means of contact. So will God. He started long ago in the Garden of Eden. Having eaten of the forbidden fruit, Adam and Eve were alienated and naked before God, who was already preparing new ways to be in touch. To Satan, God said, "Cursed are you" (Gen. 3:14), promising him enmity between his seed and the woman's seed, Jesus. He'll suffer and die but will rise again and have power over all the devil's evil.

Long ago in the wilderness, John the Baptist proclaimed, "The one who is more powerful than I [Jesus] is coming" (Mark 1:7). John said he gives people a ritual baptism for washing and helped them see their need of Jesus. But when Jesus comes, he will baptize people with the strength and power of the Holy Spirit.

From the wilderness comes a fresh word of God for each of us today. Let's put aside other Christmas preparations and go to the sparseness of the wilderness to hear the quiet footsteps of Jesus coming. He, who sees into the deepest recesses of our hearts, knowing every need, wants to make a redo, preparing the houses of our lives. He is not only knocking, but even now, is putting the desire in your heart and mine to let him in. Jesus waits there saying, "If you hear my voice and open the door, I will come in to you and eat with you, and you with me" (Rev. 3:20). Come to worship. To the table. For cleansing and forgiveness. A fresh start. I'm waiting at your door.

~ ecc

❖ MARK 1:1-18 ❖

❖ Knowing Our Place ❖

When I was a synod bishop one of my greatest problems was dealing with pastors who left a congregation or retired, but insisted on meddling in the parish. They may have had an exceptional ministry in that place. But now, with no sensitivity whatever, they conducted weddings and funerals and continued calling on parishioners without permission from the current pastor. It caused unnecessary turmoil and division.

John the Baptist was a man who knew his place. As his popularity grew it was inevitable that some "groupies" would attach themselves to him. Little wonder. His stirring preaching made him a popular figure in Jerusalem and the surrounding countryside. Droves of people admired him and thought he must surely be the promised messiah.

Along comes Jesus, his cousin and an equally commanding figure. Now crowds begin to flock to him as well, hanging on his every word. The scene that unfolds could have been easily predicted. Like rival congregations with equally "star power" preachers, tensions grew between the rival groups. Each was saying, "Our pastor is better than your pastor."

Fortunately, John knew his place. Without hesitation he urged his followers to transfer their allegiance from him to Jesus. For John, it was just that simple.

It's a good lesson for all of us as we prepare for Christmas. These hectic days can be distracting. We so easily get caught up in secondary matters, forgetting that it's all about Jesus.

John the Baptist comes with a simple but important message: "It's not about us or who we are or what we will receive for Christmas. Christ is so great that none of us is worthy to even stoop down and untie the laces of his sandals." John says: "He must increase, but I must decrease" (John 3:30). It's not easy to let go. But none of us is indispensable. No, not even a man as great as John the Baptist.

~ hwc

❖ JOHN 3:22-30 ❖

❖ Mercy or Judgment ❖

When I started teaching college students I had the idea that most of the students would remember most of what I said for most of their lives. When I administered tests at the end of the first term I stepped into the world of reality. A few remembered. Most had already forgotten. Over the next years I discovered that the only way for something to stick in a student's mind was to repeat it—and not just once.

Dr. A.D. Mattson, one of my seminary professors, understood this. Again and again we heard this pronouncement: "If God cannot rule in mercy, he will rule in judgment; but rule he will." It still sticks after more than fifty years.

This is what Advent is about. It is a strong word to us that God will rule. Yes, God's preference is to rule in mercy. But, if not, God will rule in judgment.

For this reason, when I observe Advent as it should be, I do not feel comfortable. It is a season when I hear Scripture lesson after Scripture lesson that makes me feel uneasy. They make me face up to my sin and my need for mercy.

The same goes for the church and our larger society. We invest enormous power and authority in those we elect to office. But Advent tells us that these powers are transitory. The governor of the state, the president of the country, the presiding bishop of the church, all will be forgotten in a short time. But God's mercy and judgment are forever.

During Advent we hear from John the Baptist. Can you imagine how it must have felt to stand in a crowd listening to that preacher of hellfire and brimstone? He was scathing. But here's the good news. He promised that if they repented God would have mercy. Now that's really good news. And that's what Advent is about.

~ hwc

❖ LUKE 3:1-14 ❖

❖ Take Off Your Mask ❖

Kierkegaard once said, "There comes a time when every person must unmask." As we learned on his commemoration day, that seemingly gloomy Dane was unrelenting in his insistence that we come into a direct encounter with God. To do so is frightening. But to do so is the only way to find peace with God and ourselves.

These are good words for the Advent season. The thought of being naked and exposed unsettles all of us. We want to be covered, protected, and sheltered. We want to be enveloped by all the things that make us feel comfortable, including our work, our home, our pension plan, our wardrobe, and much more.

What happens in Advent—and probably makes us want to leap over it and land safely in Christmas—is that every Bible text for every Sunday exposes us to the great reality of the Christian life—that the only thing we have for certain is the grace of God.

Jeremiah, to take but one example, lived in the worst of times. Many had abandoned any hope for the future. They had always thought of themselves as God's special people. But all had changed as they witnessed chaos on every side. Now they stood unmasked, exposed, broken, and hopeless. Along comes Jeremiah with words of hope: "In those days and at that time I will cause a righteous Branch to spring up for David; and he shall execute justice and righteousness in the land" (Jer. 33:15).

There you have it. At any given moment we may fall into despair as we unmask and see ourselves and the world around us as we really are. Painful as it is, this is necessary if we are to live in the hope that shines from Jeremiah's word. Our hope is in "the Branch" that will spring up from the roots of God's promises.

Yes, this is why we need Advent before Christmas.

~ hwc

❖ JEREMIAH 33:14-16 ❖

❖ Hope from the Prince of Peace ❖

Just before Christmas 1990 I traveled to the Middle East with a delegation of U.S. religious leaders. We were Baptist and Orthodox and Presbyterian and Episcopalian and Lutheran and Methodist and many more.

War clouds were gathering. We thought—some would say naively—that we could do something to head off the impending conflict between Iraq and the United States. My group's destination was Israel and the Gaza Strip.

We learned then what has been apparent to every student of the Middle East, namely, that the linchpin for the conundrum of conflict in the entire area is the Israeli-Palestinian stalemate. We witnessed intense hatred and animosity on both sides.

Fortunately, we also found in both communities some signs of hope. Though not large in number, there were Israelis and Palestinians who genuinely believed that a way could be found to resolve their differences.

On our return we issued a statement from our group. We warned that war in Iraq would "not establish regional stability" but only "inflame the entire Middle East."

More than two decades later our prophecy has come true. We have lost thousands of our country's finest women and men. Tens of thousands of innocent civilians, including children, are dead. Our investment of resources is driving us toward national bankruptcy.

We concluded our statement in 1990 with words of hope, words as relevant this holiday season as they were then. We stated that any resolution would "take a miracle. But in this season we are reminded that the Middle East is the cradle of miracles."

It is tempting to become pessimistic and weary in our prayers, especially when those prayers are for peace in places that seem so resistant to it. But if the babe of Bethlehem is the promised "Prince of Peace," how can we stop praying?

~ hwc

❖ ISAIAH 9:2-8 ❖

❖ MAKING ROOM FOR JESUS ❖

It's Advent. Someone important is coming! Clean house. Get food ready. But oh, the road, it's rough and full of potholes and dangerous curves. We must fix the highway so he can get safely through. Can it be fixed within a week? Jesus may come finding a sign on our heart, "Road out. Do not proceed."

Douglas Hall writes about human nature that doesn't want to admit wrong and can neither feel such feelings nor tell them to God—can neither own them nor allow others to. So what do we do when feelings are blocked, packed tight, making a hard spirit that wipes the smile off our face? It's not hidden even though we think it is. Prayer is blocked. Tenderness is gone. To justify self, we blame others. These are the gnarly roots that eat out potholes and block the road so Jesus can't get to our heart for Christmas.

John the Baptist asked the people why they flee God's wrath. Then he tells us there is a mighty one who can dig out the roots, no matter how far they have traveled. No matter how deep the potholes have become. He is able to fix the road to our hearts. In time for Christmas.

Jesus does it by winnowing and refining. I can see the woman in Tanzania holding her flat, woven, round frame and bouncing grain where with each bounce the wind blows away the chaff, leaving whole and healthy kernels ready to grind for baking bread. The Holy Spirit winnows out chaff and also refines us by fire. The firing is like what's happened to tiles from ancient cultures we see in museums. Refining fires, actually by accident was what preserved those tiles while others crumbled and decayed. The Holy Spirit, likewise, works in our hearts removing chaff and refining with fire, to make room for Jesus.

> O come to my heart, Lord Jesus, there is room in my heart for Thee (*The Hymnal* #47).

~ ecc

❖ LUKE 3:7-18 ❖

❖ Waiting and Expecting ❖

Waiting makes time long. December always seemed so very long as I was waiting for my birthday and Christmas. On a page of my tablet I made a calendar. Every day I marked off another day with an "X," which wore a hole through the paper.

Advent is a time of waiting, expectation, and preparation. Elizabeth in her old age waiting for her son to be born, the one who would "make ready a people prepared for the Lord" (Luke 1:17).

On the day Jesus was baptized, a powerful thing happened to John. He heard a voice and saw a dove descend on Jesus. He bore witness to that saying, "He on whom you see the Spirit descend and remain is the one who baptizes with the Holy Spirit. And I myself have seen and have testified that this is the Son of God" (John 1:33-34).

Stalwart, courageous John the Baptist, dedicated to the Lord, filled with the Spirit, sent by God, was now imprisoned for his witness of Jesus the Christ whom he had seen with eyes of faith. He sends his followers to ask Jesus, "Are you the one who is to come, or are we to wait for another?" (Matt. 11:3). If anyone's faith should have been secure, surely it would be John's. But now sitting in prison, he struggled with despair and doubt. Like John, we too see with fresh eyes of faith, yet yield to despair and doubt.

Luther taught us that trials are helpful actually in leading us to know the Scriptures, to come to faith, and to fear and love God. Faith flourishes only in those who are needy. And we are they.

Expect means take hold of and ahead of time. Expecting, we lay hold of something ahead of its happening. We wait, assured of what has not yet happened.

> Come, thou long expected Jesus, born to set thy people free;
> From our fears and sins release us; let us find our rest in thee
> (*LBW* #254).

~ ecc

❖ I Doubt It—but I Believe ❖

When I was a young Christian, full of simple answers to complex questions, I had little patience with Thomas, the disciple we commemorate this day. "After all," I said, "he had spent three years as a companion of Jesus, he had witnessed the miracles, and he had heard Jesus say he would rise on the third day. How could he possibly doubt that Jesus was alive?"

That was then. Now I'm getting old, having crossed over the threshold into my 80s. Now I have a few battle scars. Now, like Jacob, I've wrestled with angels and have a limp. Now I've walked the valleys of the shadows. Now I'm not so hard on Thomas.

I agree with those who say it's harder to believe than not to believe. In four days we will come to a most unbelievable day of the year, a day when we confess that the God who created all things was wrapped in the swaddling cloths of a baby. That's an affront to our reason.

Then we will move on toward another most unbelievable day—Good Friday—when we confess that this baby died on a cross to forgive the sins of the world.

Then in three days another unbelievable day when we shout, "He is risen." Isn't that too much? Is it any wonder Thomas had some reservations?

Doubt is not the opposite of faith. The opposite of faith is despair. Despair questions and then gives up. Doubt questions and then persists until there is a breakthrough. I have not found faith at the end of a perfect day. No, I have found it at the end of a day when my world had all but collapsed. There in the darkness I asked for light. And there, like Thomas, Jesus came and gave me faith. There I learned again that only the Holy Spirit can give that gift.

~ hwc

❖ JOHN 20:24-29 ❖

❖ You May Never Know ❖

"The Nutcracker Suite" at Lincoln Center. What could be more festive at this time of year? Our small children were enraptured in awe as the dancers swept across the stage. Their toes seemed scarcely to touch the floor. A memory for a lifetime.

Indeed, Tchaikovsky gave the world a priceless treasure when he composed this opera more than 200 years ago.

It may come as a surprise to know that he himself thought his work to be a failure. And so, in fact, did music critics of his day. When he died two years later he had not even the faintest idea that "The Nutcracker" would live on as a musical treasure around the world. Music is truly a universal language.

We can learn from Tchaikovsky, especially in this holy season. Did the wise men live long enough to know that they had visited the Savior of the world? Probably not. Did Joseph reach an age where he experienced the resurrection of Mary's son and share in the joy of that day? Probably not. Did any of the apostles believe their message of "good news to all people" would be embraced by believers in every land, places they could not conceive of in the first century? Probably not.

Can any of us know the impact of our witness? Certainly not.

But Christmas is a time for hope. A phone call, a note, an email message, a gift—because God stretches our influence beyond this moment, we can live in the expectation that our seemingly insignificant acts will result in some good that reaches beyond our time in this world. We may think something a failure. Others may not recognize any value in something we do. But, yes, we can live in hope, believing that God will take the seeds we plant and bring fruit beyond our imagination.

~ hwc

❖ LUKE 2:8-14 ❖

❖ We Can Know ❖

Can you believe that God became human and is our Savior? Joseph knew. Mary knew. The shepherds knew. Wise men knew. Even Elizabeth knew when Mary came to her pregnant that the child she carried was "my Lord" (Luke 1:43). And we can know, too. The Word of Life was made manifest to them. They saw with eyes of faith. The Holy Spirit gives us that gift.

At age eleven I felt afraid of God. That fear grew until one sleepless night I called my mother. She came to my bedside thinking I was ill. But no, I was afraid of God. She carefully explained how in the presence of God, who is almighty, it isn't strange that we feel afraid. But that was why out of love, God provided a way so that we would never have to be afraid. That was why God sent Jesus into the world to be our Savior.

And then she told me about a promise from God, one of her favorite Bible verses that she had memorized from 1 John 1:9, "If we confess our sins, he who is faithful and just will forgive us our sins and cleanse us from all unrighteousness." Well then, I wondered how I could be sure. She explained God will help us believe when we ask. The October full moon was shining through my window as together we knelt beside my bed praying that the Holy Spirit, given to me in baptism, would open my heart to believe this was true for me.

That was one of many awakenings when the Holy Spirit has opened the hearing of the Word to help my heart believe. What a gift!

~ ecc

❖ 1 JOHN 1—2:3 ❖

❖ THAT VERY ORDINARY GIRL ❖

Mary, the mother of Jesus, has been so highly revered that it's nearly impossible to reconstruct the real woman. For starters, she was probably a 15- or 16-year-old teenager when we first meet her, the age when it was common for girls in her day to be engaged. She lived in the nondescript village of Nazareth in the far north of Palestine, far from the bustling streets of Jerusalem. She probably didn't stand out from the other teens who walked the streets of her home town. Her family was no doubt the most ordinary we could imagine. Even today as you walk the streets of Nazareth it is hard to imagine that a world-changing event could happen to one of these innocent-looking girls.

But it did. Yes, it did. An unsuspecting young girl heard the word, "You will conceive in your womb and bear a son, and you will name him Jesus. He will be great, and will be called the Son of the Most High" (Luke 1:31-32). Is it any wonder that she was startled? This was Mary's mystical experience, so personal and so exceptional that no one else would understand it. She hears a call and she obediently replies, "Here am I, the servant of the Lord; let it be with me according to your word" (v. 38).

You and I may not be able to point to an event as unusual as the one that happened to Mary. But the pattern is the same for all of us. God comes with shocking good news, over and over again. Along with it comes an appeal for a response. We are given the opportunity to say, "I hear you, Lord. I know what you want me to do. I will do it."

Strip away all the trappings and excesses of the Christmas season and get down to the root meaning. Christmas is a time to recommit your life to God.

~ ecc

❖ LUKE 1:26-38 ❖

❖ To YOU Is Born a Savior ❖

Bill showed up at our synod assembly. Hadn't seen him since he was a child. "Can we do lunch?" he asked, "I need to talk." During college years, sensitive Bill got caught up in drugs. With high standards, he was becoming depressed over missing the boat—overwhelmed with feelings of failure. "It came to the point," he said, "I carried an instrument of death at all times. I wanted it handy if the pressure got too great. No one knew."

In the midst of such struggle, one can blame parents, spouse, or life's situation. It's a dead end road until at last saying, "Bankrupt!" That is what happened to Bill. But hope came.

One day, at life's blackest moment, he described seeing a beam of light—enough to remember things from confirmation. He decided if he were going to throw his life away, maybe throw it to God. Give him a chance. Nothing to lose. So he blurted out, "God, I can't make it! I give up! I give myself to you totally!" Then he waited to see what would happen. He described a fresh glimpse of God, coming like a miracle. "God revealed himself to me. I believed and was at peace."

Sin can rest on only two places—on our conscience or on Jesus. Our conscience knows us and is on the side of the law, accusing. It drives us to despair. No way out if we're trying to make it on our own. But we have a Christmas gift—*To YOU Is Born a Savior.*

Because Jesus lived human like us, was tempted like us, and suffered evil, he understands us. He paid the ultimate price for our transgressions so we don't have to. Martin Luther says, he descended into hell waving flags of victory over Satan.

> I lay my sins on Jesus, the spotless Lamb of God;
> He bears them all and frees us from the accursed load (*LBW* #305).

~ ecc

❖ LUKE 2:8-14 ❖

❖ Stephen, Deacon and Martyr ❖

Acts 6-7 tells the story of Stephen, "full of grace and power did great wonders and signs among the people" (Acts 6:8). As a wise, elected deacon in the early church, he was so capable that folks became enraged with jealousy, which culminated in violence. Finding witnesses who would bring false accusations against Stephen, they brought him to court where he made his courageous defense. With heightened anger they dragged him outside of the city and stoned him. As he was dying, he saw the heavens opened and he prayed, "Lord, do not hold this sin against them" (Acts 7:60). A "proto-martyr," he was one of the first of many martyrs to follow Christ. Because of his stalwart faith and love for those who persecuted him, he is highly revered in the church, and we commemorate his life on December 26.

Just before the Allies arrived, Dietrich Bonheoffer, theologian and pastor, was executed April 9, 1945, in the Flossberg concentration camp. While defending the faith, he was charged with treason for defying Hitler's nazism. His suffering exemplifies Tertullian's words, "the blood of the martyrs is the seed of the church." Bonheoffer believed Christ's gifts to us in baptism are intertwined—God's all-sufficient grace, the cross of Christ, and our call to discipleship. He teaches us to daily renew our baptism, which means examining God's will for a new day. And doing it no matter what the cost. His life and writings have been and continue to be a great inspiration for many.

We should not be surprised either that in obeying God's call we suffer the jealousy of others or their false accusations. We are to die daily with Christ and rise to newness. Even if "the fiery ordeal that is taking place among you [is] to test you" (1 Peter 4:12). God promises joy in sharing Christ's sufferings, and "you are blessed, because the spirit of glory, which is the Spirit of God, is resting on you" (v. 14).

~ ecc

❖ 1 PETER 4:12-19 ❖

❖ Dreams Change History ❖

Dreams that changed history are here within the first two chapters of Matthew. Matthew, like many other writers of Scripture, must have experienced God's guidance in dreams to have given the history-changing events center stage. Think how dramatically these dreams of Joseph and the wise men changed history.

Joseph did take Mary as his wife, giving up the need to preserve his honor. It could have been otherwise. They were betrothed when Joseph learned that Mary was pregnant, an extremely difficult situation for him. Pursuing marriage would bring great long-lasting shame to him as husband. To resolve his dilemma, he had made the decision to divorce her quietly. Until the dream.

When arrogant Herod caught wind of a child born king, he rallied his world, including the wise men, to find and destroy the child. But the wise men, after visiting the Christ child, avoided Herod, because they were "warned in a dream not to return to Herod" (Matt. 2:12).

When their family was in danger of Herod's violence, an angel of the Lord appeared to Joseph in a dream saying, "Get up, take the child and his mother, and flee to Egypt, and remain there until I tell you" (v. 13). Joseph quickly escaped with his family until bidden by a dream to return. Not to Judea, but to safety in Nazareth of Galilee.

Following each dream, notice the definite certainty. There's new courage and decisive action, even against social custom. Throughout Scripture and in the early church it was the norm for God's will to be revealed through dreams and visions. This great gift was lost to the West until recently when Carl Jung, Morton Kelsey, John Sanford, and many others since have taught us to listen to our dreams.

Dreams are like a camera capturing our inner feelings when the guard is down. Journaling it, we see a clear picture of who we are, what we must change, and the courage we have been given to act. God bless you with dreams.

~ ecc

❖ MATTHEW 1:18-25 & 2:1-23 ❖

❖ HOLY INNOCENTS DAY ❖

Herod wanted no rival to his throne, so when wise men came looking for the one born King of the Jews, he was enraged. After his search failed to find the child, Herod made his outrageous decree that all male infants under two be killed. Mothers wept. Mothers still weep for children who suffer and die as a result of war, abuse, injustice, or suicide. Our adopted son at eighteen took his life because of a painful lost identity. His death connected me to other youth who search for identity. I've traveled the country speaking to youth in assemblies and hugged scores of tearful teenagers who tell me, "I've attempted suicide because I was born gay (or lesbian) and hear mean things said about me in the church. I can't change and don't want to grow up this way." Though Andrew's reason for ending his life was different, I've assured each of them, hugging them to my mother's heart, that in the church there are also many of us who love them just as they are. And I know Jesus does.

David Weiss, in *To the Tune of a Welcoming God,* quotes a gay Notre Dame University student writing of his "daily four-year battle toward self-acceptance while driven by fear to remain in the closet." In his pain, God seemingly remained silent. Weiss went public as a GLBT ally in a newsletter: "I see now that if God keeps silent in the face of your anguish, it is only because I wouldn't lend God the use of my words."

Hear a gay person's anguishing cry and God's answer in Robert Seeley's choral, "Dialogue."

> Now I lay me down to sleep. I wonder who my soul will keep?
> Where is the someone out there who cares,
> who hears and answers my simple prayers?
>
> Restless and alone, thinking you're the only one, you're not.
> Praying in the dark, pouring out your heart, hoping I hear, I do.

God, give us words to speak for those who have no voice.

~ ecc

❖ MATTHEW 2:13-18 ❖

❖ A New Name for a New Year ❖

When Scandinavian emigrants came to the United States it was common for many to change their names. Maybe there were already too many "Petersons" in the country. At other times, such as with my paternal great grandparents, it was because their name was too difficult to pronounce or spell. Thus "Kjöllerström" became "Chilstrom."

Change of name also occurs at times in the Bible. "Abram" becomes "Abraham." "Jacob" becomes "Israel." In these instances, however, the change had to do with a new identity that springs out of an unusual experience that turns their lives in new directions.

One of the lessons we use in the post-Christmas season is Isaiah 62:1-3. It is a time of darkness in the land. People wonder why their prayers are not heard. Into their gloom steps the prophet Isaiah with a reassuring word: "You shall be called by a new name that the mouth of the Lord will give" (Isa. 62:2).

As we look back over the year and around at the condition of our world, we may be tempted to fall into despair. We may count many reasons not to be very optimistic about the New Year to come.

But God comes to us as God came to the people of Israel with words of strong hope. There is no need to go out and purchase silly hats and toy whistles, no need to stock up with alcoholic beverages for a grand New Year's Eve party. That may dull what should be the proper way to welcome a new beginning. We hear Isaiah tell us in a natural way to pull out all the stops. This is no time to repress our sense of confidence in God. It is a time to remember with thanksgiving, to sing with joy, to embrace with love. We have just welcomed the Christ child. It's a new day. Who should be happier than we?

~ hwc

❖ ISAIAH 62:1-3 ❖

❖ TRUSTING GOD ❖

"Where did this year go?" We hear words like that often at this time. Before he died, Bertil Anderson, pastor, organist, and choral director, penned some free verses that expressed his inner feelings as he neared the end of his life. He muses: "For today is the tomorrow I once worried about. Today is often the grave of yesterday's hopes."

Indeed, how many of the things we feared actually happened? From today's perspective, was it worth all the energy we wasted on them? And those bright hopes? Some blossomed into what we had dreamed would happen. But what about those that never materialized? Is it possible that we might even be grateful that they were never fulfilled?

Over and over again in the Scriptures we are urged to trust in God rather than ourselves and our own designs. That's easier to say than to do. Even when we feel confident our prayers have been answered or when God has seemed so close one day, we awaken the next with those old fears lurking around the edges of our life again. Why is it so hard to trust in God, to remember what God has already done in our lives?

The word *trust* is repeated over and over in the psalms. A few of those references might be well to pack away as we approach the threshold of a New Year:

> Those who know your name put their trust in you . . . (9:10).
>
> Trust in the Lord, and do good; so you will live in the land, and enjoy security (37:3).
>
> I trust in the steadfast love of God forever and ever . . . (52:8).
>
> [I] will say to the Lord, "My refuge and my fortress, my God, in whom I trust" (91:2).

Anderson ended his poem with these strong words:

> You who lives beyond the power of death,
> Live in me and I shall then first know that I am alive.

~ hwc

❖ PSALM 56 ❖

❖ Time to Keep or Throw ❖

It's time to move into a new year. And moving means time to get rid of accumulations and extra baggage. That certainly includes outdated and poorly fitting things in the closet and seldom or never used items in cupboards. But more importantly, as we move now into the New Year, it includes things that weigh down the spirit—resentments, anxieties, fears, dullness of spirit. It's time to reassess priorities, use of time, meaning in life, and even taking time to measure lost enthusiasm.

"Enthusiasm," from the Greek word *entheos*, meaning God-possessed, is clearly linked to our call from God, which is related to the giftedness God has given us from birth. Research tells us that the degree of job satisfaction correlates to how much we use those gifts, either in a career or in volunteer work. Ernest Becker, in *Denial of Death*, suggests that one's greatest sin is to deny using those best God-given gifts. No wonder we have such inner hunger to use our talents, and also such reward in giving them to the world.

Returning for a post-operative check-up, my foot surgeon after removing the bandage stood tall with a very satisfied look on his face saying, "I just love to fix feet!" Using your gifts gives the world something no one else can give.

So let us "lay aside every weight and the sin that clings so closely, and let us run with perseverance the race that is set before us, looking to Jesus the pioneer and perfecter of our faith" (Heb. 12:1-2).

> Take my life, that I may be consecrated, Lord, to thee;
> Take my moments and my days; let them flow in ceaseless praise.
> Take my hands and let them move at the impulse of thy love;
> Take my feet and let them be swift and beautiful for thee.
> Take my silver and my gold, not a mite would I withhold;
> Take my intellect, and use every pow'r as thou shalt choose
> (*ELW* #685).

~ ecc

❖ ECCLESIASTES 3:1-13 ❖